EX AUDITU

An International Journal for the Theological Interpretation of Scripture

VOL. 36  **2024**

Ex Auditu is published annually by Pickwick Publications, an imprint of
Wipf and Stock Publishers, 199 West 8th Avenue, Suite 3, Eugene, Oregon 97401, USA

SUBSCRIPTIONS

Individuals:
U.S.A. and all other countries (in U.S. funds): $20.00
Students: $12.00

Institutions:
U.S.A. and all other countries (in U.S. funds): $30.00

This periodical is indexed in the ATLA Religion Database, published by the American Theological Library Association, 300 S. Wacker Dr., Suite 2100, Chicago, IL 60606, Email: atla@atla.com, www: http://www.atla.com/; *Internationale Zeitschriftenshau für Bibelwissenschaft*; *Religious and Theological Abstracts*; and *Old Testament Abstracts*.

Please address all subscription correspondence
and change of address information to Wipf and Stock Publishers.

©2024 by Wipf and Stock Publishers
ISSN: 0883-0053
PAPERBACK ISBN: 978-8-3852-1190-6
HARDBACK ISBN: 978-8-3852-1191-3

Scripture quotations marked (NRSV) are taken from the New Revised Standard Version Bible © 1989 Division of Christian Education of the National Council of the Churches of Christ in the United States of America. Used by permission. All rights reserved.

Scripture quotations taken from The Holy Bible, New International Version® NIV® Copyright © 1973, 1978, 1984, 2011 by Biblica, Inc. Used with permission. All rights reserved worldwide.

EX AUDITU

An International Journal for the Theological Interpretation of Scripture

Dennis R. Edwards, Editor
J. Nathan Clayton, Associate Editor
K. C. Hanson, Associate Editor
Klyne R. Snodgrass, Editor Emeritus

Dennis R. Edwards
Seminary Dean and Vice President of
   Church Relations
North Park Theological Seminary
3225 West Foster Avenue
Chicago, Illinois 60625-4987
USA

Tel: (773) 244-6238
email: dredwards@northpark.edu
Web site: http://wipfandstock.com/catalog/
   journal/view/id/12/

EDITORIAL BOARD

Richard B. Hays, The Divinity School,
   Duke University, Durham, North Carolina
Jon R. Stock, Wipf and Stock Publishers,
   Eugene, Oregon
Miroslav Volf, Yale Divinity School,
   New Haven, Connecticut
John Wipf, Wipf and Stock Publishers,
   Eugene, Oregon

THE EDITORIAL BOARD MEMBERS AND CONSULTANTS represent various disciplines and denominations. Theological interpretation of Scripture is a task to be taken seriously by scholars who are committed to the Christian faith and tradition. However, as one editorial consultant stated: "Let people gradually get used to the idea that a sane hermeneutics is both oriented in advance toward agreement/consent and is simultaneously exigent, discriminating, critical."

EDITORIAL CONSULTANTS

M. Daniel Carroll R.
Wheaton College
Wheaton, Illinois

Simon Gathercole
University of
Cambridge
Cambridge, England

Nijay Gupta
Northern Seminary,
Lisle, Illinois

Robert Johnston
Fuller Theological
Seminary
Pasadena, California

R. Walter L. Moberly
University of Durham
Durham, England

Sujin Pak Boyer
The Divinity School
Duke University
Durham, North
Carolina

Iain Provan
Regent College
Vancouver, British
Columbia

Kevin J. Vanhoozer
Trinity Evangelical
Divinity School
Deerfield, Illinois

William H. Willimon
The Divinity School
Duke University
Durham, North
Carolina

N. T. Wright
St Mary's College,
University of St.
Andrews, Scotland

CONTENTS

Abbreviations vi
Introduction vii

Jeremiah 29 and Political Theology 1
Stephen B. Chapman

Who Can Lead a Flock of Shepherds? Paul, the Pillars, And Political Challenges in Our Churches Today 21
Timothy Milinovich

Response to Milinovich 37
Christy Randazzo

Forgiveness as the Redoubling of God 43
Colby Dickinson

Response to Dickinson 64
Kaitlyn Schiess

I Feel You: The Theo-Politics of Compassion and the Poor in Liberation Theology and Karl Barth 69
Jules A. Martinez Olivieri

Response to Martinez 85
Rose Lee-Norman

Some Texts and Our Politics 88
Vincent Bacote

Response to Bacote 102
Jonathan Wilson

Love's Domain or White Christians' Dominion? A Missiological Response to the American Culture Wars   107
Janel Kragt Bakker

Response to Bakker   128
Christopher W. Skinner

What's in a Name? Ideology and Naming   134
Kay Higuera Smith

Response to Smith   153
Bret M. Widman

Select Annotated Bibliography on Politics   159
Presenters and Respondents   164

ANNOUNCEMENT

The Covid-19 pandemic was disruptive for the Symposium on Theological Scripture hosted by North Park Theological Seminary in Chicago, Illinois. Since the pandemic, we have decided to shift from hosting the symposium and publishing *Ex Auditu* every year, to hosting the symposium every other year, and publishing *Ex Auditu* in the intervening years. This volume of *Ex Auditu*, volume 36, gathers in print the papers and responses from the September 2021 symposium, which was held online. In September 2023, the symposium was held again in person at North Park and the theme was Creation Care. The papers and responses from that gathering will be published in 2025 as volume 37 of *Ex Auditu*. Furthermore, North Park Theological Seminary is pleased to announce that the thirty-eighth Symposium on the Theological Interpretation of Scripture will be held in person February 14 and 15, 2025. The theme will be Hospitality and Immigration. We anticipate, then, that volume 38 of *Ex Auditu* will be published in 2026.

ABBREVIATIONS

Unless listed here, all abbreviations are as specified in *The SBL Handbook of Style: For Biblical Studies and Related Disciplines*, 2nd ed. (Atlanta: Society of Biblical Literature, 2014).

    JTI   *Journal of Theological Interpretation*
    JSPL   *Journal for the Study of Paul and His Letters*
    JSJSup   Journal for the Study of Judaism Supplement Series

INTRODUCTION

It seems fair to say that the political polarization in our society became more pronounced after the 2016 election of Donald J. Trump as the forty-fifth president of the United States, especially since a large proportion of professing Christians supported him. Consequently, a Symposium on Theological Interpretation of Scripture held in the fall of 2020 could provide a thoughtful and engaging backdrop for the upcoming election when President Trump vied for a second term with his main opponent being a long-time Democratic politician, Sen. Joe Biden. But alas, the Covid-19 pandemic caused us at North Park Theological Seminary (NPTS) to cancel the 2020 symposium. As we began to plan for 2021, we agreed to keep politics as the topic for discussion.

Perhaps it was providential that our delayed discussion of politics came nearly a year after the 2020 election. Not only could scholars and other participants reflect on the rise of what has been called Trumpism, they could also analyze the aftermath of that election, such as the insurrection on January 6, 2021. The essays in this volume are of course still pertinent as we experience another presidential election that is poised to be historic for several reasons.

As we geared up for our 2021 symposium, the world was hit with a Covid-19 variant and people were again falling ill in large numbers. It seemed that most planners of large, in-person gatherings had to make tough decisions. We, like others, were cautious about hosting an event where some participants had to travel from out of state to attend. We decided, therefore, to hold the symposium virtually. It was a difficult decision but seemed to be the right thing to do. Fortunately, our presenters and respondents were ready, willing, and able to engage online. We were able to have meaningful conversations even though we missed the typical collegiality and interpersonal connections our symposia are known for. I am grateful for all the participants who made the necessary adjustments to interact online.

I am also grateful for the NPTS community and for Wipf and Stock Publishers. Both groups were patient with me as I transitioned from the classroom to administrative roles at the seminary right after we held the symposium. I'm especially appreciative of Chris Spinks of Wipf and Stock, who has now gone to be with the Lord and who had long been involved in our symposium. Chris was helpful as we deliberated how best to hold the event in 2021. I take this opportunity to thank Luke Palmerlee, our former Director of Seminary Operations, who for years has been key part of

Introduction

making the symposium happen and who helped us with the logistics of a virtual conference. I would also like to thank J. P. De Neui for his detailed work proofreading and formatting the essays and responses in this volume. Stephen B. Chapman, Associate Professor of Old Testament at Duke Divinity School, was also supportive in this project with a thorough proofreading, besides contributing the first essay. Finally, thanks also goes to Nathan Clayton, Associate Professor of Old Testament at NPTS. Nathan picked up editing duties from me right as he left for sabbatical. I'm excited for the leadership Nathan provides as the new editor for *Ex Auditu*.

    Dennis R. Edwards
    Seminary Dean and Vice President of Church Relations
    North Park Theological Seminary

JEREMIAH 29 AND POLITICAL THEOLOGY

Stephen B. Chapman

Jeremiah 29:7—"Seek the welfare of the city"—is one of those increasingly few Old Testament (OT) texts retaining a regulative function within contemporary Christian theology.[1] Even if its invocation is more like an awkward habit or the memory of a once livelier discourse rather than evidence of truly robust biblical theology, the verse is still employed as a key marker within current theological conversations about the relationship between church and society. It remains part of the conceptual furniture within the Christian theological imagination, one element of the biblical grammar with which Christians continue to reflect theologically.

Theologians, rather than biblical scholars, are to be thanked for this holdover. Biblical scholars—some of them—are only starting to recognize how extensively they have been misled by a deeply held version of the genetic fallacy: where things come from does not determine what they mean.[2] But can the history of their making still provide hermeneutical cues for interpreting their present meaning and significance? Yes, but I would suggest that those cues most usefully operate in biblical studies on a broad level of historical contextualization instead of deriving from attempts to "reverse engineer" the history of a biblical text's literary formation or to reconstruct a conjectural historical context for the speech-act depicted in and/or represented by a particular biblical text.

The academic discipline of biblical studies has traditionally invested enormous energy and resources in such reconstructions, thereby privileging what is putatively

---

1. In this essay I use the NRSV for biblical quotations. I am grateful to Luke Bretherton, Walter Moberly, and Brent Strawn for reading an earlier draft and offering helpful comments on it. I hope they will forgive me for declining to incorporate all of their recommended changes.

2. The organic chemist August Kekule attributed his discovery of benzene's ring structure to a dream in which he saw a snake biting its own tail. See Malcolm W. Browne, "The Benzene Ring: Dream Analysis," *The New York Times*, August 16, 1988 (C 10). Even if the history of this discovery was more complicated, as described by Browne, the incident underscores how intentions, subjectivities, and origins do not determine essences or identities. Benzene has nothing to do with snakes, even if Carl Jung sought to enlist Kekule's ouroboros in the service of his own psychoanalytic theory. See C. G. Jung, *The Psychology of Transference*, in *Collected Works of C. G. Jung*, vol. 16, trans. F. R. C. Hull (Princeton: Princeton University Press, 1969) 168.

"early" or "original" as most important. The problem has not only been that in this way a reconstructed developmental sequence was made to substitute for the biblical books themselves,[3] but also that the mutually implicating nature of the discourse between biblical exegesis and theological formulation pulled apart, resulting in biblical scholarship without interest in theological consequences and theology without regard for biblical compatibility. Again, the blame for this regrettable situation lies mostly with biblical scholars and their preoccupation with "the world behind the text" rather than the text as such, or in Paul Ricoeur's suggestive phrase, "the world *in* the text."[4]

Thus, one might easily read multiple biblical commentaries on the book of Jeremiah without realizing that Jer 29:7 plays a major role in Christian political thought. Indeed, even in the thematic study *Israel and Empire* by Leo Perdue and Warren Carter, Jer 29:7 goes unmentioned, a puzzling circumstance suggesting that there has not just been a simple oversight but a tendentious cherry-picking of the evidence.[5] One can understand how a seemingly pro-imperial "collaborationist" text like Jer 29:7 might prove awkward within an anti-imperial approach to the OT. There is, of course, a full secondary literature on Jeremiah 29 within biblical studies. However, most of this work focuses on reconstructing the political agenda of the historical prophet (was he indeed "pro-Babylonian"? at least for one phase of his professional life?) and the original contents of his letter to the Judean exiles.[6]

But when Jeremiah 29 is invoked in the theological discussion, then it is frequently cut loose from its historical moorings and the importance given to it is disproportionate. It becomes an outsized framework for conceptualizing the ideal interaction between church and society today. Angus Paddison more or less defines "public theology" in relation to Jer 29:7.[7] James Davidson Hunter bases his view of "faithful presence within" on Jer 29:7 in his manifesto *To Change the World*.[8]

---

3. Darian Lockett, "Limitations of a Purely Salvation-historical Approach to Biblical Theology," *HBT* 39.2 (2017) 211–31.

4. Paul Ricoeur, "World of the Text, World of the Reader," in *A Ricoeur Reader: Reflection and Imagination*, ed. Mario J. Valdes (Toronto: University of Toronto Press, 1991) 491–97 (my emphasis). See also Paul Ricoeur, "Biblical Hermeneutics," *Semeia* 4 (1975) 29–148.

5. Jeremiah 29:10 appears in the index, cited in relation to Jeremiah's prophecy of seventy years. Otherwise, Jeremiah 29 is absent from consideration, and the prophet Jeremiah is presented exclusively as anti-Babylonian. See Leo G. Perdue and Warren Carter, *Israel and Empire: A Postcolonial History of Israel and Early Judaism*, ed. Coleman A. Baker (London: T. & T. Clark Bloomsbury, 2015) esp. 87–92.

6. For a fine exception by a biblical scholar, see Barry A. Jones, "Speaking to the Exiles: How the Theme of Exile in Jeremiah Addresses 21st Century Congregations," *RevExp* 101 (2004) 177–200.

7. Angus Paddison, "Theological Interpretation and the Bible as Public Text," *JTI* 8 (2014) 175–92 (178).

8. James Davidson Hunter, *To Change the World: The Irony, Tragedy, and Possibility of Christianity*

Luke Bretherton places Jer 29:7 at the center of his monograph *Christianity and Contemporary Politics*,[9] drawing on Augustine, who had already appealed to Jeremiah 29 as a way of understanding the "city of God" in relation to the "earthly city."[10] Paddison is sharply critical of what he calls "ecclesiocentric accounts" of Scripture.[11] Bretherton interprets Jeremiah 29 as advocating the formation of a "common life with pagans and oppressors," which therefore entails a contemporary "call to become part of the public life of the city to reject the false prophets who perpetuate illusions of escape into a private world of gated communities, religious fantasies centered on Christ's immanent [sic] return, or daydreams of revolution."[12] Despite their exemplary attention to Jeremiah 29, such formulations raise the concern that this one text is being pushed too far.

It must be asked why Jeremiah 29 should be selected as a controlling text over other biblical texts, especially those possessing a more negative view of cities and foreigners. After all, the Bible's other allusions to Nineveh, Babylon, and Rome hardly seem friendly or admiring. Mark McEntire has recently attempted to sketch a more positive view of cities within the Bible, but he admits upfront that his effort is a corrective to a long tradition of interpreting biblical cities as "dens of iniquity."[13] Why Jeremiah 29 rather than the book of Jeremiah as a whole?[14] Or why Jeremiah 29 instead of the Tower of Babel story in Genesis 11? Or Nahum's celebration of the fall of Nineveh? Or Isaiah's judgment against Babylon (Isa 14:3–23)? Or, for that matter, Babylon/Rome in the book of Revelation? Privileging Jeremiah 29 without sufficient

---

in the Late Modern World (New York: Oxford University Press, 2010) 276–79.

9. Luke Bretherton, *Christianity and Contemporary Politics: The Conditions and Possibilities of Faithful Witness* (Malden, MA: Wiley-Blackwell, 2010) 4 and *passim*.

10. Augustine, *The City of God against the Pagans*, trans. R. W. Dyson (Cambridge: Cambridge University Press, 1998) 19: 26.

11. His critique primarily targets the work of Robert Jenson. Cf. Duncan B. Forrester, "The Scope of Public Theology," *Studies in Christian Ethics* 17.2 (2004) 5–19, who understands public theology to be "theology which seeks the welfare of the city *before* protecting the interests of the Church, or its proper liberty to preach the Gospel and celebrate the sacraments" (6, my emphasis).

12. Bretherton, *Christianity*, 5.

13. Mark McEntire, *Not Scattered or Confused: Rethinking the Urban World of the Hebrew Bible* (Louisville: Westminster John Knox, 2019) vii. The LXX of Jer 29:7 reads "land/country" rather than MT "city." But the difference between these two lexical options is reduced if "city" is understood as a synecdoche, as suggested by W. Eugene March, "Guess Who Is Coming to Dinner? Jeremiah 29:1–9 as an Invitation to Radical Social Change," in *God's Word for Our World, Volume 1: Biblical Studies in Honor of Simon John De Vries*, ed. J. Harold Ellens et al., JSOTSup 388 (New York: T. & T. Clark, 2004) 200–210 (207). On the question of how to define "city" in the Bible, see Michael Patrick O'Connor, "The Biblical Notion of the City," in *Constructions of Space II: The Biblical City and Other Imagined Spaces*, edited by Jon L. Berquist and Claudia V. Camp, LHBOTS 490 (New York: T. & T. Clark, 2008) 18–39.

14. Worthy of consultation in this regard would be John Hill, *Friend or Foe? The Figure of Babylon in the Book of Jeremiah MT*, BibInt 40 (Leiden: Brill, 1999).

recognition of these other canonical voices amounts to an illegitimate frontloading of the argument.

Precisely because I am a Christian OT scholar, I am also suspicious of this nod to the OT by Christian theologians. Is it perhaps because they cannot find a congenial text within the New Testament (NT), as would probably be their first impulse? As Stanley Hauerwas once remarked to me: "I worry that Christians are happy to ignore the Old Testament until they want to kill someone." In other words, the hermeneutical reasons for privileging an OT text within Christian theological discourse also normally go unacknowledged and under examination sometimes betray a desired outcome that actually stands in tension with the NT. I myself would want to preserve the potential for the OT to challenge and even amend the message of the NT at certain points, instead of proceeding with the common assumption that the NT always trumps the OT. However, my present point is that such negotiation among the biblical witnesses has to be done intentionally and explicitly, with adequate reasons and criteria provided. It is not enough to move the biblical furniture around. One must offer a compelling explanation for its arrangement.

The pitfall of over-emphasizing Jer 29:7 becomes even clearer in Louis Stulman and Paul Kim's introduction to the biblical prophetic literature, in which they characterize Jeremiah as enjoining the Judean community in Babylon to "surrender its old identity in the land and accept its marginal status in diaspora in order to survive and eventually flourish."[15] The notion that Israel is to *surrender* its identity, even if only in its "landed" aspects, is rather obviously not a view found in the book of Jeremiah. The book not only stresses the need for the exiles to retain their Jewish identity, it holds out for a return to the land of Israel on the part of the exilic community (e.g., Jer 23:5–8). Nevertheless, Monica Melancthon, in the blog *Political Theology Today*,[16] builds on Stulman and Kim's work by insisting that Jeremiah 29 calls present-day readers to "move away from any 'doctrinal narcissism' and find ways to make our theology politically and socially relevant." Melancthon tips her hand a bit more than she realizes when she goes on to assert "Our theology needs therefore to be transformed into a public theology if it seeks legitimation from and by the wider society." Why theology needs legitimation from wider society is left unexplained, but Melancthon's overriding interest clearly lies in challenging the church to "address issues affecting people" on the margins of society, "those that suffer from

---

15. Louis Stulman and Paul Hyun Chul Kim, *You Are My People: An Introduction to the Prophetic Literature* (Nashville: Abingdon, 2010) 103. They cite Jer 21:1–10 and 29:4–10 in support of their interpretation.

16. Monica Jyotsna Melancthon, "Seeking the Peace and Prosperity of the City: The Politics of Jeremiah 29:1, 4–7," *Political Theology Today*, posted October 7, 2013, at http://www.politicaltheology.com/blog/seeking-the-peace-and-prosperity-of-the-city-the-politics-of-jeremiah-2914-7.

political, social and cultural insecurity and discrimination."[17] And such issues would surely be good to address.

Yet from seemingly the opposite end of the political spectrum, Bruce Baker interprets Jeremiah 29 as "investment advice" in a post for Seattle Pacific University's Center for Integrity in Business.[18] For Baker, Jeremiah 29 is a "business parable" instructing us to "bring prosperity to the city in which we live" through the creation of wealth for ourselves and our neighbors. His view finds meaning in Jeremiah for the wealthy, or at least those who want to use their wealth, while Melancthon's concern lies with the poor and the disadvantaged. What both views share is an extraction of the biblical text from its historical and literary contexts, with the result that the particularity of Israel evaporates and with it an active role for the *church* in modern society. Both Melancthon and Baker offer distinctly individualistic accounts of Jeremiah 29's message.

Here then are the horns of the dilemma: on the one side, historically oriented biblical scholarship that seems largely unwilling or unable to consider the contemporary implications of Jeremiah 29, and on the other side, theological discourse that gives due consideration to the significance of Jeremiah 29 for contemporary reflection but makes suspiciously expansive and even contradictory claims for the text's meaning. Is it possible to thread a way between these two alternatives?

Jeremiah 29

To begin afresh with the biblical text is immediately to be confronted with several imposing challenges. The first one is to determine the nature of the text itself and its boundaries. As is well known, the Greek text (or LXX) of Jeremiah is approximately 15 percent shorter than the Masoretic text (MT) of Jeremiah in Hebrew, and the two versions are arranged in a significantly different order.[19] Most critical scholars now incline to the view that Greek Jeremiah is likely a translation of an earlier version of Hebrew Jeremiah, particularly since the discovery of 4Q71 (4QJer^b) at Qumran, a version of Jer 9:22—10:21 without vv. 6–8 and 10 of the Masoretic text, just as in

---

17. See also the womanist theoethical use of Jeremiah 29 by Valerie Miles-Tribble, "Restorative Justice as a Public Theology Imperative," *RevExp* 114.3 (2017) 366–79, who locates a warrant in Jeremiah for a liberative social ethic and Black Lives Matter.

18. Bruce D. Baker, "Investment Advice to the Exiles: Seek Prosperity (Jeremiah 29:1–7)," at http://blog/spu.edu/cib/2014/10/15/investment-advice-to-the-exiles-seek-prosperity-jeremiah-291–7/.

19. Emanuel Tov, "The Literary History of the Book of Jeremiah in Light of Its Textual History," in *The Greek and Hebrew Bible: Collected Essays on the Septuagint*, VTSup 72 (Leiden: Brill, 1999) 333–84.

Greek Jeremiah.[20] Such a determination might then mean that Masoretic Jeremiah is an expanded addition of the book, produced *after* Greek Jeremiah.

This general difficulty in the interpretation of the book pertains directly to the interpretation of MT Jeremiah 29, since vv. 16–20 of that chapter are not found at all within Greek Jeremiah, and v. 15 therefore appears immediately before v. 21. Accordingly, the authenticity of vv. 16–20 has been called into question.[21] Yet several scholars have argued instead that Greek Jeremiah represents a later shortening of MT Jeremiah, either for the most part intentionally, to enhance ideological or cultural conformity,[22] or unintentionally through scribal error.[23] Currently, most scholars do lean toward the priority of the Greek text, but the question remains open and individual passages seem best evaluated on a case-by-case basis.

The specific reconstruction of Jeremiah 29's literary formation presents another stiff challenge. Ever since the work of Bernhard Duhm, much effort has gone into identifying the original "letter" of Jeremiah thought to be embedded within the chapter. Duhm believed that it had consisted of vv. 4a, 5–7, and 11–14.[24] Verses 8–10 represented a later expansion that sought to explain the lengthened duration of the exile. Subsequent scholarship has sometimes reconstructed Jeremiah's original message as lacking any concrete mention of a return, both because some scholars believe the "seventy years" motif was a secondary addition throughout the book,[25] and also because the mention of a return would have subverted Jeremiah's counsel to participate constructively in Babylonian society.[26] That is, it is thought to be more likely that Jeremiah himself described the condition of the exiles as permanent (or

---

20. For further details, see Raymond de Hoop, "Textual, Literary, and Delimitation Criticism: The Case of Jeremiah 29 in M and S," in *The Impact of Unit Delimitation on Exegesis*, ed. Raymond de Hoop et al., Pericope 7 (Leiden; Brill, 2009) 29–62.

21. Hermann-Josef Stipp, "Probleme des redaktionsgeschichtlichen Modells der Entstehung des Jeremiabuches," in *Jeremia und die 'Deuteronomistische Bewegung,'* edited by Walter Gross, BBB 98 (Weinheim: Beltz Athenäum, 1995) 225–62.

22. Georg Fischer, "Zum Text des Jeremiabuches," *Bib* 78 (1997) 305–28; Arie van der Kooij, "Jeremiah 27:5–16: How Do MT and LXX Relate to Each Other?" *JNSL* 20 (1994) 59–78; Arie van der Kooij, "Zum Verhältnis von Textkritik und Literarkritik: Überlegungen anhand einiger Beispiele," in *Congress Volume: Cambridge 1995*, edited by J. A. Emerton, VTSup 66 (Leiden: Brill, 1997) 185–202.

23. See, e.g., Jack R. Lundbom, "Haplography in the Hebrew Vorlage of LXX Jeremiah," *HS* 66 (2005) 301–20.

24. Bernhard Duhm, *Das Buch Jeremia*, HAT (Tübingen: Mohr Siebeck, 1907) 229–30.

25. Karl-Friedrich Pohlmann, "Das 'Heil' des Landes—Erwägungen zu Jer 29,5–7," in *Mythos im Alten Testament und seiner Umwelt: Festschrift für Hans-Peter Müller zum 65. Geburtstag*, ed. Armin Lange et al., BZAW 278 (Berlin: de Gruyter, 1999) 144–64.

26. See the discussion in Daniel L. Smith-Christopher, *The Religion of the Landless: The Social Context of the Babylonian Exile* (1989; reprint, Eugene, OR: Wipf & Stock, 2015) 130. Smith-Christopher accepts this view.

indefinite) rather than temporary, since if the exiles knew their situation was temporary they might not have done what he wanted.

In my view, such judgments are unnecessary and facile. I think their logic probably reflects at some level a modernist unease with predictive prophecy, even as it exhibits how critical biblical scholarship often amounts to a sort of fundamentalism in reverse by employing overly literalistic criteria of consistency and dissimilarity.[27] Accordingly, Jeremiah (either the person or the book) is only thought capable of a "stay" or "go" message, without any possible complexity or ambiguity.

Recent Jeremiah scholarship is more skeptical about whether Jeremiah's letter can be reconstructed, as well as if it even ever existed.[28] Archaeological finds have provided additional evidence of Hebrew epistolary forms and conventions.[29] Ancient Hebrew letters typically begin with addressee information and/or greetings, using standard prepositional and verbal formulae, then transitioning to the body of the message, and ending with closing greetings and signatures.[30] Yet these conventions are for the most part absent in Jeremiah 29,[31] leading to the conclusion that, at best, Jeremiah 29 may contain the memory of such a letter, with its remembered content now reformulated according to another type of format. Dennis Pardee therefore cautiously styles the bulk of the chapter as "a series of prophetic oracles stated in the narrative frame to have been sent as a letter."[32] Gerhard Büsing and Klaas Smelik likewise advise interpreting the present text according to its formal or text-immanent literary features. In fact, the most striking feature of the received form of the text is its heavy use of the prophetic messenger formula, "thus says the

---

27. Indeed, the intensive search for Jeremiah's "original" message conformed to what is now easier to recognize as a historicized account of scriptural inspiration, even if that account had shifted from explicitly theological terminology to the secular language of the prophet as Romantic poet and "genius." Gerhard Büsing, "Ein alternativer Ausgangspunkt zur Interpretation von Jer 29," *ZAW* 104 (1992) 402 n2, neatly points out how Duhm characterized Jeremiah as a "born poet" (*geborene Dichter*) but deprecated Baruch as "no great mind" (*kein grosser Geist*) and dismissed later editors as "untalented authors" (*kein Autorentalent*). See Duhm, *Jeremia*, 13, 15, and 19 (respectively).

28. Klaas A. D. Smelik, "Letters to the Exiles: Jeremiah 29 in Context," *SJOT* 10 (1996) 282–93.

29. Dennis Pardee, *Handbook of Ancient Hebrew Letters*, SBLSBS 15 (Chico, CA: Scholars, 1982); Klaas A. D. Smelik, *Writings from Ancient Israel: A Handbook of Historical and Religious Documents* (Louisville: Westminster John Knox, 1992) 116–31; James M. Lindenberger, *Ancient Aramaic and Hebrew Letters*, 2nd ed., WAW 14 (Atlanta: SBL, 2003); Lutz Doering, *Ancient Jewish Letters and the Beginnings of Christian Epistolography*, WUNT 298 (Tübingen: Mohr Siebeck, 2012).

30. Pardee, *Handbook*, 145–52.

31. Pardee, *Handbook*, 177, notes that the first line of the supposed letter is a prophetic declaration, followed by imperatives: "There are no markers of relationship . . ." He also comments that Jer 29:4–23, if in fact a letter, would be "the longest Hebrew letter about which we know anything." Cf. Smelik, "Letters," 284.

32. Pardee, *Handbook*, 177. Note that vv. 26–28 of Jer 29 are presented by the narrative as a second letter, in which the first letter is summarized.

Lord" (*kōh ʾāmar yhwh*) and the related prophetic expression *nəʾûm yhwh*.³³ "Thus says the Lord" appears nine times throughout the chapter (Jer 29:4, 8, 10, 16, 17, 21, 25, 31, 32; cf. 30:2), threading its contents together.

Büsing identifies an introduction in vv. 1–3, followed by two major units consisting of the description of Jeremiah's message in vv. 4–32 and an incorporated letter from the rival prophet Shemaiah in vv. 24–31a. The central section (vv. 4–23) is further subdivided into Jeremiah's letter itself (vv. 4b–7) and three further "supporting" sections, each introduced by the messenger formula (vv. 8–10, 16–20, 21–23).³⁴ Smelik similarly finds an introduction (vv. 1–3) and four prophetic oracles in the present Hebrew text: vv. 4–7 (with a second and third part in vv. 8–14), vv. 15–19, 20–23, and 24–32.³⁵ Even with the differing details of their analyses, both scholars give priority to the literary features of the present text and develop an understanding of the chapter as something like scribal prophecy (i.e., the notion that later hands contributed to this text in an ongoing process of interpretive writing, with the result that the present, received text is a kind of palimpsest).³⁶ There is an appealing symmetry to such accounts, especially in Smelik's version. The first prophecy in vv. 4–14 concerns the Judeans in Babylon, while the second prophecy (vv. 15–19) describes the fate of Judeans left in the land.³⁷ The third prophecy criticizes two other Judean prophets in Babylon (vv. 20–23) and the fourth prophecy (vv. 24–32) addresses Shemaiah, another such prophet, and his antipathy toward Jeremiah.³⁸ Even though all of this oracular material is directed toward the exilic community in Babylon, its focus alternates between Babylon and Judah, and by doing so emphasizes their interrelationship.

---

33. Büsing, "Ausgangspunkt," 402–3; Smelik, "Letters," 284.

34. Büsing, "Ausgangspunkt," 403–4.

35. Smelik, "Letters," 292.

36. See further Christl M. Maier, "Jeremia am Ende. Prophetie als Schriftgelehrsamkeit," *EvT* 77.1 (2017) 44–56; Wolfgang Schütte, *Israels Exil in Juda: Untersuchungen zur Entstehung der Schriftprophetie*, OBO 270 (Göttingen: Vandenhoeck & Ruprecht, 2016). Older scholarship generally discounted literary additions. It is increasingly recognized that the OT writings formed gradually in an ongoing, accumulative process and are thus best regarded as "traditional literature" rather than a documentary archive; see Konrad Schmid, *The Old Testament: A Literary History* (Minneapolis: Fortress, 2012) xiii. William McKane, *A Critical and Exegetical Commentary on Jeremiah: Introduction and Commentary on Jeremiah I–XXV*, ICC (Edinburgh: T. & T. Clark, 1986) l–lxxxiii, helped to bring about this sea change in the field with his idea of Jeremiah as a "rolling corpus."

37. The status of v. 15 is difficult to determine. In its present position, it appears to function as a swing verse between the two oracular units. For an argument that v. 15 belongs with the unit ending in v. 14 instead of introducing the next unit prophecy in vv. 16–20, see Samuel Hildebrandt, "Are God's 'Good Plans' not Good Enough? The Place and Significance of Jer 29:15 in Jeremiah's Letter to the Exiles," *JSOT* 45 (2021) 561–75.

38. Smelik, "Letters," 286.

Not only do these approaches do better justice to the received form of the text (as opposed to speculating about its prehistory), they also connect the content of Jeremiah 29 to what is arguably the main theme of Jeremiah 27–28, namely false prophecy.[39] Interpretations of Jeremiah 29 in which the prophet's political activity is described as "pro-Babylonian" have badly missed the point by assuming that the prophet's purpose was pragmatic *Realpolitik*, and that the biblical text should be read in that light.[40] The received form of Jeremiah 29 advises patience in exile not out of political calculation but as theological opposition to false prophets who are preaching cheap grace. For these false prophets, the punishment already experienced by Israel was enough, and the Judeans should therefore expect an imminent return to their land (e.g., Hananiah's oracle in Jer 28:1–4). However, for Jeremiah—Jeremiah as a literary persona rather than "the historical Jeremiah"—the punishment is not yet sufficient and thus the Judeans must prepare for a longer stay in Babylon (Jer 29:10). This rationale is a reminder that Israel's presence in Babylon is not otherwise viewed within the book of Jeremiah as a blessing, or even an opportunity for one, but as a divine punishment for disobedience (e.g., Jer 5:19–31; 9:15–16; 15:5–9; 18:13–17; 30:12–17; 52:3).

Jeremiah 29:7

Using this reframed exegetical scholarship, the content of Jer 29:7 can be reexamined and possible analogies with the present reconsidered. Two key points will be developed. The first is that exile is presented in Jeremiah 29 as a time-bound rather than permanent reality. The second is again that exile is treated in Jeremiah 29 primarily as a punishment and a threat instead of an opportunity for mission.

On both points it is especially important to engage the influential reading of John Howard Yoder, who cited Jer 29:7 as a marker of a major shift in salvation history from the theocratic, Davidic project to diasporic existence, a shift that was both permanent and missional for God's people.[41] In a key paragraph, Yoder wrote:

---

39. Douglas Rawlinson Jones, *Jeremiah*, NCBC (Grand Rapids: Eerdmans, 1992) 360; Wolfgang Werner, *Das Buch Jeremia, Kapitel 25–52*, NSKAT 19/2 (Stuttgart: Katholisches Bibelwerk, 2003) 48–49. Sometimes Jeremiah 26 is included in this grouping, but Daniel L. Smith, "Jeremiah as a Prophet of Nonviolent Resistance," *JSOT* 43 (1989) 95–107 (105 n6) points out key differences between Jeremiah 26 and Jeremiah 27–28, such as their chronological references, the spellings of certain names, and the fact that Jeremiah appears in third person description in 26 but first person in 27:2—28:4.

40. Stulman and Kim, *You are My People*, 109. Cf. R. E. Clements, *Jeremiah*, Int (Atlanta: John Knox, 1988) 172; Walter Brueggemann, *To Build, to Plant: A Commentary on Jeremiah 26–32*, ITC (Grand Rapids: Eerdmans, 1991) 32.

41. It needs to be acknowledged that Yoder's legacy is now being questioned because of his abusive personal behavior toward women. See Karen V. Guth, "Doing Justice to the Complex Legacy of John Howard Yoder: Restorative Justice Resources in Witness and Feminist Ethics," *Journal of the Society*

> More than Christians are aware, Babylon itself very soon became the cultural center of world Jewry, from the age of Jeremiah until the time we in the West call the Middle Ages. The people who colonized the "Land of Israel," repeatedly, from the age of Jeremiah to that of Johanan ben Zakkai, and again still later, were supported financially and educationally from Babylon, and in lesser ways from the rest of the diaspora. Our Palestinocentric reading of the story is a mistake, though a very understandable one.[42]

Yoder was correct that a Jewish community persisted in Iraq for many centuries. According to the U.S. Holocaust Memorial Museum, 90,000 Jews lived in Baghdad as late as the 1940s, when a series of pogroms known as the Farhud began.[43] Thirty-four Jews remained prior to the Iraq War in 2003, when the last synagogue closed. The last rabbi left the city in 2010.[44] As of 2020, four Jews still lived in Baghdad.[45] However, Yoder's historical appeal overlooks the fact that some Jews were never exiled to Babylon in the first place but remained in the land (how many is currently a topic of debate[46]), and that while some Jews did remain in Babylon, other Jews eventually returned home (how many is again disputed[47]).

Moreover, the biblical writings decisively focus on the returnees as the normative bearers of the tradition.[48] Yoder's history devalues the renewed presence of Israel in the land, the rebuilding of the Jerusalem Temple, the reestablishment of centralized

---

of Christian Ethics 35.2 (2015) 119–39; Rachel Waltner Goossen, "Mennonite Bodies, Sexual Ethics: Women Challenge John Howard Yoder," *Journal of Mennonite Studies* 34 (2016) 247–59. Even so, Yoder's reading of Jeremiah continues to be influential, as shown by the fact that it is shared by some theologians who reach conclusions quite different from his own.

42. John H. Yoder, *For the Nations: Essays Evangelical and Public* (Grand Rapids: Eerdmans, 1997) 57.

43. As posted at https://encyclopedia.ushmm.org/content/en/article/the-farhud.

44. For the details of this history, see Reeva Spector Simon, Sara Reguer, and Michael Menachem Laskier, *The Jews of the Middle East and North Africa in Modern Times* (New York: Columbia University Press, 2003); Nissim Rejwan and Joel Beinin, *The Last Jews in Baghdad: Remembering a Lost Homeland* (Austin: University of Texas Press, 2010); Marina Benjamin, *Last Days in Babylon: The Story of the Jews of Baghdad* (London: Bloomsbury, 2013).

45. According to the Jewish Refugee blog: https://www.jewishrefugees.org.uk/2020/09/sitt-marcelle-dies-leaving-four-jews-in.html.

46. See Lester L. Grabbe, *Ancient Israel: What Do We Know and How Do We Know It*, rev. ed. (New York: Bloomsbury, 2017) 219, 255; Oded Lipschits, *The Fall and Rise of Jerusalem: Judah under Babylonian Rule* (Winona Lake, IN: Eisenbrauns, 2005).

47. See Bob Becking, "'We All Returned as One!': Critical Notes on the Myth of the Mass Return," in *Judah and the Judeans in the Persian Period*, ed. Oded Lipschits and Manfred Oeming (Winona Lake, IN: Eisenbrauns, 2006); Lester L. Grabbe, "'They Never Returned': Were the Babylonian Jewish Settlers Exiles or Pioneers?" in *By the Irrigation Canals of Babylon: Approaches to the Study of Exile*, ed. John J. Ahn and Jill Middlemas, LHBOTS 526 (New York: T. & T. Clark Continuum 2012) 158–72.

48. John C. Nugent, *The Politics of Yahweh: John Howard Yoder, the Old Testament, and the People of God*, Theopolitical Visions 12 (Eugene, OR: Cascade, 2011) 157–58; cf. Stephen B. Chapman, "The Old Testament and the Church after Christendom," *JTI* 9.2 (2015) 159–83.

power structures, and the evidence that exists, even if it is limited, that other diaspora communities continued to look to Jerusalem for advice and approval (e.g., the "Passover Letter" sent to Elephantine in 419 BCE).[49] Yoder likewise advances a dismissive view of Ezra and Nehemiah, alleging that they "each reconstituted a cult and a polity as a branch of the pagan imperial government."[50] The problem, of course, as Peter Leithart has trenchantly observed, is that the Palestinocentric reading "is the *canonical* account, which does not dismiss Ezra and Nehemiah as agents of a pagan empire but rather sees them as fulfilling authoritative prophecies, *Jeremiah's* prophecies not least."[51] Indeed, it is striking how little prominence the postexilic biblical writings give to the ongoing presence of a Jewish community in Babylon. The book of Jeremiah articulates a clear vision of a restored Davidic monarchy (Jer 23:5; 30:9; 33:15-17) within the land of Israel (30:1; 31:8, 16-17, 27-28).[52]

In Jeremiah 29 the stress falls primarily on the need for Israel to survive an extended period of exile by boosting its population size and, through participation in Babylonian society, gaining new insights into God's character and ways. *Israel* is the central focus of the chapter, not Babylon. The exiles are to build houses, plant gardens, and bear children, so that they "multiply there, and do not decrease" (Jer 29:6). *Multiplying* is just as important to the message of this chapter as welfare seeking. The text itself does not specify that its language of "taking wives" and "giving daughters" authorizes intermarriage with the Babylonians, although such an interpretation has been offered.[53] However that question is adjudicated, Israel's survival remains the prime concern. There is no indication that the exiles are to assimilate or that the divine goal is for them to produce a hybrid Jewish-Babylonian culture. To the contrary, God's injunction to "seek the welfare of the city" is framed in reflexive terms: "for in its prosperity you shall prosper." The purpose of social participation is for the Jewish community to survive and flourish.[54]

---

49. See further Melody D. Knowles, *Centrality Practiced: Jerusalem in the Religious Practice of Yehud and the Diaspora in the Persian Period*, ABS (Atlanta: Scholars, 2006). Pilgrimages to Jerusalem and donations to the Jerusalem Temple continued in the postexilic period. However, a divide between East and West did open up within Judaism because of the Babylonian exile, and this divide greatly widened after the destruction of the Second Temple in 70 CE. See Arye Edrei and Doron Mendels, "A Split Jewish Diaspora," *JSP* 16.2 (2007) 91-137.

50. Yoder, *Nations*, 74.

51. Peter J. Leithart, *Defending Constantine: The Twilight of an Empire and the Dawn of Christendom* (Downers Grove, IL: IVP Academic, 2010) 296 (his italics).

52. Leithart, *Constantine*, 295.

53. March, "Guess Who," 205-6. March points to 2 Kgs 24:13-17 as evidence that the exiles were largely male and without numerous single females, but this is an argument made from silence ("There is no suggestion that any large number of unmarried females were included among the company deported.").

54. Smith, "Jeremiah," 104. Cf. Waldemar Janzen, "John Howard Yoder's Ecclesiology: As Seen by

The biblical text similarly implies that a longer stay of exile will be necessary not only because of God's determination to destroy old Israel (see Jer 27:8, "until I have completed its destruction"),[55] but because of the people's need to learn the true meaning of "whole-hearted" obedience (Jer 29:13). Only once the exiles have learned such unrestricted obedience will a return to their homeland be possible. As Jer 29:12–14 declares, "*Then* when you call upon me and come and pray to me, I will hear you ... I will let you find me, says the Lord, and I will restore your fortunes and gather you from all the nations and all the places where I have driven you, says the Lord, and I will bring you back to the place from which I sent you into exile."[56] One stated reason for its exile is precisely Israel's refusal to listen to God's servants the prophets (Jer 29:19). A crucial spiritual need for the exiles is thus to hear God's word (Jer 29:20) and learn to judge rightly between true and false prophets, in keeping with the theme of Jeremiah 27–28.

In sum, Jer 29:7 is both less radical and more radical than many contemporary interpreters would have it. It is less radical because the exiles are not told to live in Babylon permanently or to adopt Babylonian customs or to cease being Jews. They are to remain resident aliens and their liminal social situation is further depicted in the books of Daniel and Esther. The experience of exile is presented primarily as a punishment and a training ground for the exiled Judeans before they have a go at rebuilding their own country and maintaining their identity in it. Jeremiah 29:7 is more radical because unlike the situation of Christians in the modern West, the exiles were defeated captives, without the rights of citizens, outside their own land, in the country of their military conquerors.

Contemporary Appropriation

So does Jer 29:7 have any relevance for current discussions in political theology? I believe so. Even though the main focus of the biblical text is on *Israel's* survival and spiritual well-being, the text's perspective cannot be adequately described as merely utilitarian or self-interested. To the contrary, Jer 29:7 acknowledges what Bernd Wannenwetsch has called "a genuine interwovenness of welfare."[57] The emphasis is

---

an Appreciative Critic," in *The Church Made Strange for the Nations: Essays in Ecclesiology and Political Theology*, ed. Paul G. Doerksen and Karl Koop, Princeton Theological Monograph Series (Eugene, OR: Pickwick, 2011) 36–51 (46 n. 50): "the exhortation to seek Babylon's welfare is ultimately motivated by Israel's need for survival rather than by a 'missionary concern' for Babylon."

55. A related motif is that Babylon has its own prescribed end within the divine plan (Jer 27:7, "until the time of [Nebuchadnezzar's] own land comes").

56. My emphasis. "Then" is one interpretation of the initial *waw*-consecutive verb, which could also be rendered simply as "and." Either way, a sequence is presumed.

57. Bernd Wannenwetsch, "'For in its welfare you will find your welfare': Political Realism and the

on Israel as God's elect people and chosen instrument, but there are accompanying convictions about God's universal sovereignty and the ultimate purpose of Israel's election as being the repair of the entire world:[58] "For Jeremiah, his summoning of the people to genuine political participation was based on his confidence that eventually all human societies (gentile, like the Babylonians', included) were under the reign of one and the same God, whether they knew this or not."[59] God has a plan in place for Babylon too (Jer 25:13–14) and all the peoples of the world (Jer 25:15–26). Even in times of imperial domination, therefore, there can still be constructive engagement by God's people in the structures of society, not for the sake of the empire but for the sake of God's reign.

This aspect of the biblical presentation is encapsulated in the Hebrew verb "seek" (*drš*) in Jer 29:7. Rather than some vague injunction, the Hebrew verb in this context likely introduces a technical phrase for cultic oracular activity. "Seek the welfare"—literally, "peace" (*'et-šālôm*)—of the city" would then mean specifically to request a *shalom*-oracle on behalf of the city (see Jer 38:4).[60] That such an oracle could transpire at a distance from Jerusalem and apart from the Jerusalem Temple may itself be significant.[61] Yet the linguistic usage articulates the text's overall perspective quite precisely: it is Israel's ongoing existence and worship life that counts, but Israel's worship can and should be directed toward the flourishing of all human society. This interpretation is strengthened by the parallel directive to "pray to the LORD" on the city's behalf (Jer 29:7; cf. 29:12). Such close attention to the language of the text highlights how the terminology of Jer 29:7 ironically becomes secularized in many theological discussions by being taken to refer to "seeking" and "peace" in general, exemplifying an attitude of "neutral moral goodness."[62] Put differently, what many proposals for political theology advocate is an account of Christian theology *without a doctrine of election*. This is a problem because then Christian political action is either limited to individuals, or some other group, such as the state, is invested

---

Limits of the Augustinian Framework," *Political Theology* 12.3 (2011) 457–65.

58. For a discussion of "repair of the world" as a traditional conviction in Judaism, see Gilbert S. Rosenthal, "Tikkun ha-Olam: The Metamorphosis of a Concept," *JR* 85.2 (2005) 214–40.

59. Wannenwetsch, "For in its welfare," 464.

60. Jonathan P. Sisson, "Jeremiah and the Jerusalem Conception of Peace," *JBL* 105 (1986) 429–42. His insight is accepted in Leslie C. Allen, *Jeremiah: A Commentary*, OTL (Louisville: Westminster John Knox, 2008) 321. It has also been argued that the term *shalom*, which was used as a greeting (in both oral and written contexts), is suggestive of a letter form. See Smith, "Jeremiah," 97.

61. Helga Weippert, "Fern von Jerusalem: die Exilsethik von Jer 29,5–7," in *Zion—Ort der Begegnung; Festschrift für Laurentius Klein zur Vollendung des 65. Lebensjahres*, ed. Ferdinand Hahn et al. (Bodenheim: Athenäum Hain Hanstein, 1993) 127–39.

62. Karl Barth, *Church and State*, trans. G. Ronald Howe, Church Classics (Greenville, SC: Smyth & Helwys, 1991) 81.

with salvific agency. In the end, Jer 29:7 warrants the view that the church not only has a responsibility to improve the administration of justice within society but to become a just community.[63]

In my judgment, the uses to which Jer 29:7 is being put in contemporary political theology tend to underplay the corruptive dimension of politics and the state[64] as well as the proper missional witness of biblical faith.[65] Political theologians are often reacting appropriately to the privatization of faith enforced within neo-liberal politics, on the one hand, and, on the other, the bourgeois solipsism of many current faith communities. But I believe these theologians are insufficiently alert to the ways in which a focus on social engagement can undermine the church's attention to the vitality of its own tradition. Part of the reason may be that such theologians do not think they need to attend to the health of the church, especially if they are coming from an established church continuing to operate with cultural status, legal advantage, and social privilege.[66] For those of us in disestablished "free" churches, however, the vitality of the contemporary church is an urgent concern. And, in fact, even established churches are becoming more like free churches today because of their waning social cachet and influence.

Social justice is also of course an urgent concern. But the prior question is: how will Christian advocates for social justice be created? The Rev. Dr. Martin Luther King Jr. did not spring into action fully formed, like Athena from the forehead of Zeus. Nor did King discover social justice in a book or university syllabus. He was raised in a preacher's family with two devout Christian parents and grew to maturity within the faith community of Ebenezer Baptist Church in Atlanta, Georgia. Although it remains little known, his given name was actually Michael King, like his father. But his father took to calling himself Martin Luther King, particularly after he participated in the 1934 Baptist World Congress in Berlin (Germany) and

---

63. Stanley Hauerwas, *Against the Nations: War and Survival in a Liberal Society* (Notre Dame, IN: University of Notre Dame Press, 1992) 75.

64. Wannenwetsch, "For in its welfare," 461.

65. Nigel Biggar, "Seek the Welfare of the City: A Response to *Christianity and Contemporary Politics*," *Political Theology* 12.3 (2011) 453–57 (457): "But if a form of activity does not move agents to embrace God, and eventually to profess belief in God, then how on earth is it a *witness*? This needs much more explication, otherwise the significance of theological belief is reduced to that of one of many diverse and equal matrices of neighbour-love—and we are returned thereby to a form of liberal Protestantism" (his emphasis).

66. E.g., the argument of Biggar, "Seek the Welfare," 455–56, that an establishment of religion can "keep Christians honest" by forcing them to abandon "negative stereotypes of the world" and exercise pastoral responsibility for all members of society. However, Biggar conflates "Anglicans" and "Christians" in his argument, thereby eliminating from consideration the prejudicial effect of establishment on non-Anglican Christians as well as non-Christians.

encountered the Reformation legacy of Martin Luther more closely.[67] (Two uncles of Michael King Sr. were also named Martin and Luther.) So both he and his son gradually became known as Martin Luther King, Senior and Junior, although among some close associates they remained known as "Big Mike" and "Little Mike."[68] The point is that Martin Luther King Jr.'s own name is a tradition-bound construct signaling his deep embeddedness within a web of historical social relations, the Christian tradition, and, yes, the church.[69]

If theologians do not attend to the question of Christian formation, even the most winsome account of political theology will find itself without any takers. Where will the people come from who actually *want* to be both theological and political, who will possess the Christian virtues and character necessary for constructive, transformative political activity and advocacy in wider society? Especially at the cost of suffering and possible loss of life? Without this kind of formation, Christians will only replicate the cultural mindset and political manners of current society.[70] The question is not *whether* people will be formed but *how* they will be formed and according to what pattern.[71] Because the Bible's prophetic tradition is so often invoked as a warrant for social action, it is important to observe that the biblical prophets not only critique injustice but strive to create greater justice through rehabilitated social practices and institutions.[72] There is thus a danger in focusing on *performative* uses of Scripture to the exclusion of *formative* uses of Scripture. Scripture not only

---

67. Taylor Branch, *Parting the Waters: America in the King Years, 1954–63* (New York: Simon & Schuster, 1988) 43–44.

68. Martin Luther King Sr. *Daddy King: An Autobiography* (New York: Morrow, 1980) 26, 87–88. King Senior attributed the name change to a request from his father, James Albert King, who had apparently always considered his son's given name to be Martin Luther, after his two brothers. King Junior was also sometimes known to family members and friends as "M. L."

69. For more on the ecclesial dimension of King's political activities, see Richard Lischer, *The Preacher King: Martin Luther King, Jr. and the Word that Moved America*, updated ed. (New York: Oxford University Press, 2020).

70. For a powerful account of the church's failure to provide adequate spiritual formation for moral action by Christians, see Joshua T. Searle, *Theology after Christendom: Forming Prophets for a Post-Christian World* (Eugene, OR: Cascade, 2018). Unfortunately, Searle does not propose much in the way of a constructive alternative.

71. See further John M. Lewis, "The Church and the Formation of Political Conscience," *RevExp* 73.2 (1976) 191–204; Kaitlyn Schiess, *The Liturgy of Politics: Spiritual Formation for the Sake of Our Neighbors* (Downers Grove, IL: InterVarsity, 2020); Scott Aniol, "Changed from Glory into Glory: The Liturgical Formation of the Christian Faith," *Journal of Spiritual Formation and Soul Care* 14.1 (2021) 48–71.

72. Terence E. Fretheim, "The Prophets and Social Justice: A Conservative Agenda," *WW* 28.2 (2008) 159–68; Daniel Pryfogle, "Seeing a New Thing: The Prophet Must Prophesy for the Institution," *Baptist News Global* (July 12, 2019); https://baptistnews.com/article/seeing-a-new-thing-the-prophet-must-prophesy-for-the-institution/#.YQbcCEApA2w.

instructs Christians in how to live out their faith, it inspires them and instructs them in how to become Christians and be part of the people of God.

The stories of Joseph, Daniel, and Esther would be especially profitable as Bible studies for an "exilic" church in post-Christendom society.[73] These stories offer more textured strategies for participation within a foreign host culture than Jeremiah 29, precisely because they stay alert to the ever-present danger of cultural accommodation. It is instructive that Judaism developed the thrust of Jer 29:7 into a rabbinic dictum: *dĭna' dəmalkŭta' dĭna'* or "the law of the land is the law."[74] This formulation foregrounds the limiting aspect of Jeremianic teaching (i.e., not to violate secular law, when to submit to gentile courts, etc.) more than its positive thrust (i.e., how to contribute constructively to gentile society).[75] But Jeremiah 29 does encourage positive contributions and, as Yoder rightly noted, the history of Judaism provides many impressive examples of doing so. Judaism has traditionally enriched a wide variety of host cultures, yet without attempting to take over those cultures and dominate them—partly, to be sure, because of imposed legal restrictions and anti-Jewish prejudice. But domination, it must be said, became instead the Christian pattern.

This Constantinian temptation lingers on, both wittingly and unwittingly, in some proposals for political theology, both liberal and conservative. Both camps reach first for action by the state and changes to federal policy.[76] The biblical vision is different, I would suggest, and no less political although more "sectarian."[77] True, a

---

73. See further Daniel L. Smith-Christopher, *A Biblical Theology of Exile*, OBT (Minneapolis: Fortress, 2002); Luke Bretherton, *Hospitality as Holiness: Christian Witness amid Moral Diversity* (Burlington, VT: Ashgate, 2006) 128–32.

74. Menachem Lorberbaum et al., eds, *The Jewish Political Tradition: Volume 1, Authority* (New Haven: Yale University Press, 2000) 431.

75. Francois-Xavier Licari, *An Introduction to Jewish Law* (Cambridge: Cambridge University Press, 2019) 143–53.

76. At one level this focus on the state likely stems from a pragmatic determination that only the state still appears to have the power to effect social change. The lack of viable intermediary social associations, networks, and institutions constitutes a "missing middle" in contemporary U.S. society. See Marc J. Dunkelman, *The Vanishing Neighbor: The Transformation of American Community* (New York: Norton, 2014); Robert D. Putnam, *Bowling Alone: The Collapse and Revival of American Community*, 20th anniversary ed. (New York: Simon & Schuster, 2020). Just for this reason, a crucial task for the contemporary church is to assist in efforts to restore local communities. See further Robert D. Putnam and Lewis M. Feldstein, with Dan Cohen, *Better Together: Restoring the American Community* (New York: Simon & Schuster, 2004); Robert D. Putnam and David E. Campbell, *American Grace: How Religion Divides and Unites Us* (New York: Simon & Schuster, 2010); Wayne Gordon and John M. Perkins, *Making Neighborhoods Whole: A Handbook for Christian Community Development* (Downers Grove, IL: InterVarsity, 2013).

77. The term "sectarian" is unfairly used as a smear by some. It also frames the issue at stake in a one-sided fashion. For an early step in the direction of its rehabilitation, still well worth reading, see George A. Lindbeck, "The Sectarian Future of the Church," in *The God Experience*, edited by Joseph P. Whelen (New York: Newman, 1971) 226–43.

fully sectarian ecclesiology is not a viable option, since for the Bible *withdrawal* from the world remains an abdication of responsibility. What the Bible instead promotes is the construction and maintenance of a contrast community that will instruct and inspire wider society by the beauty and surpassing justice of its example, even as it strategically engages that society in order to provide a living witness to God and God's purposes in the world.[78] *The Bible's political program is God's people, Israel.*[79] For Christians, this is the task and mission of the church as the New Israel.[80] As Jacques Ellul famously challenged his fellow Christians: "How can we be the question that God puts to the world?"[81] The task of the church is not only to *do* something but to *be* something.

This fundamentally Jewish perspective is taken up and affirmed within the NT as a call to exist as a "body" of believers (e.g., 1 Cor 12:4–31) and simultaneously as a religious duty of loyalty to the pagan/secular state (e.g., Matt 22:21; Rom 13:1–7; 1 Pet 2:13–17). That duty of secular loyalty expresses itself characteristically in prayer (1 Tim 2:1–4), just as in Jeremiah 29. Yet there is also found within the NT the notion, shared with Jeremiah 29 as well, that the household of faith is deserving

---

78. Reinhard Hütter, *Suffering Divine Things: Theology as Church Practice* (Grand Rapids: Eerdmans, 2000) 170–71, has protested against an account of the church as contrast community, arguing that then society provides the basic reference point for the church's self-understanding and the church is locked into an exclusive stance of resistance. This point is well taken, but I would go a step farther by affirming the internal pluralism of both church and society, with the consequence that there will be multiple, *ad hoc* quarrels and alliances between various groups within church and society, and with the memberships of those groups in many cases being overlapping. In such contexts, "againstness" cannot be the exclusive criterion of faithfulness. Yet when the church is faithful to its Lord, the biblical witnesses anticipate opposition and hostility from the nations alongside the nations' repentance and salvation. See the formulation of George A. Lindbeck, *The Church in a Postliberal Age*, edited by James J. Buckley (Grand Rapids: Eerdmans, 2003) 159: "[The church's] role is instrumental: it exists in order to witness to the nations. It does this, however, not primarily by striving to save souls or to improve the social order, but by being the body of Christ, the communal sign of the promised redemption, in the time between the times."

79. Janzen, "Yoder's Ecclesiology," 47, makes the point that the book of Ruth paints almost the opposite picture of the one in Jeremiah: "Naomi and Ruth return from 'diaspora' (Moab) to the 'promised land' (Bethlehem) and experience the protections and care of a Torah-abiding community (observing the laws of inheritance, gleaning, and levirate marriage), and therewith the leading of God within the frame of the Abrahamic blessing of land and descendants, while the Davidic monarchy appears as a promise for the future." What unites the centrifugal movement of Jeremiah and the centripetal movement of Ruth is their common rootedness in the particularity of Israel.

80. With this identity the church properly does not seek to replace Jewish Israel but to extend it. See Frank Spina, "Israel as a Figure for the Church: The Radical Nature of a Canonical Approach to Christian Scripture," in *The Usefulness of Scripture: Essays in Honor of Robert W. Wall*, edited by Daniel Castelo, et al. (University Park, PA: Eisenbrauns, 2018) 3–23; Demetrios E. Tonias, "Fulfillment in Continuity: The Orthodox Christian Theology of Biblical Israel," *Review of Ecumenical Studies* 11.2 (2019) 209–36.

81. Jacques Ellul, *The Politics of God and the Politics of Man*, trans. Geoffrey W. Bromiley (Grand Rapids: Eerdmans, 1972) 142.

of special care (Matt 25:40; Gal 6:10), even as Christians and Christian leaders are liable to more severe punishment when they betray their vocation (1 Cor 6:8; Heb 10:26–31; Jas 3:1). In the NT, the way to peace and justice in society is still through the people of God.

Viewed comprehensively, somewhat differing perspectives on the Babylonian exile exist throughout the OT, but they all view it negatively.[82] However, even though the exile as a historical event concludes with the return of some Judeans to Yehud and the reestablishment of the Judean community and its institutions, there emerges within the postexilic biblical writings an unexpected, ongoing typology of exile. It turns out that once Israel is back in the land, an exilic consciousness lingers.

In Ezra 9, in a prayer before the returned community in Jerusalem, Ezra surprisingly declares "we are slaves," even as he thanks God for extending "steadfast love before the kings of Persia, to give us new life" (Ezra 9:9). Israel's return has not entirely ended its oppression. Likewise in Nehemiah 9, Ezra prays to God, "Here we are, slaves to this day—slaves in the land that you gave to our ancestors to enjoy its fruit and its good gifts. Its rich yield goes to the kings whom you have set over us because of our sins; they have power also over our bodies and over our livestock at their pleasure, and we are in great distress" (Neh 9:36–37). The return from Babylon has not fully resolved Israel's political situation, with the result that the postexilic Judeans remain like slaves or exiles, only now in their own land.[83]

This extended sense of exile is also on display in Daniel 9, in which Jeremiah's predicted seventy years of exile (Jer 25:11–12; 29:10–14) are lengthened to seventy

---

82. Isaiah M. Gafni, *Land, Center, and Diaspora: Jewish Constructs in Late Antiquity*, JSPSup 21 (Sheffield: Sheffield Academic, 1997) 21. See further John Kessler, "Images of Exile: Representations of the 'Exile' and 'Empty Land' in Sixth to Fourth Century BCE Yehudite Literature," in *The Concept of Exile in Ancient Israel and its Historical Contexts*, edited by Ehud Ben Zvi and Christoph Levin, BZAW 404 (Berlin: de Gruyter, 2010) 309–51; Nicholas G. Piotrowski, "The Concept of Exile in Late Second Temple Judaism: A Review of Recent Scholarship," *CurBR* 15.2 (2017) 214–47. There may be a hint of a more positive assessment in Deut 8:1–10, which regards Israel's forty years in the wilderness as a time of redemptive chastisement prior to entering the promised land. There is also a sense in which Israel's exodus from Egypt is "for" the nations (e.g., Exod 7:5; 9:14–15; 15:14–17). Both of these traditions might show the influence of later reflection on Israel's exilic experience. On post-biblical understandings of exile, some of them positive, see Gafni, *Land*, 24–40.

83. For additional examples, see Adele Berlin, "The Exile: Biblical Ideology and Its Postmodern Interpretation," in *Literary Construction of Identity in the Ancient World: Proceedings of the Conference Literary Fiction and the Construction of Identity in Ancient Literatures: Options and Limits of Modern Literary Approaches in the Exegesis of Ancient Texts, Heidelberg, July 10–13, 2006*, edited by Hanna Liss and Manfred Oeming (Winona Lake, IN: Eisenbrauns, 2010) 341–56, esp. 351: "exile came to be understood not merely as a historical event in the past but as an existential mode of being." See also Michael A. Knibb, "The Exile in the Literature of the Intertestamental Period," *HeyJ* 17 (1976) 253–72; Bob Becking et al., *From Babylon to Eternity: The Exile Remembered and Constructed in Text and Tradition* (Oakville, CT: Equinox, 2009); Ehud Ben Zvi and Christoph Levin, eds., *The Concept of Exile in Ancient Israel and Its Historical Contexts*, BZAW 404 (New York: de Gruyter, 2010); Martien A. Halvorson-Taylor, *The Metaphorization of Exile in the Hebrew Bible*, VTSup 141 (Leiden: Brill, 2011).

"weeks" of years (Dan 9:24–27).[84] From this vantage point, Jeremiah's injunction to "seek the welfare of the city" can indeed be viewed as counsel extending beyond the immediate circumstances of its initial speech-act situation.[85] If exile persists in some fashion, then seeking the welfare of the exilic host culture can persist as well.[86] In the OT's postexilic literature, however, the primary force of that counsel is directed to Israel's well-being within the context of an Israel restored to its land but nonetheless subsisting as a disempowered minority under foreign domination.

Remarkably, an exilic sensibility continues into the NT. The letter of James, directed to Christians, is addressed to "the twelve tribes of the dispersion" (Jas 1:1). The letter of 1 Peter is similarly addressed to "the exiles of the dispersion . . . who have been chosen and destined by God the Father and sanctified by the Spirit to be obedient to Jesus Christ and to be sprinkled with his blood" (1 Pet 1:1–2a; cf. 17).[87] With such formulations, early Christians are acknowledged to retain an exilic identity and this identity becomes a canonical one.[88] Their exilic condition is no longer time-bound and no longer an expression of punishment. Exile or diaspora has instead become a typological and permanent dimension of Christian existence.

The Christian Bible as a whole is thus strongly exilic in its overall orientation and thrust, and a typology of exile frames the Bible's understanding of political action on the part of the people of God.[89] The writer of 1 Peter develops this point of view, drawing on the legacy of Jeremiah: "Beloved, I urge you as aliens and exiles to abstain from the desires of the flesh that wage war against the soul. Conduct

---

84. *Pace* Steven M. Bryan, "The End of Exile: The Reception of Jeremiah's Prediction of a Seventy-Year Exile," *JBL* 137.1 (2018) 107–26.

85. John Hill, "'Your Exile Will Be Long': The Book of Jeremiah and the Unended Exile," in *Reading the Book of Jeremiah: A Search for Coherence*, edited by Martin Kessler (Winona Lake, IN: Eisenbrauns, 2004) 149–61.

86. Thus, there is ultimately room to develop a stronger account of Yoder's "Jeremianic shift," one that would be framed canonically and typologically rather than historically in the way that Yoder attempted. It would need to be able to credit landedness as well as landlessness and not dismiss the reality of postexilic Israel. See further John Howard Yoder, *The Jewish-Christian Schism Revisited*, edited by Michael G. Cartwright and Peter Ochs (Scottdale, PA: Herald, 2008); Peter Ochs, *Another Reformation: Postliberal Christianity and the Jews* (Grand Rapids: Baker Academic, 2011).

87. See Andrew M. Mbuvi, *Temple, Exile, and Identity in 1 Peter*, LNTS 345 (New York: T. & T. Clark, 2007); Friedrich Wilhelm Horn, "Christen in der Diaspora: zum Kirchenverständnis des 1. Petrusbriefs," *KD* 63.1 (2017) 3–17.

88. See further James M. Scott, ed., *Exile: Old Testament, Jewish, and Christian Conceptions*, JSJSup 56 (Leiden: Brill, 1997); Merril Kitchen, "Another Exile: 'Jesus and his brothers' in the Gospel of Matthew," *ABR* 59 (2011) 1–12; Timo Eskola, *A Narrative Theology of the New Testament: Exploring the Metanarrative of Exile and Restoration*, WUNT 350 (Tübingen: Mohr Siebeck, 2015); James M. Scott, *Exile: A Conversation with N. T. Wright* (Downers Grove, IL: IVP Academic, 2017).

89. Rodney Clapp, *A Peculiar People: The Church as Culture in a Post-Christian Society* (Downers Grove, IL: InterVarsity, 1996); Stanley Hauerwas and Will Willimon, *Resident Aliens: Life in the Christian Colony*, exp. 25th anniversary ed. (Nashville: Abingdon, 2014).

yourselves honorably among the Gentiles, so that, though they malign you as evildoers, they may see your honorable deeds and glorify God when he comes to judge" (1 Pet 2:11–12). Crucially, this idea of conducting oneself honorably, with its evident concern about wider society, is not offered as a strategy for winning social approval but as a means of encouraging non-Christians to come to know God (cf. Matt 5:13–16).

Perhaps the clearest vision for how the early church could live out its Jeremianic heritage is found in the Letter to Diognetus (5.1–17), usually dated to the second century CE:

> Christians are distinguished from other[s] . . . neither by country, nor language, nor the customs which they observe. For they neither inhabit cities of their own, nor employ a peculiar form of speech, nor lead a life which is marked out by any singularity . . . But inhabiting Greek as well as barbarian cities . . . and following the customs of the natives in respect to clothing, food, and the rest of their ordinary conduct, they display to us their wonderful and confessedly striking method of life. As citizens, they share in all things with others, and yet endure all things as if foreigners. Every foreign land is to them as their native country, and every land of their birth as a land of strangers . . . They pass their days on earth but they are citizens of heaven. They obey the prescribed laws, and at the same time surpass the laws by their lives. They love all . . . and are persecuted by all. They are unknown and condemned; they are put to death, and restored to life. They are poor, yet make many rich; they are in lack of all things and yet abound in all; they are dishonored, and yet in their very dishonor are glorified. They are evil spoken of, and yet are justified; they are reviled, and bless; they are insulted, and repay the insult with honor; they do good, yet are punished as evil doers.[90]

What is both striking and sobering about this ancient vision of Christian community is how distinctive that community was once held to be, so that the truth and the power of its beliefs came from the character of its example.

---

90. For convenience, I cite the text as it appears in Hunter, *Change*, 284–85. I have shortened it slightly. For a critical edition, see Clayton N. Jefford, ed., *The Epistle to Diognetus (with the Fragment of Quadratus): Introduction, Texts, and Commentary* (Oxford: Oxford University Press, 2013). It is unclear how much the letter's description of the Christian life is a statement of fact and how much it is wishful thinking.

WHO CAN LEAD A FLOCK OF SHEPHERDS? PAUL, THE PILLARS, AND POLITICAL CHALLENGES IN OUR CHURCHES TODAY

Timothy Milinovich

Introduction

There are three things that Americans are taught from childhood not to talk about in pleasant company—sex, religion, and politics. For this reason, the confluence of political or moral topics within religious contexts can have awkward results for leaders and worshippers alike. What is religious, what is moral, and what is political can sometimes become amalgamated into an individual's own concept of what is right and wrong, regardless of what their faith community believes. But in a society that is continuously fractured by competing narratives in the larger culture and social media, church leaders might ask how they can delve into issues like war, social justice, abortion, poverty, and so many other issues that affect not only their faithful in the pews, but the traditions and concepts understood as central to the gospel?

This article will examine Paul's account of his meetings with the Jerusalem Pillars in Gal 2:1–14 to see whether and how those events could shed light on how pastors operate in churches during politically sensitive times today. This can relate to issues-based politics, which are very visible from the pulpit and billboards, but also the watercooler level of politics that can be present in any workplace or area where power is a commodity, including churches.

The text of Gal 2:1–14 offers a unique set of examples from early Christianity by which to examine church leaders disputing culturally sensitive topics in various modes or formats. Circumcision and dietary codes were issues that demonstrated complex intersectionality with cultural identity outside the faith community, but also impacted traditional operations and narratives within the community as well.

The ways these topics were addressed in an increasingly heterogenous community as the gospel spread—while the leadership remained largely homogenous—created new challenges not unlike the societal changes our own churches' environments might encounter today.¹ Galatians 2:1–14 offers glimpses of these interactions in five different settings, albeit from one participant's perspective. But this article will look at how the models offered may still be gleaned for how similarly intersectional topics can be discussed in faith communities today.

To do this, the first section outlines the key points of Paul's rhetorical argument in the text. The second section offers evidence that there was more tension between Paul and Jerusalem than is often considered in modern scholarship. In the third and main section, I treat the major events in 2:1–14 and the letter itself from the perspective of power dynamics. Lastly, I will draw out observations from Paul and the Pillars' political interactions—the good and the bad—that can help modern pastoral leaders and workers consider pathways to addressing these issues in their own churches.

Context for Galatians 2:1–14

The content of Galatians 1–2 is well-traveled, but some comment here will offer basis for our analysis further below. Paul narrates four major events in the opening of his letter to the Galatians: his calling (1:11–17), his first meeting with Peter and James in Jerusalem (1:18–20), a second meeting with the Pillars involving the "false brothers" (2:1–10), and the Antioch incident (2:11–14).

In addition to these, we can surmise at least three other events pertinent to the content and audience's reception of the letter. Paul had founded the community with Barnabas (4:12–16). New missionaries arrived after Paul's departure teaching circumcision (4:17–20).² And, lastly, Paul was made aware of the community's re-

---

1. Circumcision, for example, was central to some first-century Jewish groups' concepts of covenant identity and practice, as were certain practices of dietary codes or table fellowship. See Paul Fredriksen, "God Is Jewish, but Gentiles Don't Have to Be: Ethnicity and Eschatology in Paul's Gospel," in *The Message of Paul the Apostle within Second Temple Judaism*, edited by Frantisek Abel (Lanham, MD: Lexington/Fortress Academic, 2020) 3–30; David A. Bernat, "Circumcision," in *EDEJ*, 471–74; Bradley B. Blue, "Food Offered to Idols and Jewish Food Laws," in *DPL*, 306–10.

2. The discussion of the identity of Paul's opponents is complicated by the lack of textual evidence and the vituperative rhetoric he uses to describe them (see George Howard, *Paul: Crisis in Galatia: A Study in Early Christianity* SNTSMS 35 (Cambridge: Cambridge University Press, 1990 1–19. On the challenge of invective, see A. B. Du Toit "Alienation and Re-Identification as Pragmatic Strategies in Galatians," *Neot* 26 (1992) 279–95. Some scholars consider Paul's description of the opponents to be informative despite its polemical nature; John M. G. Barclay, "Mirror-Reading a Polemical Letter: Galatians as a Test Case," *JSNT* 10 (1987) 73–93; Thomas R. Schreiner, *Galatians* (Exegetical Commentary on the New Testament; Grand Rapids: Zondervan, 2011) 39–51. A growing number of scholars, however, point to the polemical rhetoric as requiring some caution in the interpreter in reconstructing the identities and ideas of the opponents. See Hans Dieter Betz, *Galatians: A Commentary on Paul's Letter to the Churches in Galatia* (Hermeneia; Minneapolis: Fortress, 1989) 80–85; James D. G. Dunn, *The Epistle to the Galatians,* BNTC (Peabody: Hendrickson, 1993) 50–51; and Nina E. Livesey,

ception of the teachers' message. Presumably, the teachers were at least partially effective to elicit such a dramatic response in the form of a pastoral intervention from one of the communities' founding apostles, in the text now known to the world as the letter to the Galatians.[3]

Like many persuasive orators, Paul initiates his argument with a story, and in this case, it is his own. His major talking point—that he gained his gospel from God and not from any other human—is so indissolubly linked to his autobiographical data, that it is hard to tell where the narrative content ends and the rhetorical intention begins. By his own account, Paul did not approach any leaders within the Christ movement from whom he might have learned the gospel. Not until three years after his call did he stay with Peter for fifteen days in Jerusalem and meet with James as well (2:18–20). He did not return until fourteen years later when, after guided by a revelation, he went up with Barnabas and Titus to explain to the Pillars the gospel God had revealed to him (2:1–5).

He describes an intense debate from challengers within the Jerusalem church, whom he refers to as "false brothers," over Titus, his uncircumcised gentile co-worker.[4] Paul states proudly that he and Barnabas held their ground on this point, and the false brothers were repelled. Instead, the Pillars sided with Paul and Barnabas on the matter and gave them their right hands of fellowship (2:9).

But things quickly shifted. Later, after Peter and Paul had been in Antioch and been participating in mixed table fellowship, Peter abruptly changed and drew back after people from James arrived (2:11–12). Paul found this move unacceptable and called him out in front of the community for his hypocrisy. Yet Paul's stance, while as presumably valiant as he had been in Jerusalem, was not as successful. Barnabas, who had stood firm with him against the false brothers, and "the other Jews," were now carried away by Peter's hypocrisy (2:13). Paul, who had claimed to have been set

---

Galatians and the Rhetoric of Crisis: Demosthenes—Cicero—Paul (Salem, OR: Polebridge, 2016) 1–20.

3. The timespan between Paul's last visit and the emergence of the crisis in Galatia remains undetermined but what is clear is that these new teachers had a significant impact on the communities he and Barnabas established there. See David A. deSilva, *Galatians*, NICNT (Grand Rapids: Eerdmans, 2018) 10–15.

4. The majority of scholars view the false brothers as Christian Jews, with some seeing the designation of "false" as rhetorical and others, like Schreiner (*Galatians*, 124–25) seeing in it a theological designation or condemnation. Their relationship with the Pillars is disputed and complicated by the passive *pareisaktous* (2:4) that implies they were "smuggled in" by one or more of the Pillars (Diod. Sic. *Hist.* 12.41.4; 15.61.4; see Ben Witherington, *Grace in Galatia: A Commentary on Paul's Letter to the Galatians* [Grand Rapids: Eerdmans, 1998] 136). Craig S. Keener, *Galatians: A Commentary* (Grand Rapids: Baker Academic, 2019) 120: "Although this passage's *fake siblings* are surely not Paul's opponents in Galatia . . . from a literary standpoint they prefigure them, and from a historical standpoint they may have influenced them."

apart from his mother's womb, now stood ideologically opposed to his coworkers in the faith and physically alone.

It remains unclear how much time passed since the Galatians had last seen their founding missionaries when the new teachers who preached circumcision arrived. It is also difficult to determine how Paul's fallout in Antioch may have impacted his standing throughout the Jerusalem-Antioch network, including those he had founded among its satellite churches, or whether the new missionaries were affiliated with Jerusalem or Antioch in any way. Whatever transpired, and however Paul heard of the challenge, he now responds with a pastoral intervention that stands out as one of his harshest letters.

Paul's Relationship with the Jerusalem Pillars

Before engaging the politics of Paul's interactions with the Pillars in Jerusalem, it is worth delving into the delicate question of their relationship. Scholars have, by and large, concluded that Peter and Paul's differences never overflowed to the point of contention or division. There have been detractors to this view, most notably F. C. Baur,[5] and there are a growing number of nuanced arguments that place blame on Peter or James to explain the tension between Paul's mission and Jerusalem.[6] But, for the most part, the majority opinion holds that Paul and the Jerusalem Pillars had a good working relationship at the time of writing Galatians and throughout Paul's ministry.[7]

What this state of research leaves aside, however, is the polemical nature of Gal 2:1–14.[8] In a forthcoming book, *The Campaign Rhetoric of Paul*, co-author T. J.

---

5. Ferdinand Christian Baur, *The Church History of the First Three Centuries*, 3rd ed., trans. Allan Menzies (London: Williams & Norgate, 1878) 46; C. K. Barrett, "Cephas and Corinth," in *Essays on Paul* (Philadelphia: Westminster, 1982) 28–39; Michael D. Goulder, *St. Peter vs. St. Paul: A Tale of Two Missions* (Louisville: Westminster John Knox, 1994); Gerd Lüdemann, *The Acts of the Apostles: What Really Happened in the Earliest Days of the Church* (Amherst, NY: Prometheus, 2005).

6. Franz Mussner, *Der Galaterbrief* (Freiburg: Herder, 1974) 24–27; Raymond E. Brown and John P. Meier, *Antioch and Rome: New Testament Cradles of Catholic Christianity* (Mahwah: Paulist, 1983) 36–38; Dunn, *Galatians*, 91–95; Jacob Neusner, "What, Exactly, Is Israel's Gentile Problem? Rabbinic Perspectives on Galatians 2," in *The Missions of James, Peter, and Paul*, edited by Bruce D. Chilton and Craig A. Evans, NovTSup 115 (Leiden: Brill, 2005) 275–312.

7. The majority of studies on the Antioch Incident find little or no break between Paul and the Jerusalem establishment. Markus Bockmuehl, *The Jewish Law in Gentile Churches: Halakhah and the Beginning of Christian Public Ethics* (Edinburgh: T. & T. Clark, 2008) 49–83; Markus Zetterholm, "The Antioch Incident Revisited," *JSPL* 6 (2016) 249–59; Douglas A. Campbell, "Beyond the Torah at Antioch: The Probable Locus for Paul's Radical Transition," *JSPL* 4 (2014) 187–214; William R. Farmer, "James the Lord's Brother, According to Paul," in *James the Just and Christian Origins*, ed. Bruce D. Chilton and Craig A. Evans, NovTSup 98 (Leiden: Brill, 1999) 133–53.

8. Betz, *Galatians*, 5–7.

Rogers and I outline how Paul uses military metaphors throughout the narrative in which he describes his interactions with the false brothers and the Pillars in 2:1–14, thus characterizing the false brothers and the Pillars equally as antagonistic forces in the story he is crafting before his Galatian audience.[9] To support the political reading further below, I will summarize this argument regarding the tension between Paul and the Pillars in the limited space of this section.

Across two scenes and within the span of fourteen verses, Paul uses eight terms or phrases that are either used in military contexts or are primarily military in meaning, to describe his interactions with the false brothers, and this imagery continues when describing his interactions with the Pillars (2:6–14). He describes the false brothers as infiltrating, being sneaked in, and spying during his meeting with the Pillars (*pareisaktous, pareiserchomai, kataskopeō*, 2:4), and himself and Barnabas as not yielding to their plans to enslave the gentiles (*katadouloō, eikō*, 2:4–5).[10] The Pillars then offer their right hands to him and Barnabas, a gesture with deeper military implications that we will discuss in more detail below (*didōmi dexian*, 2:9–10). Then, in Antioch, hostilities are renewed when Peter succumbs to fear of the circumcision and Paul feels compelled to oppose him (*antistēmi kata prosōpon*, 2:11) while Barnabas is carried away like spoils of war (*sunapagō*, 2:13) by his hypocrisy.[11]

One of the largest obstacles to interpreting Gal 2:1–14 as polemical is the translation gloss in 2:9, "right hand of fellowship," which, ubiquitous in translations and commentaries, has become so engrained in our minds and imaginations, that it may well be impacting how scholars interpret the rest of 2:1–10 in critical circumstances. In the notes on 2:9 in his commentary on Galatians, e.g., Richard Longenecker lists a host of citations from Josephus to support how this phrase is "an idiom of the day for pledging friendship or acknowledging agreement," and then continues to expound on the extent of the "mutual fellowship and partnership" that Paul shared with the Pillars.[12] But there is a problem with this assertion. Not one of those seven citations Longenecker offers actually speaks to friendship. They all refer to combat situations,

---

9. Timothy Milinovich and T. J. Rogers, *The Campaign Rhetoric of Paul* (Lanham, MD: Lexington/Fortress Academic, forthcoming).

10. Betz (*Galatians*, 88–90) was the first scholar to identify military aspects in Paul's language in Gal 1–2. See also Dunn, *Galatians*, 97–101; Witherington, *Grace*, 135–40; Schreiner, *Galatians*, 124–26. On *katadouloō*, see Roy E. Ciampa, *The Presence and Function of Scripture in Galatians 1 and 2*, WUNT 2/102 (Tübingen: Mohr Siebeck, 1998) 157–58, and Witherington (*Grace*, 137), who adopts the view of Betz that this is political language, but goes further to connect it to the social category of conquest.

11. Roy Ciampa (*Presence*, 157–58) and Philip F. Esler (*Galatians* [New Testament Readings; London: Routledge, 1998], 65), publishing in the same year, appear to have reached this conclusion regarding *kata ton prosōpon* independently of one another.

12. Richard N. Longenecker, *Galatians*, WBC 41 (Waco: Word, 1998) 58. Josephus, *B.J.* 6.318–320, 345, 356, 378; *A.J.* 8.387; 18.328; 20.62.

and in six of the seven the aggressor offers the right hand to show it was empty and as a promise not to harm the other while terms are discussed. It is in no way "friendship" or "unity" in those instances.

In contrast to previous studies that examine the word *dexias* in isolation, our research narrows this scope to the concept of *offering* the right hand, particularly as Paul fashions the construction.[13] As a point of comparison, consider that an *olive branch* by itself generally signifies the idea of peace, whereas *extending an olive branch* specifically presumes a situation of conflict into which peace must now be inserted.

Surveying the extant Greek literature found that this construction is used in a military setting by a nearly 4:1 ratio and with three common traits.[14] The "right hand" is not a sign of friendship, but of a cessation of violence, meaning it presumes the existence of hostility already in the relationship. The party offering the right hand is always either the aggressor or the party with a perceived intention to aggress. And by this gesture, the aggressor or stronger party is expected to cease hostilities for an agreed time.[15]

Incorporating this new data set into an analysis of 2:9, alongside the polemical context and other military terms throughout 2:1–14, compels us to set aside the traditional understanding of "unity" between Paul and the Pillars and reconsider the right hand given to Paul, and therefore his relationship with the Pillars and 2:1–14 as a whole, in light of the three common threads described above. On this reading, Paul is presenting to the Galatian audience that 1) he viewed his relationship with the Pillars before 2:9 as marked by hostility; 2) the Pillars initiated this hostility; and 3) the Pillars agreed to cease hostilities before breaking their own agreement in Antioch.

---

13. Ernest D. W. Burton, *A Critical and Exegetical Commentary on the Letter to the Galatians*, ICC 35 (New York: Scribner, 1920) 95, e.g., incorporates various uses of *dexias* into his analysis without accounting for Paul's particular construction. This leads to citations of Gen 24:2, 9, as when Abraham made his slave swear to him to complete a mission using his right hand, being included to justify a friendly reading of Paul's encounter with the Pillars.

14. See Milinovich and Rogers (*Campaign Rhetoric of Paul*, forthcoming) for further lexical and statistical data regarding the military language in 2:1–14.

15. When employed as a military gesture, an offered right hand broadly communicates an intention to cease existing hostilities. It can be extended from a conquering force to a subjugated city or army as a peace offering (Polyb., *Hist.*, 5.54.8; 1 Macc 11:62), or granted as assurances to individuals who have reason to expect harm (Diod. Sic., *Hist.* 17.38.3; Aristotle, *Athenian Constitution* 18.6). It can be requested by a conquered city or army to concede victory to their attackers and initiate terms for surrender (Xen., *Cyropaedia* 4.2.7; 1 Macc 6:58; 11:66; Josephus, *B.J.* 6.378), or it can be offered by an attacking force to terminate an unsuccessful siege (1 Macc 6:58). Presumptive victors can offer it to a lesser force as an assurance of safety to initiate negotiations (Xen., *Anabasis* 2.5.3; Josephus, *A.J.* 18.326, 328), or as a condition for surrender (Josephus, *B.J.* 3.31). It can also be exchanged between opposing forces to agree mutually to a cessation of hostilities (Xen., *Anab.* 1.6.9; 2 Macc 12:11).

Based on the text, the polemical tone, and the total of eight military terms and phrases that is shared with both false brothers and the Pillars within a complex battle sequence that stretches across the narrative of Paul's encounters with the Pillars in Jerusalem and Antioch in 2:1–14, Rogers and I conclude that Paul at least sought to portray the Jerusalem apostles as adversaries to his audiences in the Galatian churches when he composed the letter for his rhetorical purposes.

Politics between Paul and the Pillars

So if Paul and the Pillars in Jerusalem—Peter, James, and John—had conflict with one another over cultural political issues while Christianity was still in the cradle, we should not think such conflict strange to the hallowed halls of our churches. In fact, we should accept such behavior as all too human and rather common in any corporate entity.

Early church leaders came to blows, metaphorically at least, over circumcision of gentile converts and table fellowship between Jewish and gentile members. In both topics, leaders were arguing over cultural identity markers that were visible, rooted in narratives of their tradition, and tied also to those of their eschatological future. The question becomes, how can we deal with similar political issues of our own time effectively, and with the politics of power dynamics that play out in social groups like churches, in a manner that is constructive and conducive to the gospel?

It is important to isolate here what I mean by "political" since the term itself can have many meanings, many of which can be negative. Here I mean political in the watercooler "politics" that can exist in any group of people or contingency that is public. To the question, why do churches, places of holiness and the sacred, become politicized, the answer is not so difficult. Churches involve politics because churches are full of people. And that's what politics is: it's the culmination of the people and their lives, their narratives, their fears, their hopes, and their conflicts coming together in one sequence of social chemical reactions and combustions.

One can see these on display in Gal 2:1–14, as well. Observations and methods on specific figures can be limited by the genre of polemical rhetoric and extent of evidence, so here I will look at the meetings as general models that took place and how topics were addressed within them in terms of structures and process. First, in 2:1–5, there is discussion of an immediate issue before an authoritative body (2:1–5). Second, which is connected to the first, but separated for purposes of analysis, is the attempt to resolve a dispute through agreed distinction of jurisdictions and terms (2:6–10). Third, as if an immediate referendum on the second example, is a dispute on jurisdictions from that resolution (2:11–14). And fourth, is the pastoral intervention of the letter itself.

With the increase of sociological, socio-historical, and empire-critical methods in Pauline studies in general, there have been several that have contributed to the study of power dynamics in cultural, gender-oriented, imperial, or house church model lenses.[16] Even studies that remain largely theological or traditional in their approaches have needed to confront the dynamics of how Paul was or was not subordinate to the Pillars in bringing his gospel to them, or of the status of Peter and James in relation to one another and the Jerusalem community or its Antiochian network.[17]

This approach borrows broadly from this constellation of studies with an emphasis that has a growing interest but is rarely fully articulated in so many terms in Galatians studies. We will consider the conflict situation between Paul and the Pillars as it relates to two critical limited resources: 1) the identity of the subjects (Paul, Peter, James) to identify as leader (i.e., who can lead the flock of shepherds) and therefore have their vision shape the future of the movement they are attempting to serve; and 2) the gentile believers themselves as the third party whom these subjects are competing to persuade—in the general sense, it would be implied gentile believer; but for the letter, there is also the specific interest in persuading this audience to support Paul's vision and away from another. The matter becomes a conflict over a scarce resource in which, once the subjects determine there is little room for compromise, becomes a game with only a zero-sum result as the possible outcome.

The first form of dispute that we see manifest, as portrayed by Paul, is that between himself and the false brothers in Jerusalem. Spirited deliberation takes place before an authoritative body, the Pillars. At their core, all meetings are inherently political. Who is invited, who is leading, who sets the agenda, who is able to speak and when—all of these are decisions made before the meeting that give agency and impact the deliberations within its proceedings.

Whether or not circumcision was on the agenda before Paul arrived, his interest in having a private audience is itself a political move. Being an outsider, meeting

---

16. Davina Lopez, *Apostle to the Conquered: Reimaging Paul's Mission,* Paul in Critical Contexts (Minneapolis: Fortress, 2010) 1–56; Peter Oakes, *Galatians,* Paideia (Grand Rapids: Baker, 2015) 1–21, 64–80; Philip F. Esler, "Making and Breaking a Covenant Mediterranean Style: A New Perspective on Gal 2:1–14," *BibInt* 3 (1995) 285–314; Pheme Perkins, *Abraham's Divided Children: Galatians and the Politics of Faith* (Harrisburg: Trinity, 2001) 48–56; Harry O. Maier, *Picturing Paul in Empire: Imperial Image, Text and Persuasion in Colossians, Ephesians and the Pastoral Epistles,* (London: Bloomsbury, 2013) 35–61; Bruce W. Winter, *Divine Honours for the Caesars: The First Christian Responses* (Grand Rapids: Eerdmans, 2015) 226–40.

17. E.g., F. F. Bruce, *Galatians,* NIGTC (Grand Rapids: Eerdmans, 1982) 117–34; Longenecker, *Galatians,* 50–52; J. Louis Martyn, *Galatians,* AB 33A (New Haven: Yale University Press, 2004) 236–45.

with the Pillars would elevate Paul's stature and that of his gospel to the gentiles and his opponents.[18] Having other voices there helps to alleviate this pressure for the Pillars in three ways. (1) They are no longer giving Paul a private audience—and thus not conferring immediate authority to him. (2) They have an opposing voice to balance out his position. (3) And they have a third party who can act as witness to any testimony Paul might say about the meeting. The Pillars, being the authoritative party, chose a moderate pathway, allowing both sides to walk away with a sense of accomplishment. Titus, the focal point of the discussion, was not required to be circumcised at that time.

It is notable, however, that there is also no mention of a blanket declaration by the Pillars at this juncture regarding other gentiles' foreskins—only Titus's. If there had been such an explicit declaration to this effect from the Pillars as is seen in Acts 15, this would be a key point in this letter to mention that. But all that Paul mentions in 2:3 is that Titus was not compelled to be circumcised at that time. Meaning the Pillars did not find it necessary for Titus to be circumcised during that specific visit.

There are positives to this model, but also too many negatives. The authorities have too much control over the agenda, and the end is more focused on a zero-sum win than a dialogue of constructive growth or development. Paul's techniques were also less than useful. Arriving by way of revelation is essentially admitting one showed up uninvited and adds unwanted pressure onto the very party you are looking to persuade.

The next approach, while technically at the same meeting, can be distinguished by topic and attendees. The authorities offer terms of peace based on distinguished jurisdictions (2:6–10). Peter was to preach to the circumcised while Paul was to preach to the uncircumcised. This maintains consistency with the previous topic of circumcision, but still does not offer any explanation over whether or not Paul's gentile converts would be free from the question of circumcision. Instead, as above, Titus seems to be an isolated matter and the more general question of what happens with the numerous other gentile converts remains an open question.

The division of mission fields between circumcised and uncircumcised is vague. Dividing mission fields does not in itself grant Paul authority in that area, yet Paul or his churches could reach such a conclusion as a general victory for his gospel in all situations and for all of his gentile converts. Perhaps this is how he took it. Perhaps this is how the Pillars intended it. Perhaps neither is the case.

---

18. Esler (*Galatians*, 130) and Oakes (*Galatians*, 65) note that Paul's action of bringing his uncircumcised gentile co-worker to a meeting in Jerusalem could have been considered a kind of challenge to Jerusalem or the false brothers.

What is clear is that the jurisdictional division can create immediate challenges in communication and relationships. If the Pillars are leaders in the circumcision mission, is Paul to be a leader in the gentile mission parallel to the Pillars in Jerusalem? This would be a tremendous elevation if that were the case. Paul's account of the event helps with this impression, but it nonetheless gives evidence to the vulnerability that such vague phrasing could create.

The other problem this creates is that the resolution is not realistic. One group is to go to Jews and the other to gentiles. But what about communities that are both? Who has jurisdiction there? This lack of clarity and unrealistic resolutions—or, rather, resolutions that immediately fall apart with exceptions at the next meeting—doom these terms of peace from the start. Even if Paul and the Pillars entered this agreement in good faith and felt that they were now acting with some authority to give voice on disputes in areas where their converts were involved, it was unlikely either was prepared for what would transpire later in Antioch when another dispute about gentiles and Jewish traditions arose in mixed company.[19]

At Antioch, the context moves from private discussion to public confrontation and from a theoretical discussion to a leadership dispute on public display. The topic has shifted at this point from circumcision to table fellowship. While the context of Jewish/Gentile relationships within traditional identity markers remains, the dynamic has changed. By Paul's account, Peter had been staying at Antioch and abiding by the rules of inclusive fellowship until representatives from James arrived in town. At this point, Peter withdrew from fellowship with the gentile believers, and Paul felt compelled to confront him.[20]

Peter could suggest to James's people that this form of inclusive fellowship is preferred here, but as with Titus, he moves for a moderate and temporary solution that offers little substantive change.[21] After James's people leave, presumably, things

---

19. Douglas A. Campbell, *Framing Paul: An Epistolary Biography* (Grand Rapids: Eerdmans, 2014) 179–81, has argued that the Antioch incident (2:11–14) preceded and necessitated the meeting in Jerusalem (2:1–10) mainly to assuage the unresolved problem with the Pillars that 2:14 leaves open. But this argument would problematize Paul's assertion that he went up to Jerusalem according to a revelation (v. 2) and essentially reorganizes the text to fit the interpreter's preferred reconstructed narrative of a peaceful resolution between Paul and the Pillars.

20. The exact nature of Peter's withdrawal and his motives continues to be debated. Here I take the general view that Peter separated from table fellowship with the gentiles, breaking with his regular practice of eating with them. See James D. G. Dunn, "Echoes of intra-Jewish Polemic in Paul's Letter to the Galatians," *JBL* 112 (1993) 459–77; Dragutin Matak, "Another Look at the Antioch Incident (Gal 2:11–14)," *Kairos* 6 (2012) 49–59. Whatever Peter's internal process for making this decision, it was this noticeable break in his pattern that, for Paul, became a threat to the gospel; for our purposes, it indicates a decision made for the purpose of maintaining a specific stature in the communities in Antioch and Jerusalem (whatever that may have been) that was publicly visible and, therefore, inherently political.

21. Martyn (*Galatians*, 244) avers that Paul blames Peter more than James for the problems in

can go back to the way they were. But the downside to this move is that everyone knows that it is just a temporary action. It is political theater designed to appease a particular audience. Paul attempts to capitalize on this moment with a substantial risk/reward ratio. If he is persuasive, he may convince the entire Antiochian community to his overall gospel. But if he is wrong, he may end up putting his mission back several steps and running, as he said he feared he would do, in vain.

If the event was as dramatic as Paul implies in his narration, it would no doubt have left an impression on the community that witnessed the interaction. But that impression would not have been a positive one for Paul's political capital. As he reports, even without noting Peter's response, Barnabas and the other Jews (and possibly even some gentiles in Antioch) were persuaded to Peter's side. This does not need to mean that they felt Peter was entirely correct. It may mean that, in this instance, Paul's reaction was so counterproductive that even his most trusted ally, Barnabas, left him and sided with Peter.

It probably does not require much analysis to conclude that this model should not be followed in regular pastoral practice. As with the imperative meeting by a revelation in 2:1–5, this dialogue relies too much on performance rather than constructive dialogue. The issues can easily be lost in talking points or a zero-sum accounting of who is winning or losing. In the end, everyone lost in this scenario. Peter lost a great ally; Barnabas lost a coworker; Antioch lost a missionary; and Paul's network in Antioch was severely damaged for a time, if not for a lifetime.

Finally, we can consider one other leadership event recorded in the letter itself. If we consider that Paul has received word of new teachers in Galatia and is now writing to respond to that effect, then the entire letter operates as a kind of pastoral intervention. To be sure, this letter is not written to Peter or the Pillars, or even to the antagonists. The addressees are clearly the Galatian believers. But the Pillars and antagonists operate as "rhetorical opponents" within the letter, as foils to which Paul sets himself in comparison, and against whom he proves the validity of his gospel and his apostleship. He is, in other words, engaging these rhetorical opponents and their ideas in front of the Galatian audience and forcing them to choose between himself and his opponents, the false teachers who have arrived and presumably taught circumcision to the Galatians. This is then both pastoral in expression and a kind of campaign speech; Paul is setting before his audience an ultimatum to choose him or his opponents as their leader.

The letter offers many political challenges for Paul, as indicated by many of its harsher (and unnecessary) comments about the law being clarified in Romans

---

Antioch because Peter could have chosen a more moderate path that satisfied James's people and maintained his practice of table fellowship with the gentiles.

(3:21—8:39).²² He takes unnecessary shots at potential allies that do not need to be made (Gal 2:6-14), insults his audience (3:1), and buries some of his better arguments under weaker ones (3:2-6). Scholars note that the Galatians are mentioned in 1 Cor 16:1 to support Paul's pitch for the Corinthians to contribute to his collection, but not in his later pitches in 2 Cor 8-9 and Rom 15:26, raising the question of how many of his Galatians believers felt this letter fell short of its initial main goal to win them back.

But the other question might also be asked of what the Galatians gained from this letter spiritually or pastorally. This is a challenging question to ask, post-Augustine and post-Luther, who so elevated and revered this letter. But for a Galatian gentile convert, pondering the gospel of Paul and the teachings of the Jewish-Christian missionaries, who sounds more sincere and viable as a spiritual leader?²³ The individuals who preach Christ and tradition, or the person who confronted Peter at Antioch, and whose own mission partner sided against him?

It would not be too difficult for those with affinities for the new teachers to deduce Paul's separation of faith and works of the law as a false dichotomy. Clearly, the teachers who taught circumcision believed in Christ and felt that God's covenant would give the gentiles grace, too. And Paul's gospel is not exactly free of Jewish customs: he is still requiring ethical vigilance, sexual morality, and avoidance of things like idolatry and witchcraft that certainly sound familiar to Jewish legal traditions (5:16-19). He even encourages the Galatians to fulfill the kernel of the Jewish legal ethic (5:14). Arguably, his attacks on the opponents and the law are more about branding his opposition and defining himself in an effort to persuade a third party than they are a substantive theological discourse. By the textual evidence of 2 Cor 8-9 and Rom 15:26, it remains plausible that, despite its success among Paul's base, a sufficient number of Galatian churches responded negatively enough that he felt he could no longer include them in his pitch to others to contribute to the collection.²⁴

---

22. Keener, *Galatians*, 120.

23. DeSilva (*Galatians*, 22-26) notes that "who the Galatians can trust" becomes a major issue for the tone and argumentation of the letter.

24. Keener (*Galatians*, 45) views the use of 2 Cor 8-9 and Rom 15:26 as an argument from silence, but this is not entirely accurate. It is unlikely for Paul to have the same lapse of memory twice after listing them in a previous pitch. This is compounded by the fact that Galatia is the only church mentioned in 1 Cor 16:1, and they are the example Paul gave of how the Corinthians are to gather the collection. It is in Paul's best interests to include them in his directions to the Corinthians. The absence of the Galatians in both 2 Cor 8-9 and Rom 15:26 indicates that Paul felt he would be harmed by including them—perhaps because not enough of them were remaining for him to claim them as the exemplary community for his collection that they had been when he wrote 1 Corinthians.

Relevance for Today

So what can be gleaned from these examples for our churches today? We deal with cultural issues that are wrapped in theological and practical concerns on a regular basis. It is noteworthy that there are things that these models can show us to do, and that they can also show us not to do.

People Are Political

We should not be surprised to find the plight of human conflict in our churches. But constructive dialogue about how to worship, and how to practice one's faith, is no less devotional than any prayer or good work. The key part here is that it needs to be constructive and instructive. We need to be willing to foster dialogue and differing opinions without taking on a militaristic atmosphere. We also need to back away from the tendencies that anxiety can lead us to to push for a quick answer now rather than a better resolution tomorrow. These anxieties that are at the core of our individual selves can exacerbate our social interactions, and explode in our communities, and so we need to be careful that we keep our eye on the horizon.

At times my students or diaconate candidates lament that it can be difficult to preach or listen to sermons where political situations come up in their parishes. I encourage them that politics in their churches are evidence there are people in the pews, and that's a good thing. To be sure, it can be challenging to try to thread the needle as a pastor in a community with divergent views on a topic. But the gospel was never an easy message, nor was preaching it an easy task. They could have done anything on a Sunday morning, but they came to your church. So give them something for them to consider. Challenge them with the message of the gospel—not just your own ideas or talking points from the news, but challenge them to consider what the gospel means in the world today and in their lives today.

Communication Is Key

The same anxieties and desires that want a zero-sum victory also sometimes prefer vague terms to keep the narrative that way. Clarity can take away victory from those who would presume to hold it. But that is all the more reason why communication must always be pursued, resolutions agreed upon, and then everyone must agree that they have agreed to those resolutions and what they mean. Because what resolutions seem to mean under one set of circumstances one day might look slightly different the next, and having a clear sense of who you are working with can help to clarify previously unseen challenges. Communication and relationships are essentially the same thing. Following up with those with whom you met, maintaining the connection, and ensuring that the agreement stands as time passes, is a way of keeping trust among all parties involved and keeping the relationship solid. This strength will then be able to withstand pressure more effectively when new challenges arise.

Public Theatrics Make for Bad Politics, and Even Worse Pastoral Care

Many who are drawn to ministry tend to have an interest in performance. This talent or drive can make them good preachers and/or offer an "it" factor to lead, even when they are not standing behind a pulpit. But that tendency is also something that needs to be kept in check when working with the ministry team and with the community.

What or who decides what is appropriate regarding the level of intensity or visual effect when communicating the gospel over politically sensitive issues? This can differ from community to community. This in itself can become its own topic of discussion and can be addressed by the group's own statement of mission and articulation of the gospel within its own charisms. For both Peter and Paul in Antioch, the emphasis on performance is focused on the short-term and often for individual success. Rarely do communities gain from drastic performances. The initial sense of relief or victory can be deceptive, as both apostles learned after Antioch.

The Flock Suffers When the Shepherds Fight

There is a difference between constructive disagreement and outright conflict. The first can offer a complementary benefit or building up of a body. The latter is more often destructive. Since we only have Paul's account, it is hard to tell who is more at fault for the conflict that arose between them. But it is fair to say that the conflict between Paul and the Pillars was counterproductive for everyone involved. Jerusalem lost one of their top fundraisers. Antioch lost one of their best missionaries. And the churches Paul would establish possibly lost out on developing a closer network with the base in Syria and Cilicia.

However, disagreements among your pastoral team take place, it is very possible your church members will hear about them. As a leader, it is important to maintain your level of patience and how you go about the process. Focus on the issue on the table rather than the people in the chairs. Encourage your team to do the same. It is important to note here that disagreements are not the problem. It is how your pastoral team resolves the disagreement that matters. Members of a congregation can benefit from seeing a disagreement within the pastoral team resolved calmly and with helpful dialogue.

It Should Never Be about You, the Pastor

Peter's withdrawal from table fellowship was more about protecting his appearance than the community's growth. And, likewise, when he is least effective in Galatians, Paul is talking about the opponents, and his conflict with the Pillars, or himself. When he is at his best, he is talking about his relationship with the Galatians and what they share in Christ. This is also a critical part of politics in churches today. It shouldn't matter what your politics are as an individual. What matters is your congregation and what they need as individuals. Every one of your families is hurting—maybe of similar things, maybe of different things. But at many tables there are empty chairs, or bills piling up, or loved ones who are not returning. And in this epidemic of crises people will seek a signal of solace. That signal isn't the pastor. The signal is always the gospel. The question is how you help to amplify that signal to the community. It seems Paul had it better in a later letter that we imitate and amplify the gospel best when we become translucent and let the light of the gospel shine through us (2 Cor 4:5–6). In other words, pastors and ministers of care serve the world best when they forget themselves and remember who they are serving.

Conclusion

So there are three things we are told not to talk about in pleasant company: sex, religion, and politics. One of the reasons for this distinction is that people are fragile and revealing this information to unfamiliar individuals would make one too vulnerable. But that also points to another reality: all three of these are key parts of our identities and make us very vulnerable. That means talking about them requires a special sensitivity and precision.

The goal of this article was to consider how political strife found between Paul and the Pillars in Jerusalem—the cultural issues and the internal competition for who can be identified as leader and whose vision will shape the movement—could benefit how we pastor churches in politically difficult times today. We know politics will not go away. It will be in our churches, in and among our church members, and within our pastoral teams. The question becomes what kind of dialogue we foster and how we proceed to nurture those differences within the community.

So when people in your community want to discuss how political or cultural issues play a role in our churches today, or how our churches can make a statement on them, or how prayer services or worship or Bible studies could be used in service of social justice or police reform or addiction or dealing with the pandemic, or any number of other issues we deal with today, be mindful of how it can be done, and how it should not be done. Be mindful of the power principles at play and how the powerless can be given a voice. And be mindful of how time is your greatest resource.[25]

And, at the same time, there may be individuals who come up to you after a sermon or a Bible study who say that they came to church to get away from politics. Thank them for coming and for their comment, and let them know the church is always open for silent prayer. And if they were moved enough to come and speak with you about it, then maybe there is something more they would like to talk about. Is it politics they don't like, or just that particular topic? Is there a topic they are interested in hearing more about? And now you have a dialogue rather than a confrontation.

Political dynamics and political issues will always be with us in our churches, but the mission remains the same as it did before. Preach the gospel. Sometimes even with words. And work together for the building up of all in Christ.

---

25. One caveat would be this: because there are parts of the Bible that have been used to harm others; while I would encourage you to nurture discussion of ideas, there are some ideas that self-disqualify. If a person's main argument is harmful or demeaning against a particular group of people within or outside the community, then that should be pointed out, and more appropriate ideas welcomed and encouraged.

RESPONSE TO MILINOVICH

Christy Randazzo

It would be an understatement to say that I resonate with Dr. Milinovich's warning about the topics to be avoided in pleasant company—politics, religion, and sex. I often state that as a political theologian, two of these topics are literally my job, which can make dinner parties somewhat complicated, to put it mildly. When I add on the fact of the physical presentation that often accompanies my nonbinary gender identity, I far too often find that I am a walking embodiment of everything which, as Milinovich reminds us, tends to cause offense in what some might term "polite society"! It is from this social location that I speak, asking the challenging question: what, actually, *is* "political"?

This question can be dismissed as simply a minor semantic game, with the assumption that whatever definition one holds is the most inherently obvious one. Yet, as Milinovich argues, our definition of this word foregrounds our entire conceptual framework, establishing the boundaries of acceptability and necessity across potentially the entire scope of human interaction: from our understanding of "justice," to our approach to the economic structures of our society, and even finally to our conceptions of the human person (again, an issue of which I am rather painfully aware). This is not a minor concern, dismissed as mere partisan bickering and deal-making. I'd argue that the sweep of the biblical tradition assumes the existence of a divine being intimately engaged with the fundamental questions of human existence, often with a very clear intent towards which this being would care to frame the human experience. In that vein, therefore, God is inherently and unavoidably "political," so concomitantly, the biblical witness must be as well. By limiting our understanding of the "political" to simply the actions of political parties, we actually run the risk of failing to comprehend the gospel itself.

Moving even farther, we cannot simply bracket the "political" out from our understanding of, and approach to, the issues of personal pastoral concern which are so often the core aspect of the lives of our church communities. As that old canard states, the "personal is political": unavoidably so. Our congregants' ability to access—or lack of ability, as is often the case—the healthcare they require is an inherently political question, as are not only the potential reasons behind the vast differentials of access, but also the causes of the illnesses and diseases from which they suffer. While Leviticus demands that we provide for the needs of the poor, the widows, and the orphans, it also demands that we continuously right the injustices which cause the poverty and alienation which create the populations which we are then called upon to serve.

I need not belabor this point any further, save to insist that when we make efforts to not cause conflicts within our congregations so as to diminish the pastoral benefits that religious community, ritual, and teaching can offer—under the fear that discussing likely contentious and challenging issues will create rifts in our communities—we risk simply offering a Band-Aid when what is actually required is a surgeon. We do not create rifts when we address the lived reality of our congregations; we simply uncover the rifts and conflicts which were already extant.

Therefore, I truly appreciate Milinovich's fierce—and I'd argue vitally necessary—intervention here with the interpretive tradition of Gal 2:1–14. I especially appreciate his deft dismantling of the interpretive tradition which has sought to view the "right hand of fellowship" in 2:9 as an inherently amicable or even friendly gesture, which is then used as the main lens through which to interpret the entire conflict itself. As Milinovich insists, this reading ignores the rather strident and even sarcastic tone which colors Paul's relation of this series of events, which due to the timing of the writing of this letter after the events which Paul describes, would at the very least speak to a rather less than amicable relationship between Paul and the Pillars. Milinovich carefully builds his argument by asking us to imagine the events as they occurred, offering some intriguing ways to set this scene in our mind's eye, and then asks us to consider whether the traditional reconciliatory interpretation actually holds any water. Through a very careful reading of the text, Milinovich presents what I find to be a rather persuasive argument that not only must we not ignore the rather militaristic framing Paul ascribes to this series of incidents—and thus to what can only be understood to be his own ferocious response to the actions of the "spies" and "betrayers" —but that we must reassess the Letter to Galatians in the light of conflict and human frailty, and begin to learn the lessons it teaches us about how to approach conflict in our communities.

At this point, I must confess that I feel rather marked by my own methodological, theological, and ecclesiastical commitments, commitments which necessarily frame my response to this paper. I have served in parish ministry for many years, and I have training in both the practice and theology of peacemaking, particularly in situations of inter-Christian conflict. I am also a political theologian who spends a great deal of time considering the Biblical witness from the lens of applying its lessons and teachings to issues of political import, specifically peacemaking, political reconciliation, and ecological concerns. It is from that perspective that I can offer my own response to the theses put forth in this paper. Simply put, I find Milinovich's five lessons—the ones which conclude his paper, which he gathered from the series of conflicts in Gal 2:1–14—both insightful, and also puzzling.

1. People Are Political

As I've already mentioned above, this claim seems to not only be absolutely true, but nigh on obvious, almost to the point that it is so foundational that it is akin to air, water, and food: it just *is*. Actually, I'd argue that the very fact that Milinovich felt compelled to not only mention this, but to spend a great deal of space exploring this argument, demonstrates that it is akin to a core truth of the human condition because isn't it true that we tend to forget those things which are so true and consistent and foundational that they become the furniture of our lives? This then begs the question: how do we effectively foreground the truth that politics simply *are*, without falling into the trap of minimalist definitions of politics?

2. Communication Is Key

This is another truth that is so foundational that it has actually somehow slipped into the realm of cliché. The absolute tragedy of this is that we seem to be singularly incapable of remembering this simple truth: we actually need to *talk* to each other in order to ever hope to be understood. One point I do feel compelled to mention, however, is that communication is not an inherently beneficial good. One can just as easily communicate manipulatively as communicate truthfully; Milinovich helpfully points out the possibility that Paul's emotional state could quite easily have impacted his ability to present the most accurate and "truthful" account of the events which transpired, and as the paper notes ruefully, Paul's gloss on the event very likely closed off doors for future relationship with his community in Galatia, and may have caused permanent damage to the relationship between Paul, the Galatians, and the Antioch community. John Paul Lederach, one of the foremost theorists in post-conflict reconciliation and religious peacemaking, claims that reconciliation is the place which exists at the point where peace, justice, mercy, and truth all meet. As Milinovich notes, the multiple failures of everyone in this incident demonstrates a general lack of mercy, justice, and most unfortunately, truth amongst all involved. As we have so painfully been reminded recently: silencing the truth, even if out of a concern for comfort, ultimately poisons our witness, and simply ensures the continued presence of injustice, sometimes at the heart of Christianity. I wonder: is Milinovich being too harsh on Paul here, as he seemed to fervently believe that he needed to right what he understood to be an injustice? What is the role of the angry expression of righteous truth, and how do we determine that we are actually seeking justice . . . and not just personal relief?

3. Public Theatrics Make for Bad Politics, and Even Worse Pastoral Care

On the point of the role of "public theatrics" in the life of a congregation, I find my own religious tradition—the Religious Society of Friends, also known as Quakers—most illuminating, as it provides a helpful lens for exploring Milinovich's concerns about ensuring that the roles of prophet and pastor don't bleed together to such a degree that the pastoral care of one's community is left behind. Friends have a long history of responding to the prophetic urge to speak the truth of God's will for God's people to those in power, even to those in power in their own communities. Friends have learnt that the prophetic needn't always arrive in an immediately unpalatable package, yet that defining the limits of "palatability" is inherently a question of power, and thus that any action which might curtail or even simply critique those in power is likely to be deemed "unpalatable" or "unacceptable" by default.

The challenge I find in Millinovich's argument here is that justice is often embedded in the concerns to which pastoral care is often addressed, and not only theodicidic questions of the role of divine justice. A notable example of a Quaker who held pastoral care and the prophetic impulse in balance would be John Woolman, the noted eighteenth-century American abolitionist and proto-environmentalist. He employed a diverse variety of tactics in his efforts to abolish slavery amongst Quakers. Some were quite "theatrical" in their efforts to publicly shame Quakers who enslaved their fellow humans, including his well-known refusal to consume any products connected to the slave trade, whether that be literally any product made with sugar, or any piece of clothing made from cotton or dyed with indigo. Woolman would even refuse to ride in carriages, due to the mistreatment of horses and the stablehands who cared for the horses. These efforts certainly caused widespread consternation and shame, yet they were also pastoral in that they stemmed, for Woolman, from a sincere care for the spiritual health and moral well-being of his fellow Friends. Woolman's "theatrics" were quite successful, in that during his lifetime Quakers across the Anglo-American Quaker community moved to abolish the enslavement of human beings within the Friends' community, and to take a corporate stand for universal abolition. Would this political, moral, and spiritual outcome have occurred without the stinging challenge of Woolman's prophetic "theatrics"? It's certainly a question worth engaging with.

4. The Flock Suffers when the Shepherds Fight

The challenge that Milinovich offers here is that once shorn of our understandable desire to agree with the giants of our theological history—Augustine in particular—that the founders of our religious tradition were generally in theological agreement, we might actually allow the power of another interpretation to take root: that conflict is baked into the very fabric of our tradition, and that even the apostles weren't in agreement about the way that the gospel should be understood, interpreted, and applied, and finally—perhaps *most* heretically, that maybe such conflict is not only ok, but a core element of the work of the gospel.

Another connection I find with my Quaker tradition is that the rituals of our communities can often serve to paper over conflict. While they might offer a temporary solution to conflict by giving us the ability to engage in the work of our communities, the truth of the conflict will continue to fester underneath. For example, when I sit on the bench in my meeting house, in expectant waiting worship, listening for that still, small voice of the Light of Christ to speak within, I could spend many, many, MANY years waiting to ever listen to the experiences, beliefs, and truths of those who join me on the same benches, week after week. We share the community of ritual, we all join together at coffee hour, and we even wrestle with the intricacies of money, bills, and policy decisions in our monthly Meeting for Worship for Business, and yet not only does this whole ritual of communication bracket off what is considered acceptable topics of conversation, it also serves to silence voices which might challenge the stability of community.

This begs the question: while it might not be a good thing to go three rounds about table placement in front of the entire congregation, which truths, which conflicts, which voices do we silence when we are so cautious in our public expression of conflict? As Milinovich so rightly proclaims: power dynamics exist *everywhere*, including and especially in church. Does Milinovich's caution lead him to pull his punches just when they truly need to land, especially in our necessary dismantling of unjust power dynamics, again especially in our churches?

5. It Should Never Be about You, the Pastor

On this point, I can definitely agree: the leadership of the church must insist on not imposing their own personal perspectives on the congregation. I would take this in a slightly different direction, however, by making the statement that by necessity and design, for *every* Christian, the gospel must be our primary perspective, never another ideological framework. While parties, economic ideologies, etc. will all obviously inform and shape our perspectives on political issues—again, insisting on the most generous definition of "politics"—the Gospel must be the foundation upon which we rest. Yet, here's the fundamental challenge: as I stated above, the Christian biblical witness is irretrievably, inextricably, unavoidably political, and demands that we align ourselves to its politics. If the personal is political, then inherently the political is personal: is Milinovich actually calling us to strive to remove our persons from the political? It is on this point that I find myself most puzzled.

FORGIVENESS AS THE REDOUBLING OF GOD

Colby Dickinson

God Redoubled

The metaphysical act of redoubling is as firmly in place today as it was when the Jewish people once sought to unite themselves as a nation under the protection of the "king of kings" and "lord of lords"—phrases which only increased in prominence through their subsequent liturgical usage. Only redoublings such as these (e.g., locating the "X of X") place one in a meta-position that eliminates all competitors and achieves something like a universal status. The abstraction brought about by the act of redoubling is what in fact guarantees sovereignty—an autonomous position removed from ordinary existence. God, in this sense, is not just a deity like other deities, but the true embodiment of an ancient monarchical title that functioned as a political and abstract ideal: the idealized king amongst all other actually existing kings. The title is as abstract, hence idealized, as it is self-legitimating, precisely through its attempt to position itself above all other existing, earthly kingships. Though the term was used in an ancient Near Eastern context for centuries to describe the autonomy of kings, and their alleged superiority over every other, rival sovereign claim, it was appropriated by Christianity alongside other redoubled Hebrew descriptors, "lord of lords" and "god of gods" (Deut 10:17), in order to demonstrate the unique sovereignty and majesty of its God (Rev 19:16).

The descriptors "king of kings" and "lord of lords" are not just straightforward attempts to assert divine or political sovereignty, however. In the case of the God of Judaism, and insofar as this figure becomes the model for monotheism in the West, God's being is established upon a consistent foundation of redoubling through God's declaration of God's own being—that is, through God's ability to call God's own self into being. The very name of God preserves this (redoubled) tautological structure: *'ehyeh 'ăšer 'ehyeh*, or "I am that I am" (Exod 3:14). This phrasing of God's identity before Moses, his servant, can be translated in a number of ways, including "I will be what I will be" or "I will become what I will become," though each translation retains the tautological or circular nature of the declaration as it exists in parallel form to the redoubled titles of the "king of kings" or "lord of lords." Essentially, God declares God's own self to be God's foundation for existence through a name that is a statement of God's autonomy and sovereignty: God will be the sole source capable of defining God's own self. There can be no rival claims and no other possible sovereign beside God. To say "I am who I am" is therefore structurally the same thing as to say that one is the "king of kings." Not only is this a definition of divine sovereignty, it is the mark of political forms of sovereignty through a specific act of conceptual abstraction at the same time.

Complete autonomy is the *sine qua non* of sovereign being. To be defined in relation to something else would make one dependent upon that something else. If, for example, and as Plato himself would wrestle with, the Good defines God's being, then God would appear to be subject to the conditions of goodness, thereby limiting God's autonomy and ability to deviate from a normative sense of the Good. God must be entirely independent of all qualifiers, except insofar as God could be said to be the culmination, or end point, of all qualities. In other words, God cannot be reduced to any human quality or attribute (e.g., thought), though God could be the excessive and invisible foundation for any quality (e.g., Aristotle defined God as the "thought of thought," which Anselm reinvigorated in his ontological argument for God's existence). Historically and throughout the course of theological speculations on divine being, there are long lists of such qualifications regarding divine nature, though they all affirm the main point that God cannot be the human quality we recognize (e.g., the Good), though God must be the foundation of that quality (e.g., the goodness of the Good). To declare God to be the king of kings, lord of lords, god of gods, or the goodness of the Good is to enact the process of redoubling as a form of abstraction in order to achieve a sense of transcendence through the establishment of universal abstraction itself. This removal from the ordinary through a redoubled abstraction is characteristic of what ancient Israelite political theory shares with Platonic thought: the formulation of an Idea as an abstracted ideal that exists only insofar as it is abstractly, invisibly, and immaterially a conceptual absolute.[1]

The characteristics of sovereign power that are on display in Aristotle's redoubled definition of divine being—that a deity must somehow embody the "thought of thought"—are structurally found in an ancient religious context. The fact that an offshoot of Judaic thought, Christianity, would eventually merge its theological

---

1. It is worth noting that, for Sartre, the absolute and violence have an intimate connection. As he put it, "Every violence even is produced, lived, refused, accepted as *the absolute*." Jean-Paul Sartre, *Critique of Dialectical Reason*, vol. 2, trans. Quintin Hoare (London: Verso, 1991) 31.

speculations almost seamlessly with forms of Greek metaphysics concentrated on philosophical acts of redoubling should consequently come as little surprise.

Modern Redoubling

To talk about the act of redoubling as an abstraction that grants sovereignty through its apparent autonomy is to describe the inaccessibility of sovereignty itself, of God's inaccessibility as much as a monarch's being set apart from everyday existence. What we are talking about when we talk about God in the modern era, according to Jean-Luc Marion, is not necessarily the notorious "death of God" that Nietzsche once proclaimed, but rather the unending inaccessibility of God.[2] There is, he notes, a great deal of confusion permeating multiple discourses (and in numerous disciplines) when we contemplate even the possibility of divine existence. What Marion makes clearer, however, is that, quite often, when we speak publicly of God, we are really speaking about ourselves, projecting our own desires onto an invisible divinity, all the while creating idols of God.[3] His reasonable suggestion is that, when speaking about divine things, it is perhaps best to remain apophatic in one's conjectures, offering up only hazardous suggestions as to what God is *not* rather than speculating, and so projecting, our all-too-human ideas onto the divine.

It is for this reason, Marion will contend, that every conceptual atheism is actually a provisional position, as any atheist critique of divine being can only address one of many existing conceptualizations about God, with each concept itself still subject to apophatic critique and deconstruction. Every refutation of God, he reasons, only contests one particular idea of God, which was itself inadequate according to long-standing apophatic criticisms of divine being.[4] What we witness in a contemporary, critical context then is not the same as the modern "death of God" paraded triumphally by rational iconoclasts through the streets of Western Europe. We are no longer subject to the reductionistic and short-sighted "death of God"; rather, we behold the "death of the death of God," as he puts it, a negative redoubling that signals the end of a specific strain of critique.

As he demonstrates with reference to the Christian tradition specifically, to critique our ideas *about* God is more or less built into the nature *of* God. Christianity depicts this reality insofar as it posits images of the divine that represent an impossible representation, quite literally through its formulations of the Trinity, a Godhead that cannot be comprehended by any suitable, reasonable framework

---

2. Jean-Luc Marion, *Negative Certainties*, trans. Stephen E. Lewis (Chicago: University of Chicago Press, 2015) 51.

3. Marion, *Negative Certainties*, 54.

4. Marion, *Negative Certainties*, 55.

of human understanding. The impossibility of representing God registers itself as the counter experience *of* God that is yet contained *within* God—a sign that a redoubling is certainly taking place.[5] Relying upon arguments commonly deployed to illustrate how atheism is only a position to be taken in response to theism, Marion points out how, to deny a particular idea of God, you first have to have an image of God to react against.[6] Marion's twist on this logic is that he is not claiming that every atheist is merely taking a reactionary stance against an established, historical theism. Instead, he is suggesting that the idea of God, as of an idea of the infinite, permeates human existence so thoroughly that we cannot remove the question of God from our thoughts, even if we can eliminate the historically accumulated knowledge of God embedded in organized religion. Consequently, the question he takes up is a question regarding the nature of both the possible and the impossible as they are dialectically situated within human thought. It is God's impossibility, the seeming impossibility of God's existence even, which makes the question of God forever possible.[7] (It is the act of redoubling itself, I will argue, that is primarily responsible for our inability to rid ourselves of the divine being.)

It is, for Marion, the possibility of an impossibility that creates a space for God within human existence, just as it will be the apparent impossibility of forgiveness that makes possible the transformative reality of forgiveness within a person's life, as he continues the line of inquiry.[8] The link to forgiveness is here more than emblematic in relation to the divine. The impossible, which becomes possible to think in the figure of God, is the "concept above all concepts," he will go on to claim, and we encounter God, the absolute "concept of concepts," when we try to transgress the impossible, which forgiveness helps us to perceive.[9] It is easy to imagine how we come immediately up against the notion of divine being at the same moment that we experience forgiveness, as both God and forgiveness present themselves as impossibilities that humans yet inevitably encounter over and again *within* their lived realities.

As Marion will subsequently take up in his assessment of God and forgiveness, we repeatedly subject ourselves to the paradoxical logic of forgiveness wherein what *must* be an impossibility (the act of forgiveness itself, which can never be presumed or taken as a given) must yet *become possible* if humanity is to achieve any sense of being-together. The paradoxical nature of this formulation for how forgiveness

---

5. Marion, *Negative Certainties*, 56.
6. Marion, *Negative Certainties*, 58.
7. Marion, *Negative Certainties*, 60.
8. Marion, *Negative Certainties*, 62.
9. Marion, *Negative Certainties*, 63–64.

works thus structurally bears a parallel with our historical understanding of a divine being wherein the infinite is said to be experienced through the finite, just as the finite is our gateway to the infinite.[10] It is the possibility of God imposing God's own impossibility upon humanity that becomes the hallmark of the concept of God, which is, ideally speaking, the "concept of the concept."[11]

What potentially also reveals itself within Marion's argumentation, however, is that, if forgiveness and divine being have a structural parallel, what prohibits us from assuming that the same onto-theological mistake that humanity once made concerning God's (non)existence—confusing the "Being of beings" with an actually existing ontological divine being, as Heidegger once deduced—is not replaying itself within a new framework of forgiveness?[12] If God is the "concept of concepts" for Marion, as it was once the "Being of beings" for Heidegger, what prevents us from reading forgiveness as the "concept of concepts" preceding divine being? Though our human desire to illustrate the impossible becoming possible through a divine figure may speak to the alleged presence of God, wouldn't we have to concede that the all-too-human act of forgiveness, precisely in its parallel formulation to divine being, grants us a new perspective by which to glimpse our own humanity, and not any supposed divine being? This question seems to follow directly on the heels of one of the oldest Platonic quandaries regarding God's relationship to the Good, as I have already noted: is God dependent on the Good, or the Good dependent on God?

Marion is to some degree aware of the possibility of mistaking the conceptual absoluteness of God—God being the "concept of the concept," as with Aristotle's original metaphysical speculation that God was the "thought of thought"—with forgiveness. He attempts to deal with this problem when he reasons that, if omnipotence is bound by the limits of impossibility, this binding must be dismissed because it appears to limit God, otherwise the framework of reason would be imposed on God, and a deistic paradigm alone would be left standing.[13] Omnipotence, as such, appears to limit divine power and so must be rethought.[14] What we witness in this argument is a revitalization of metaphysics—a defense of the "Being of beings"—through Marion's turn to forgiveness and the "givenness of the gift."[15]

10. Marion, *Negative Certainties*, 66.

11. Marion, *Negative Certainties*, 69.

12. Martin Heidegger, *Being and Time*, trans. Joan Stambaugh (Albany, NY: State University of New York, 1996).

13. Marion, *Negative Certainties*, 71–72.

14. Marion, *Negative Certainties*, 77.

15. This is an argument that needs to be made much more in-depth in light of Marion's earlier conjectures about a "God without being" in his *God Without Being: Hors-texte*, trans. Thomas A. Carlson, Religion and Postmodernism (Chicago: University of Chicago Press, 1991).

More Modern Redoublings

What Marion addresses is very much at the center of those conceptual-philosophical acts of redoubling that attempt to isolate and elevate conceptual abstractions to the point of creating a metaphysical, and even political-theological, platform for the legitimation of divine being and human institutions alike. Metaphysics, throughout its long history, has been littered with notions of divine being merged with conceptual, redoubled abstractions, in order to justify divine being as the "highest of the high," the source of all forgiveness (necessarily akin but distinct from political pardon, an act which indicates one's sovereign position).

Hegel's formulation of God as the concept of the concept, for example, may have been an instance of what William Desmond has called a "counterfeit" God in that it is not a position taken on divine being so much as it is a logical redoubling in an attempt at absolute mastery, or a mastery of the absolute.[16] For Desmond, such acts are what truly define the history of metaphysics, as they are an attempt at taking a position outside of or beyond (*meta*) whatever established perspective seems to govern our world. Thus, they are efforts toward providing one's own foundations beyond whatever concept or authority had seemed to limit them. Redoubling becomes, from this point of view, a metaphysical tactic of the highest order.

Hegel, we can note, determined in his *Science of Logic* that the absolute is formed through its ability to be self-positing, an "absolute self-mediation" that defines its existence as substance.[17] It is a reflective movement that posits itself through its enacted self-reflection. Substance, however, is what is presupposed by the Notion, and so taken up *within* the Notion, allowing the Notion to come into its own being through the presupposition of substance.[18] When substance becomes the cause of itself, it enters into a new identity, one forged in a freedom raised above, but not separate from, its substantiality, and this is the freedom of the Notion itself.[19] In short order, the abstraction that takes place in the self-positing of substance is what

---

16. William Desmond, *Hegel's God: A Counterfeit Double?* (Aldershot: Ashgate, 2003). On the metaphysical implications of Hegel's positing the "concept of the concept" as the Absolute, see Robert B. Pippin, *Hegel's Realm of Shadows: Logic as Metaphysics in* The Science of Logic (Chicago: University of Chicago, 2019).

17. G. W. F. Hegel, *Science of Logic*, trans. A.V. Miller (Atlantic Highlands, NJ: Humanities Press, 1969) 555.

18. Hegel, *Science of Logic*, 577. From the perspective of Giorgio Agamben, the presupposition of substance is precisely what makes Hegelian thought an exemplary metaphysical effort. I will, however, argue that, though there is a certain correctness to Agamben's critique of Hegel, redoubling, and metaphysics, there is also a negative redoubling to be found in both Hegel and Agamben that functions at the same time to negate the metaphysical constructs humanity yet continues to produce. See Giorgio Agamben, *The Use of Bodies*, trans. Adam Kotsko (Stanford: Stanford University Press, 2016).

19. Hegel, *Science of Logic*, 582.

gives rise to the Notion, or Concept. The duality of substance and Notion that we usually understand it to be is in fact an illusion, because their opposition, though apparent throughout, is only a sign of their being present in each other: "in thinking and enunciating the one, the other also is immediately thought and enunciated."[20] Substance gives rise to the Notion, which, in turn, is what we consider to be the identity of the self, the "I," or self-consciousness to be, what we often take, as substance relating to an ephemeral Notion, to be the soul—or what Aristotle had defined as the "form of all forms."[21]

It is here in Hegel's thought, with his definition of soul, that we can see how the presupposition of substance by the Notion is what gave rise to metaphysics—hence the reference to something ethereal and theological like the soul—but also simply to consciousness itself through the process of abstraction and the positing of a dimension of universality within human thought. Soul is a conceptual attempt to articulate the absolute relation itself, that which cannot actually be expressed except in the relationship between substance and Notion. This is why Hegel can argue that the Notion is not yet itself "fully a soul."[22] The Notion, we are cautioned, is not complete, as it has not yet risen to the level of the Idea, though it has presupposed, or subjugated, being and essence in its positing of itself as the absolute.[23]

If the Idea, for Hegel, is the concept of the concept, or the notion of the notion—models of abstraction that are but merely forerunners of Heidegger's "Being of beings"—it is interesting that the Notion itself ultimately comes about not through a positive metaphysical gesture of redoubling as abstraction, but through a negative process of redoubling that abstracts, but in a subtly different way, causing us to reread any "positive" redoublings. So many interpretations of Hegel turn upon readings and misreadings of this particular aspect of redoubling.

Essence is identified as the first negation of being, or what Hegel will call illusory being, while the Notion is the second negation, or the negation of negation, "being that has been restored as the infinite mediation and negativity of being within itself."[24] We abstract from our essence in order to conceive of a Notion. This is how redoubling, as an act of abstraction, puts us at once beyond our essence—transcends it, if you will—while also being something fundamental to who we are at the same time. It is not, however, the establishment of a "superior" being (e.g., a supposed

20. Hegel, *Science of Logic*, 582.
21. Hegel, *Science of Logic*, 583, 585. On Aristotle's claim that the soul was the "form of the form," see the commentary offered in Jan Patočka, *Plato and Europe*, trans. Petr Lom (Stanford: Stanford University Press, 2002) 193.
22. Hegel, *Science of Logic*, 760.
23. Hegel, *Science of Logic*, 587, 591.
24. Hegel, *Science of Logic*, 596.

deity who embodies the *Being* of beings), but an abstraction that reflects a new perspective on what is already present, hence giving rise to consciousness itself as merely a process of reflection upon an already existing substance.

What he is accessing is the "Notion of the Notion," an establishment of the universality of the Notion that is achieved only through the Notion's relation of itself to itself through negativity.[25] What takes place is a positing of absolute self-identity in the process of a redoubled negation. The universal is unbounded in relation to identity, or the identical, which is the result of the first negation only, what he calls "illusory being." This is what Hegel labels a "free power," "free love," or "boundless blessedness," but also a "creative power" that speaks only of an absolute liberation in that the Notion, as the negation of negation, does not take on a new identity through the activity of negation, but rather experiences a freedom without violence, a recognition of otherness within the self that is treated as one's own self.[26] This is how the self "returns to itself" while also transcending itself at the same time.[27]

Though representational thinking would express a separation between the universal and the particular, as also between the other and the self, the negation of negation present in his formulation of the Notion "contains their opposition and at the same time contains it in its ground or unity, the effected coincidence of each with its other."[28] The sublation of the other that nonetheless does not impede the Notion from identifying with itself as a free Notion forms the "preservation and retention" of identity formed through the first negation that is yet still present after the second negation or mediation.[29] This configuration is what leads Hegel to use phrases such as "the finite is infinite, one is many, the individual is the universal."[30] These statements appear as inadequate, though, as Hegel points out, the thinking of contradiction is actually the "essential moment of the Notion."[31] In his words, "Formal thinking does in fact think contradiction, only it at once looks away from it, and in saying that it is unthinkable it merely passes over from it into abstract negation."[32] This formal contradiction is itself sublated by the second negation of the first negation, what gives life to a free being.[33] The negation of negation, the other of the other, becomes a positive, identical, universal, as the Notion carries with it all that it once

25. Hegel, *Science of Logic*, 601.
26. Hegel, *Science of Logic*, 603, 605, 843.
27. Hegel, *Science of Logic*, 603.
28. Hegel, *Science of Logic*, 620.
29. Hegel, *Science of Logic*, 822, 834.
30. Hegel, *Science of Logic*, 834.
31. Hegel, *Science of Logic*, 835.
32. Hegel, *Science of Logic*, 835.
33. Hegel, *Science of Logic*, 836.

contained, not losing anything, only "enriching and consolidating itself."[34] It is an end returning to its beginning, a circular achievement that is also what he will term the "circle of circles."[35]

The Idea, for Hegel, is a combination of the Notion and objectivity, but not as something that can be achieved once and for all, or as that which can be a goal set before oneself to achieve; rather, the Idea is always *beyond* us.[36] The truth that can be articulated from this perspective is one that is only possible insofar as the Notion is joined to reality, just as soul is joined to body.[37] If the Notion does not relate to its own self, there is only a "dead, spiritless spirit, a material object" before us. The Idea is rather Life itself, and consequently an "absolute universality," one that transitions into cognition itself.[38] Cognition is in fact the Idea relating itself to itself—what is very similar to the "thought of thought," as Aristotle had defined divine being.[39] The Notion, when immersed purely in itself, is subjectivity, but when it is placed in objectivity, becomes the Idea or Life itself.[40] What Hegel proposes goes beyond traditional metaphysical speculations regarding the spirit or soul, delving straight to the heart of the dynamics of consciousness itself and the misperceptions of the self relating to itself as it gives rise to a metaphysical sense of the beyond.[41] In this manner, however, the beyond is nothing more than the result of the internal processes of consciousness coming to life.

Aristotelean metaphysics was premised on the concept of God as thought thinking itself, but Hegel corrects this speculation as he describes the Idea, *not* God, as a "pure thought" thinking itself, the "self-determination of apprehending itself."[42] Just as metaphysics might once have described divine being, but which now characterizes the processes of human existence, Hegel is able to express how "the logical Idea has itself as the infinite form for its content."[43] What we have been looking at in the processes of redoubling is ourselves as we come to recognize ourselves as who we are—a statement paralleled by the only suitable definition of the human being as the being who is capable of recognizing itself *as* a human being.

---

34. Hegel, *Science of Logic*, 836, 840.
35. Hegel, *Science of Logic*, 842.
36. Hegel, *Science of Logic*, 756.
37. Hegel, *Science of Logic*, 756.
38. Hegel, *Science of Logic*, 760, 763–64.
39. Hegel, *Science of Logic*, 774.
40. Hegel, *Science of Logic*, 775.
41. Hegel, *Science of Logic*, 775.
42. Hegel, *Science of Logic*, 825.
43. Hegel, *Science of Logic*, 825.

Humanity Redoubled

The definition of humanity as the only species of animal capable of recognizing itself as a human being, hence positing itself through an act of self-reflexive awareness and redoubling, is the lesson analyzed extensively by Giorgio Agamben in his study on the border between human and animal, *The Open*.[44] What Agamben critiques, in this context as in so many others, is the propensity of humanity to establish a metaphysical legitimation for its own existence through its capacity for abstraction, or what is made manifest in humanity's definition of itself through a redoubled process. Following Heidegger closely in his criticisms of such acts of redoubling, Agamben commits himself to undermining the logic of presupposition wherein the anthropological machinery, as he puts it, subdues the substance of life—or form-of-life—that resists being inscribed into a particular conceptual schema. Metaphysics has been complicit for too long with positing specific "natures" of humans, animals, and gods alike. When Agamben consequently opposes Hegel, he does so on the grounds that he is indebted to a form of dialectics that reinscribes metaphysics at its core. What he misses, however, is the way in which, for Hegel, dialectics proceeds only through a negative redoubling, a "negation of negation" that actually parallels Agamben's own philosophical musings.[45]

Hegel's emphasis on the negation of negation actually shares a powerful structural affinity with Pauline thought, at least according to Agamben's reading of Paul's Letter to the Romans.[46] This is a key interpretation, as it allows us to see how Pauline Christianity both does and does not respond to the positive acts of redoubling that grounded Judaic conceptions of divine existence. Rather than thus re-assert the "king of kings" abstractions as a means to sovereign power, Paul's second-level internal division (into flesh/spirit) of a primary-level social division (of Jew/Gentile) produces a context wherein being a Christian, for Paul, means being willing to subject oneself to a "death with Christ" that is, in reality, a "division of division itself," as Agamben phrases it. One's social, political, and religious identities, always predicated upon existing, pre-formed divisions (or categorizations) between persons and

---

44. Giorgio Agamben, *The Open: Man and Animal*, trans. Kevin Attell, Meridian: Crossing Aesthetics (Stanford: Stanford University Press, 2003). Agamben's critique of this definition is the subject of this particular study, which attempts to point beyond this privileging of the human species above all other lifeforms.

45. The same misreading could be applied as well to Agamben's reading of Adorno on dialectics, which misses a fuller elaboration of what negative dialectics entails, as well as Adorno's reading of Hegel, which turns on the possibility of a negative redoubling. For more on this topic, see my chapter on "Theodor W. Adorno" in *Agamben's Philosophical Lineage*, ed. Adam Kotsko and Carlo Salzani (Edinburgh: Edinburgh University Press, 2017) 219–29.

46. Giorgio Agamben, *The Time that Remains: A Commentary on the Letter to the Romans*, trans. Patricia Dailey, Meridian: Crossing Aesthetics (Stanford: Stanford University Press, 2005).

groups, are torn from within by a second division between the flesh and the spirit, which hollows out every first-order division, rendering them inoperative. Being a Jew no longer means simply adhering to the outward signs of "Jewishness"; it means locating an internal Jewish spirit (or soul, I might add) that is universal and abstract, but not in the sense of creating a politically sovereign being. In fact, what appears to be the spirit of true faith, for Paul, is the recognition that one's external identity has died, and that only the abstract universality of Christ remains when all else has disappeared, placing one outside of the social and political divisions of our world and leaving one to wonder if Paul was approaching some sort of relativistic renunciation of all labels and identities (e.g., what we witness in his suggestions that "there is neither male nor female" to his ability to "be a Jew with the Jews" and yet to "be a Gentile with the Gentiles").

Asking how the concept of the concept relates to the negation of negation, in a Hegelian context, is essentially the same as asking how the monarchical title king of kings relates to the Pauline division of division. There is an abstraction that is performed, one that may lead to justifications for transcendence from materiality and so legitimizing sovereign power, but this same abstraction brought about by an act of redoubling, if seen in negative terms—as the negation of negation or the division of division—leads to an abstract universalization that never fully achieves sovereignty in temporal, political terms, or, more accurately, only achieves subjectivity, consciousness or a sovereignty of the self insofar as it never reaches a complete identity with itself. There is always an otherness within the self that cannot be mastered, only approached through a negative redoubling that avoids creating a positive redoubling as an explicit attempt at mastery and dominance *through* abstract universalizing.

In a negative redoubling, the concept of the concept, just as with thought thinking about itself, never fully reaches an end in and of itself as it is undermined by the negative redoubling which haunts it. There is a tautological circularity within a (negative) redoubling that may continue to strive for completion but will never fully achieve it. This situation is why Hegelian redoubling, which recognizes both positive and negative efforts at redoubling, shares its processes with more contemporary theoretical interventions such as Pierre Bourdieu's attempts at "objectifying objectivity," Bruno Latour's "relativizing relativity" and Étienne Balibar's "secularizing secularity."[47] Each of these processes is never-ending, always striving for that which is out of reach, but which we should never stop trying to achieve. In that sense, each of these efforts shares with Derrida's efforts to "democratize democracy," but also to

47. See Étienne Balibar, *Secularism and Cosmopolitanism: Critical Hypotheses on Religion and Politics*, trans. G.M. Goshgarian (New York, Columbia University Press, 2018); Pierre Bourdieu, *The Logic of Practice*, trans. Richard Nice (Stanford: Stanford University Press, 1990); and Bruno Latour, *We Have Never Been Modern*, trans. Catherine Porter (Cambridge: Harvard University Press, 1993).

locate a "religion without religion," which seeks to embody a (spectral) messianicity without (historical) messianism, these negative markers which likewise strive for a justice which can never be fully enacted in this world.[48]

Revisiting Forgiveness

I want to return to the topic of forgiveness that we saw a moment ago in Marion's work, as it helps to illuminate the stakes today for conceiving of divine being, because forgiveness, due to its impossibility and yet necessity, mirrors well the processes of redoubling that I have isolated and examined. Vladimir Jankélévitch, in his book *Forgiveness*, sets the stage for a further framing of the act of forgiveness as what pushes the boundaries of the possible. As he describes it, the event of forgiveness is always unreasonable, or "without reasons."[49] Forgiveness, like love, is without reservations, introducing an absurd conundrum into one's life while also instituting a new life as a sort of second birth.[50] Both forgiveness and love act "even though" they should not, against reason, as an "insanity" even, causing us to see how forgiveness, like faith, is a paradoxical wager (Pascal) that believes despite the absurdity of its belief. Giving reasons for forgiveness are as irrational as those given for faith.[51] Indeed, if one had reasons to forgive, it would not be forgiveness (or faith). Forgiveness is gratuitous, like love, though it is not love, nor does it change into love, though we do end up with the possibility of loving the one we forgive through the act of forgiveness itself.

Forgiveness, in this way, evinces a "reason without reasons," what we see in a love whose grounds are ultimately groundless. Such gestures are akin, I would add, to Kant's definition of the sublime as a "groundless ground" or "lawless law."[52] These negative redoublings are part of the positive redoubling that grounds the ungrounded in the act of forgiveness, as in the act of love, something that Jankélévitch makes clear when he speaks of how love "renders what it loves lovable."[53] What is being said here helps us to see how the "concept of the concept" or the "thought of thought" can be identified with a divine being, as it is the act of loving itself that is identified with the one who loves and the one who receives, meaning that it is theoretically understandable if we tend to associate the "givenness of the given" (Marion) with the

---

48. See, among other places in his writings, Jacques Derrida, *Specters of Marx: The State of the Debt, the Work of Mourning and the New International*, trans. Peggy Kamuf (London: Routledge, 1994).

49. Vladimir Jankélévitch, *Forgiveness*, trans. Andrew Kelley (Chicago: University of Chicago Press, 2005) 119.

50. Jankélévitch, *Forgiveness*, 98–99.

51. Jankélévitch, *Forgiveness*, 106–7, 130.

52. Immanuel Kant, *Critique of the Power of Judgment*, ed. Paul Guyer, trans. Paul Guyer and Eric Matthews (Cambridge: Cambridge University Press, 2000).

53. Jankélévitch, *Forgiveness*, 146.

"Giver" whom we imagine to be the source of all that is given to us. If one renders the object of their love lovable through the love they give, through a "groundless ground" or a "reason without reasons," there is the establishment of a subjectivity through the act itself, as if one could not separate the act from the subject who is also the object. As Jankélévitch describes matters, our love transforms the one we love, without end, so that the faults of our beloved "become qualities" of what we love in them—what he refers to as the process of crystallization in Stendhal's writing. Faith therefore crystalizes, like love, producing forms of the beloved and the lover alike.[54]

Forgiveness involves forgiving the unforgiveable, just as love involves loving the unlovable. Loving the unlovable, of course, means loving the enemy and so establishes itself, he suggests, as the "paradoxical order of charity" while also demonstrating how forgiveness, like God, is a *causa sui*.[55] It is the ability to be a cause of one's own self through the acts of forgiveness and of loving that will remind us of the process of redoubling wherein someone becomes their own foundation. Hence, he continues, we observe how forgiveness forgives because it forgives, with no other explanation needed or allowed, just as love loves because it loves, *without reasons*. There is undoubtedly a circular logic at play in these formulations, but this circularity *is* the spontaneous nature of love and forgiveness. It is the clinamen, Jankélévitch notes, the movement of a wholly contingent event that we cannot control. This state of things is why forgiveness suspends the old order and creates the new, offering humanity salvation and resurrection at the same time.[56]

Within these processes we encounter the "supernaturality of forgiveness," an alteration of the orientation of our relations, that yet never stops, not even with the creation of a new order.[57] Hence forgiveness is itself unending, eternal, and part of a perpetual peace, an act of "forgiving one time" for all time, extending "unlimited credit" to the guilty. Though one may wonder what need there is for divine forgiveness when one simply beholds the infinite, impossible supernaturality of the act of forgiveness itself, we are nonetheless faced with a human phenomenon that can be summarized as "the inexplicable, the unjust, the mysteriously great feats of Forgiveness."[58] It is without a hint of irony that Jankélévitch predicates both omnipotence *and* impotence to forgiveness, through the *coincidentia oppositorium* that gives it its nature—reflecting a Hegelian motif at its core.[59]

54. Jankélévitch, *Forgiveness*, 147.
55. Jankélévitch, *Forgiveness*, 95.
56. Jankélévitch, *Forgiveness*, 148–49.
57. Jankélévitch, *Forgiveness*, 154.
58. Jankélévitch, *Forgiveness*, 155.
59. Jankélévitch, *Forgiveness*, 164.

In Marion's analysis, the impossibility of God as a fundamental question haunting humanity throughout the centuries neatly overlaps with the structural impossibility of forgiveness. This is an overlap that might have historically given rise to the idea of God as well, as Marion's replaying of Heidegger's ontological difference between Being and beings becomes one between givenness and the gifts that are actually given. Any gift, reduced to givenness, "accomplishes itself with an *unconditioned* freedom," he will state, so that the giver must disappear for the gift to appear, and this is when it paradoxically becomes a gift.[60]

Just as every particular, actually existing being masks the abstract concept of Being behind it, so too does every gift conceal the abstract sense of givenness behind it—a parallel that invokes Heidegger and the ontological difference between Being and beings, which is what the distinction between the gift and givenness is directly based on.[61] In a way that further illuminates how negative redoubling merely affirms positive redoubling, Marion demonstrates how sacrifice, the negative element, returns the gift to givenness itself, to "dwell in its [the gift's] totality." Sacrifice—or, as I would define it, a negation of what had already been divided from ordinary life, or a "negation of negation" then—returns to the gift its givenness and so makes visible "the process of givenness itself" (the positive act of redoubling that so often leads to metaphysical speculation on divine existence).[62] Sacrifice, so to speak, re-gives the gift, "as a gift given up, an abandonment of which no possession any longer masks the provenance and hides the status as given. *Sacrifice effects the redounding [la redondance] of the gift in the giving up.*"[63] Marion explicitly calls forth the act of redoubling as both that which comes back upon itself in order to ground itself, but also as a *redundancy*, an extraneous redoubling that adds nothing more to the substance that is already given to us.

Sacrifice and forgiveness, he argues, each "consists in a repetition of the reduction of the gift to givenness."[64] What he highlights is the "evidence of givenness and, within it, that of the giver redoubled," or what takes place by "repeating the very process of giving the gift, by redoubling the givenness of the gift, so that this *redounding [redondance]* of the giving event submerges its own result and becomes more visible than what it gives in the eyes of the recipient himself."[65] The regiving of the gift is only possible through forgiveness because "Forgiveness, by elevating to power the

---

60. Marion, *Negative Certainties*, 121–22.
61. Marion, *Negative Certainties*, 125.
62. Marion, *Negative Certainties*, 127.
63. Marion, *Negative Certainties*, 127.
64. Marion, *Negative Certainties*, 144.
65. Marion, *Negative Certainties*, 145.

process of givenness of the same and prior gift, submerges the given gift and the gaze of the recipient through the evident glory of this remade, repeated, restated, and *redounding* act of giving." Forgiveness forces one to recognize "for the first time" the originally given gift. As such, he concludes, "*Forgiveness assumes the gift, because it consists in its redounding.*"[66]

For Marion, who might be said to rehabilitate the positive metaphysical side of things through recourse to religious notions of sacrifice, only God "can forgive everything, precisely because he has created everything," and so appears as merciful because of his transcendence. Everything appears as a gift to God, through a type of the negative certainty perceived through the impossibility of God that is yet a possibility.[67] Marion's quest, as in his other writings, is to demonstrate, however, how he can access a space that makes room for God without invoking metaphysics. Metaphysics, he claims, does not know the event of forgiveness, because metaphysics speaks of causes, whereas the event appears without cause.[68] The event, then, mirrors divine being in that it gives itself by itself. Hence, every causal explanation or reason given is "powerless" against the event.[69] What he is tracing the contours of, once again, is a saturated phenomenon in which the intuition overflows the concept.[70]

Though I am less certain that a metaphysics is not smuggled in through the back door in his writings, Marion's focus on counter-experiences, which attest to saturated phenomena, allows him to take up the possible-impossible manifestation of the divine, though allegedly without engaging in a positive redoubling that grounds metaphysical-sovereign propositions like "king of kings."[71] There is a negative certainty, he wagers, that arrives in one's knowledge so that certainty can never be claimed about the other who remains entirely other. In this context, certitude becomes an obstacle to knowing, and we live in bad faith if we only try for positive knowledge—a point that resonates with Hegel's juxtaposing positive and negative acts of redoubling.[72] Searching for an "infinite finitude" means that thought cannot avoid the paradoxes of redoubling.[73] Rather, the paradox of thought is to want to discover something that thought cannot think—a negative redoubling that parallels

---

66. Marion, *Negative Certainties*, 146.
67. Marion, *Negative Certainties*, 147.
68. Marion, *Negative Certainties*, 182.
69. Marion, *Negative Certainties*, 183.
70. See, for example, Jean-Luc Marion, *In Excess: Studies of Saturated Phenomena*, trans. Robyn Horner and Vincent Berraud, Perspectives in Continental Philosophy (New York: Fordham University Press, 2004).
71. Marion, *Negative Certainties*, 205.
72. Marion, *Negative Certainties*, 206.
73. Marion, *Negative Certainties*, 207.

the negation of negation instead of reinscribing us within a metaphysical attempt to think the thought of thought. We are brought then to a place where we are forced to realize, in classic Hegelian terms, that *both the thought of thought and what thought cannot think are the same thing, both wholly unthinkable to the human mind.*

The event, as with forgiveness, only evidences a negative certitude. There is a want for more complexity, and a shunning of reductive views. There is a recognition that the search for positive knowledge only (reason, objects, definitions) is limited and misses the fuller picture made viewable through the actually existing realities of our encounters with negative certitudes. Forgiveness allows for possibilities, new possibilities in (positive) history, through the intrusion of the impossible into the realm of the possible. Forgiveness thus lets us see how other, complex narratives can proliferate and be heard, but can never be exhaustive; hence we must always apologize for not allowing enough complexity to be heard.

Substitution

Nicolas De Warren, in his book *Original Forgiveness*, shares with both Jankélévitch and Marion in portraying forgiveness as an absolute foundation, as the "promise" before promises, that is the condition for freedom itself.[74] It is not hard to see why so many have defined God as the source of both freedom and forgiveness. Freedom is locatable within forgiveness, in fact, because forgiveness is "an originating power in powerlessness, the anarchy of all beginnings," or what De Warren will also call the "anarchy of redemption."[75] As we have already seen, the negativity of forgiveness appears through its being a possibility of the impossible, for forgiveness must appear as impossible or it would not be possible to forgive.[76] Forgiveness is, as Marion stressed continuously, an impossible possibility. Though we are once again poised to ask what place there is for divine forgiveness or unconditional forgiveness when humans engage in the impossible possibility of forgiveness, we are forced to witness the "anarchic availability of forgiveness" as it is not dependent on any alleged "divine presence."[77] It is itself without grounding or principle; it is "unpredictable" and "uncontrollable." The "anarchy of forgiveness," as he terms it, is without guarantee, a replacement of the traditional divine will, which is notoriously unpredictable, appearing to favor some and disfavor others, offering solely its divine, mysterious judgment. Divine pardon, seen from this light, is not true forgiveness, but rather

74. Nicolas De Warren, *Original Forgiveness* (Evanston, IL: Northwestern University Press, 2020) 2.
75. De Warren, *Original Forgiveness*, 5.
76. De Warren, *Original Forgiveness*, 45.
77. De Warren, *Original Forgiveness*, 159.

what has been utilized historically to legitimate divine (monarchical) sovereignty. The problems of theodicy and divine election are concerned with justifying divine rule as it is bound up with positive acts of redoubling, not the actual conditions and relationships involved in forgiveness.

We encounter the act of redoubling in De Warren when he turns to investigate how a Levinasian framework for freedom and responsibility emerges through one's responsibility for another, an "immemorial" responsibility for the other that pre-exists our memory.[78] Like the promise before all promises, there is a "pastness" in our responsibility for the other that was never itself present. We cannot feel nostalgia for such origins, and they do not promise salvation like the narratives of fatherlands or religious traditions.[79] It is an anarchic and interrupting force, traumatic even, to be called to one's responsibility through such means.

What De Warren points toward uniquely in the context of forgiveness is the primacy of substitution wherein one is bound to the other through responsibility for them, a process of binding and unbinding where the Other is always a "missed encounter" that "opens the possibility of any and all encounters."[80] Like the substitution of one thing for another in metaphor (which Derrida describes so eloquently in his essay on redoubling, "White Mythology"), Levinas puts forth a notion of substitution that retains a proximity to the Other while also introducing a distance from the Other at the same time, thereby avoiding fusion or identification with, absorption *into*, the self.[81] The "subjectivity of the subject," he will find, is only possible through a substitution that is also an act of expiation, of letting the other remain *as* wholly other in their otherness. Expiation unites identity and alterity, yet this expiation is not what we normally think of when we consider forgiveness.[82]

Substitution is not to be understood according to a logic of gift or exchange, but rather as what takes place when we perceive that original forgiveness is not an act or an action, but "the subjectivity of the subject in its inspiration toward the Other—its openness—and investiture of the Good in being in the world."[83] Though the Good is transcendent, for De Warren, with there being no outside of the Good, even though the Good is "beyond being," it is not to be aligned with divine being, but rather with what is inescapably human.[84] We cannot escape standing before the (idea of the)

78. De Warren, *Original Forgiveness*, 202–3.
79. De Warren, *Original Forgiveness*, 204.
80. De Warren, *Original Forgiveness*, 205–8.
81. De Warren, *Original Forgiveness*, 212. See also Jacques Derrida, "White Mythology," *Margins of Philosophy*, trans. Alan Bass (Chicago: University of Chicago Press, 1982).
82. De Warren, *Original Forgiveness*, 213–14.
83. De Warren, *Original Forgiveness*, 231.
84. De Warren, *Original Forgiveness*, 241.

Good which exposes our shame.[85] An act of redoubling occurs, moreover, when we consider how, before the Good, we are ashamed of our shame: there is an "unbearable shame at the shame of one's unjustifiable existence," which calls us to be responsible for the other while, at the same time, we run the risk of misidentifying the source of the shame and blame it on the other.[86] We indulge "the shameless dream of being absolutely self-forgiving for one's own shameful existence," while simultaneously hearing a command for hospitality to the other.[87] It is this split within the experience of being human that reminds us of both the positive (metaphysical) attempts to overcome our limitations through abstraction (the egotistical possibility of being self-forgiving) while also moving through the negative redoubled aspects of our being ashamed at our shame—the only real way to move forward so as not to risk attempting a false mastery of oneself.

Overcoming our fundamental human condition of feeling shame at the shame that is felt standing before the Good, as before the Other, is what enables us to relinquish our quest for sovereignty and mastery over the other. We are, much like Paul had once found a way past the social dualities that structure our world, able to disable master/slave relations, to become rather a "servant to the servants," "to command to command" without sovereignty or authority, to invoke a "powerless glory" that allows us to "command to be commanded," as De Warren puts it. The strength that appears in weakness that Paul once identified as the key to Christian identity becomes apparent once again through the substitution of oneself for another, through responsibility for the other, which Levinas had once described as a state of being always engaged in forgiving the other for holding us hostage in our responsibility to them.[88] Feeling that the other is "two faced" insofar as we feel responsibility for them but also a rage towards them, we recognize the act of substitution as what fundamentally makes us human—the "subjectivity of the subject"—wherein we remain subjects split from within, the barred subject who both is and is not.[89]

What we genuinely encounter in this space is that we are left facing a self that interrupts itself, but also where one finds that one's shame is expiated in an original

---

85. De Warren, *Original Forgiveness*, 239.
86. De Warren, *Original Forgiveness*, 240.
87. De Warren, *Original Forgiveness*, 232.
88. De Warren, *Original Forgiveness*, 233.

89. De Warren, *Original Forgiveness*, 235. Another route to these same conclusions could be made through the work of Paul Ricoeur, whose work on metaphor in relation to metaphysics arguably dovetails with his suggestions about fundamentally understanding "oneself as another." See Paul Ricoeur, *The Rule of Metaphor: The Creation of Meaning in Language*, trans. Robert Czerny, Kathleen McLaughlin, and John Costello (London: Routledge, 1977); and *Oneself as Another*, trans. Kathleen Blamey (Chicago: University of Chicago Press, 1995).

forgiveness that precedes us, much as Marion had described sacrifice earlier.[90] This "anarchy of original forgiveness" is the "anarchy of Goodness" that remains a mystery to us always, even as we rely upon it to establish our sense of self in the first place insofar as it measures the "subjectivity of the subject."[91]

Conclusion

Søren Kierkegaard, in his *Works of Love*, offers us another angle from which to view these same lines of thought on the act of redoubling. In ways that parallel Levinas's definition of substitution, for example, Kierkegaard describes the neighbor as the one close to oneself, so close that they are actually a "redoubling" of the self, as he puts it.[92] Our proximity to the "other," he finds, is what tests the selfishness of self-love, which, for its part, cannot stand this redoubling. The command to love one's neighbor as oneself comes "as close as possible" to self-love without actually being it, issuing a summons to each individual, at the same time, to love themselves in the right way, for without a proper self-love, one cannot love the neighbor either. The self is called, then, not to further abstract itself in a bid for universal autonomy and sovereignty—to be lord of itself as a "king of kings" among all other humans. Rather, the redoubling is a negative one, a self divided by the other who is nonetheless still the self (and yet also always *not* the self as we define it to ourselves).

In its infinite capacity, love finds that it must remain in the infinite to be love.[93] That is, when love dwells exclusively on itself and not on the infinite, it is out of its element, and makes itself an object to itself. Hence, self-love, in order to be love, must be rooted in an infinity that is beyond the finite boundaries of the self. We are reminded by Kierkegaard that finite time is divided into three phases (past, present, future), though eternity simply exists.[94] Moreover, he will go so far as to claim that a temporal object cannot "redouble" or engage in "redoubling"; it is the eternal that redoubles within an individual, in both outward and inward directions, and in such a way that the inward and outward are seen as the same thing—an almost Hegelian formulation that Kierkegaard would no doubt bristle upon hearing. This is a significant point to make, however, as this distinction describes how redoubling itself is a process of the infinite and of transcendence.

---

90. De Warren, *Original Forgiveness*, 245.

91. De Warren, *Original Forgiveness*, 246.

92. Søren Kierkegaard, *Works of Love*, ed. and trans. Howard V. Hong and Edna H. Hong, Kierkegaard's Writings 16 (Princeton: Princeton University Press, 1995) 21.

93. Kierkegaard, *Works of Love*, 181.

94. Kierkegaard, *Works of Love*, 280.

The eternal has characteristics of its own, but it is also "in itself" with these characteristics in a way that the finite cannot be. Hence love, as rooted in the redoubling of the infinite, both is and is what it does. This is the core trait of redoubling, as he puts it, for the eternal is in itself at the same moment that it goes out of itself. There is a "returning" and an "outward going" that are the same thing. To love makes one the lover and makes the beloved the beloved at the same time.

Love must remain disinterested in the finite—again because a redoubling always puts itself at a remove from the existing being—so that it might remain love. Love is therefore always a "redoubling" of itself in an infinite context, as would be every sound description of spirit. Kierkegaard's turn inward—a position that will eventually prompt him to declare that "truth is subjectivity"—moves away from the external and to the internal, which is actuality.[95] Inwardly, to love God is to love people and vice versa. To extend the inwardly occurring notion of substitution (as redoubling) that much further, what we do to people, we do to God and this is what God does to us in turn. To hate others is therefore to hate God. In its biblical form, we make God "hard-hearted" by hating others. As such, God becomes a pure like for like: if anger is in us, then God is anger in us. If we are merciful, then God is merciful too: "God's relation to a human being is at every moment to infinitize what is in that human being at every moment."[96] There is an echo that is also a description of redoubling. God redoubles our actions "with the magnification of infinity."

What Kierkegaard calls the Christian "like for like," the act of redoubling that takes place between God and human actions, exposes the false "soft" forms of love that Christians might be tempted to spread, those sentimental forms in pursuit of happy days without self-concern.[97] Turning away from the external to the internal not only highlights the role of one's conscience, then, it also demonstrates the redoubled nature of faith.[98] When he reminds us that the biblical mandate is to "let it be done for you as you believe," there is no security, for everything is done for you only as you believe it to be.[99] You forgive only as you are forgiven and you are to be forgiven as you forgive others.[100] Hence, as he puts it, "your forgiveness is your forgiveness," "the forgiveness you give is the forgiveness you receive." Again, we are left to wonder what role the divine actually plays in these formulations other than

95. Kierkegaard, *Works of Love*, 384. On the nature of "truth as subjectivity," see too his *Concluding Unscientific Postscript to* Philosophical Fragments, 2 vols., trans. Howard V. Hong and Edna H. Hong, Kierkegaard's Writings 12 (Princeton: Princeton University Press, 1992).

96. Kierkegaard, *Works of Love*, 384.

97. Kierkegaard, *Works of Love*, 376.

98. Kierkegaard, *Works of Love*, 377.

99. Kierkegaard, *Works of Love*, 379.

100. Kierkegaard, *Works of Love*, 380.

as a guarantee of forgiveness taking place, for this is Christianity's like for like: God does for us what we do for others.[101]

In short order, the movement from the "positive" sovereign redoubling of the "king of kings," "thought of thought," or "concept of the concept" is undermined from within by a "division of division" or "negation of negation" that prevents absolute sovereignty from accruing even as it allows subjectivity—and even consciousness itself, Hegel would add—to form. Christianity would seem to exist already in the heart of Judaism, just as Christ dwells in the heart of God, as an illustration of these dynamics: a positive redoubling that must always be accompanied by a parallel negative redoubling. What this means, in political terms, is that every gesture toward sovereign authority will create its own limitations, no matter how much it resists exposing them to view, though to threaten the eradication of sovereign authority entirely is as implausible as it is impossible, since the forces that deconstruct its power are dependent upon its existence in the first place.

---

101. Kierkegaard, *Works of Love*, 383.

RESPONSE TO DICKINSON

Kaitlyn Schiess

Colby Dickinson has produced a compelling account of the metaphysical act of redoubling as it impacts notions of divine sovereignty, Pauline subversions of social divisions, and forgiveness as both an impossibility parallel to the impossibility of God and as a source of human salvation and resurrection. In his essay, Dickinson identifies the language "king of kings" and "lord of lords" that describes God in Scripture as a kind of redoubling that serves to not only relativize competing authorities but to legitimize an autonomous and abstract sovereignty removed from ordinary life. He helpfully explicates this rhetorical tactic through modern accounts of redoubling, as well as through a contrasting example of negative redoubling in Paul's description of the flesh and the spirit and an identification with the death of Christ. The conclusion identifies parallels between the inaccessibility of God and the paradoxical logic of forgiveness, in order to ultimately describe the redoubling between God and human actions in forgiveness.

There were a few themes I found particularly helpful in the context of a conversation about the Bible and the political sphere. The notion of sovereignty through autonomy, and self-referential or tautological declarations of authority, is resonant with modern Western notions of sovereignty. Is that due to its relationship to the predominant scriptural depiction of sovereignty, or are there features, such as the concept of God's holiness or the relationality of the incarnation, that might actually mitigate against this concept of sovereignty? Secondly, Dickinson's contrast between abstraction and encounter through lived realities is more than a useful set of categories for thinking about sovereignty but also a helpful lens for thinking about the nature and import of political theology. Finally, Dickinson illustrates the relationship between theological conceptions of sovereignty, forgiveness, and human identity, and the way those concepts inform or heighten political, social, or generally metaphysical conceptions. His parenthetical note about the relationship between forgiveness and political pardons highlights the inherently theological nature of our political concepts and conversations (resonant with Marion's argument that an idea of the infinite permeates human existence).

While there are many other themes to explore in Dickinson's paper, this response will focus on a few questions and observations intended to extend the arguments in the paper and draw out how they might inform both theological interpretation of Scripture and concrete political proposals.

First, I appreciate Dickinson tying a larger discussion of the nature of divine sovereignty to not only Aristotelean or modern conceptions of divinity in the context of redoubling, but to the specific textual feature of the language of "king of kings." His connection between the metaphysical legitimation of divine sovereignty and metaphysical legitimation of unitary political sovereigns is obviously not without precedent, but the specific use of redoubling clarifies that connection in a unique way.

It is not entirely clear, however, if the biblical language "king of kings" plays quite the extensive role, textually, that Dickinson's argument requires. The language might indicate the "idealized king amongst all other actually existing kings" in the context of the host of other communal beliefs of the people of Israel, but the language itself (and thus the tie to redoubling) does not necessarily bear all the weight of legitimating sovereignty. For one, the language is used a couple of times in Scripture to refer to human kings (Artaxerxes in Ezra 7:12 and Nebuchadnezzar in Daniel 2:37), complicating the extent to which the language was used by the Jewish people to guarantee an abstract and transcendental sovereignty.[1] While "lord of lords" and "god of gods" is used in Deuteronomy, and "king of kings" is used to describe Christ in the New Testament, "king of kings" is only used in its Mesopotamian context to refer to human kings of other nations in the Old Testament. There is also the purely exegetical question if *melek malkayya'* is truly a "redoubling." The repetition of the noun is a form of superlative in Hebrew, and there is a long tradition of understanding various other divine names as forms of the superlative as well.[2] It could of course be an instance of both a redoubling and a superlative, but the grammatical nature of the language and its use in the Old Testament might undermine the exegetical support for Dickinson's connection to "redoubling." Finally, there is some tension between the description of redoubling as producing abstract, autonomous authority "removed from the ordinary existence" and the broader scriptural witness of God entering into mundane human experiences throughout the history of Israel,

---

1. Interestingly, this designation is never used of Israelite kings, which does present a separate question about the relationship between theological and political concepts of sovereignty for Israel uniquely, as opposed to similar ancient Near Eastern contexts.

2. Marc Zvi Brettler, *God Is King: Understanding an Israelite Metaphor* (London: Bloomsbury: 2009) 30.

the incarnation notwithstanding. Would the Jewish people, or the later Christian community, resonate with redoubling as a guarantee of sovereignty, when their communal stories about their God were often as tangible and earthy as God planting a garden, regretting God's decisions, or wrestling with a human?

More than harping on the exegetical specifics of the "king of kings" reference, I am interested in how Dickinson's use of the phrase as the starting point for this study might illuminate some other questions about theological interpretation of Scripture. Given the strong place the specific wording "king of kings" plays in the study, does that suggest anything broader about biblical interpretive strategies?

Secondly, in pursuit of understanding how a study like this might impact theological interpretation of Scripture, might there be some connection between Dickinson's account of autonomous divine and human sovereignty and the self-referential sovereignty of Scripture in Christian communities? Particularly for communities that treat Scripture as an almost (if not entirely) autonomous authority, less tethered to an account of revelation and more rooted in a foundationalist epistemology, this study might identify either some explanations for that tendency, or useful criticisms of it. As Dickinson's work is in part an account of the way divine authority is described in Scripture, and its relationship to strategies of legitimating human authority, this should be a fruitful place for asking how Scriptural authority is conceived of by Christian communities. If there is a relationship between theological conceptions of divine sovereignty and political conceptions of human rulers' sovereignty, is there also a relationship between those theological and political conceptions of authority and the legitimizing or justifying logic of scriptural authority over particular communities?

Third, I am curious about the relationship between the redoubling in "king of kings" and the negation of negation in the Pauline description of the division of the flesh and spirit as opposed to preexisting social divisions. Dickinson says that Paul's willingness to subject himself to a "death with Christ" is a response fundamentally opposed to a re-assertion of the "king of kings" abstraction as a means of gaining sovereign power. How does Paul's division, one that still performs a universalizing abstraction, avoid creating a political sovereign being? The difference between redoubling and negative redoubling is compelling but would benefit from a more direct application to the theological concerns at play. What is the relationship between Paul's relativizing of all social divisions and identities, and the political status of the early church? Is there a larger tension between Jewish conceptions of sovereignty in the context of a national identity and Christian conceptions of divine sovereignty that do not trade on "external identities"? Finally, Paul uses a comparison between divine and human authority to ostensibly encourage submission to government authorities in Rom 13:1–6; what relationship does this account of authority have to Paul's "division of division" in death with Christ?

Another area for discussion is Dickinson's description of the inaccessibility of sovereignty, God's inaccessibility, and public speech about God. He describes Jean-Luc Marion's argument that public speech about God is very often a projection of human desires unto an invisible deity, connecting Marion's apophatic proposal with the inaccessible doctrine of the Trinity, a formulation that cannot be comprehended by human understanding. The impossibility of representing God is a question of public communication, as is the nature of projecting our own desires unto descriptions of God and thus creating idols. This portion of the paper identifies not only the dialectic of the possibility and impossibility of God, but the uniquely difficult nature of public speech about God. As there is a relationship between theological concepts of sovereignty and political justifications of sovereignty, it would be interesting to explore how that relationship is shaped by the unique difficulties of public speech about God, especially public speech about God that is intended to inspire political action. Is there a possibility of negative certainty, a recognition of the limits of the search for positive knowledge, inspiring or informing public speech about God?

Lastly, I appreciate Dickinson's concluding pages on the structural parallels between the possibility of an impossibility that creates space for God within humanity, and the impossible possibility of forgiveness that creates transformative potential for human communities. This seems like a fruitful ground for discerning more concrete political applications. Does this parallel indicate something unique about forgiveness that has materially and socially transformative potential? Does the suspension of the old order and creation of the new that forgiveness performs have concrete political implications? De Warren's account of original forgiveness as the foundation for human relationality hints at the power an account of forgiveness could have in grounding human communities, but this could be given more concrete application. Can original forgiveness cultivate a kind of trust within human communities that could shape political proposals differently than those grounded in original sin or progressive accounts of history? As another example, the Pauline exhortation against vengeance in Rom 12:17–21 has some parallels to Kierkegaard's "Christian 'like for like'" account of forgiveness, but with more material, if not political, implications. These comparisons have important latent possibilities for transformation in political systems, especially when it comes to Dickinson's striking portrayal of Kierkegaard's thought on neighbors, proximity, and self-love.

In short, Dickinson's probing insights on the sovereign redoubling of "king of kings" and the way a negation of negation undermines that absolute sovereignty provide fertile ground for continuing to think more concretely about the relationship between biblical language and political acts of legitimation, as well as the creative political potential of forgiveness. It provokes many important questions, chief among them what the relationship between metaphysical justifications of sovereignty in Scripture and human justifications of sovereign authority means for how we read, interpret, and apply the Bible in the realm of political activity.

I FEEL YOU:
THE THEO-POLITICS OF COMPASSION
AND THE POOR IN LIBERATION THEOLOGY
AND KARL BARTH

Jules A. Martinez Olivieri

> The LORD is compassionate and gracious...
> His mercy endures forever.
>
> Ps 103:8; 100:5

Introduction

A notable characteristic of Hellenistic theologies in classical antiquity is that gods are not expected to be compassionate. In Greek tragedy, compassion was a unique human emotion that the gods could not fully replicate: a quality that allowed humans to empathize with the suffering of others.[1] In contrast, a treasured confession in the early Christian communities in the Graeco-Roman milieu became a point of theological distinction: "Lord, have mercy on me or on us!" It was a common supplication for the poor and sick people who came to Jesus asking for healing. For instance, in the Gospels, we find reports of two blind men screaming at Jesus: "Have mercy on us!"; a Canaanite woman: "Have mercy on me!" (Matt 20: 30–31); Bartimaeus shouting, "Son of David, have mercy on me!" (Mark 10: 47) and ten lepers pleading "Jesus, Master, have mercy on us!" (Luke 17: 13). These scenes of mercy or compassion dramatically portray what is part of ancient Israel's sacred memory in Exodus tradition: YHWH shows compassion towards a people who are suffering and cries out for help. The Creator delivers them from the brink of genocide and leads them towards a life of dignity and a covenantal relationship. Compassion or mercy is a moral practice expected from human relations in the Torah (Exod 34:6). As a social virtue, it is embedded in the Hebrew law, where the rights of orphans,

---

1. C. F. Alford, "Greek Tragedy and Civilization: The Cultivation of Pity," *Political Research Quarterly* 46 (1993) 259–80.

widows, and foreigners are defended (Cf. Deut 14:28–29; Lev 19: 14, 33–34). It is in the prophetic oracles and covenantal prosecutions of the prophets for whom the true religion does not consist of offering sacrifices, but in doing good, establishing law, and practicing justice.[2] In fact, in the prophetic traditions, one of the names of God is "justice" or "righteousness," as Jeremiah affirms: "And this is the name by which he will be called: 'The LORD is our righteousness'" (Jer 23:6b).[3]

Given the prominent role of God's compassion in scripture, it is salient that divine and human compassion do not have a more prominent role in contemporary theology in English, working on the connections between theology, politics, and ethics. There are certainly exceptions to this. For example, post-holocaust theologian Johannes Baptist Metz was not only a prominent political theologian, but also known as a theologian of *compassion*. In Metz's account, divine compassion is God's "participatory perception of the suffering of the other, as active remembrance of the suffering of the other," and can thus provide narrative content for a politics of remembrance and justice.[4] Recently, Walter Kasper has also approached the topic of mercy in light of Roman Catholic theology and ministry, describing mercy as "the externally visible and effective aspect of the essence of the God who is love," and therefore "the fundamental divine attribute."[5] Oliver Davies adds to the European voices proposing that compassion is a virtue related to the human telos, since it is "an essential part of what it is to be a creature of the Triune God" and hence it is indispensable for Christian anthropology.[6]

Shifting our attention to Latin America, liberation theologians have paid significant and consistent attention to the themes of compassion and mercy, as inherent

---

2. See further Walter Brueggemann, "Scripture: Old Testament," in *The Blackwell Companion to Political Theology*, ed. Peter Scott and William T. Cavanaugh (Malden, MA: Blackwell, 2004) 7–22.

3. In this essay I use the NRSV for biblical quotations.

4. As cited in Hille Hasker, "Compassion as a Global Programme for Christianity," *Concilium* 4 (2001) 56. See further J. B. Metz, "Compassion: Zu einem Weltprogramm des Christentums im Zeitalter des Pluralismus der Religionen und Kulturen," in *Compassion—Weltprogramm des Christentums: Soziale Verantwortung lernen*, edited by J. B. Metz et al. (Vienna: Herder, 2000) 9–8. Also, Jürgen Moltmann in his account of divine solidarity with humanity seeks to reinterpret the triune nature of God by proposing the inclusion of human history, with its suffering and experiences of god-forsakenness, into divine life. For Moltmann, what transpires in human history ontologically affects God. Moltmann's work offers an account, however provocative and controversial, of divine affections and relational suffering which puts God's compassioned solidarity at the forefront of divine promissory history. See Jürgen Moltmann, *The Crucified God: The Cross of Christ as the Foundation and Criticism of Christian Theology*, trans. R. A. Wilson and John Bowden, Twentieth Century Religious Thought (Minneapolis: Fortress, 1993).

5. Walter Kasper, *Mercy: The Essence of the Gospel and the Key to Christian Life* (Mahwah, NJ: Paulist, 2014) 94.

6. Oliver Davies, *A Theology of Compassion: Metaphysics of Difference and the Renewal of Tradition* (2003; reprint, Eugene, OR: Wipf & Stock, 2016) xii, 249–252.

in the logic of Christian life, God's gospel, and theology. In Latin American theology, the work of theology involves a critical appraisal of the praxis of the church facing the suffering of the impoverished. One of its most vital contributions to the catholicity of the faith is its hermeneutical and ethical posture: the preferential option for the poor and compassion as necessary criteria for Christian praxis. First and second-generation theologians like Gustavo Gutiérrez, Jon Sobrino and Leonardo Boff have argued that "compassion" or "mercy" (often used interchangeably given the overlapping semantic range in Spanish of *compasión* and *misericordia*) are more than acts of empathy and pity that seek to alleviate someone else's misery. Instead, compassion is the public expression of the demands of love, shaping all Christian lives that follow Jesus's ethos and pathos in the presence of the kingdom of God. Compassion and mercy are to God's love what God's holiness is to divine otherness, as emphasized in the following biblical texts: "You shall be holy, for I the LORD your God am holy" (Lev 19:2b); "Be merciful, just as your Father is merciful" (Luke 6:36).

As compassion is seen in God's own revelatory acts to rescue people, more work is needed to locate the prevalence of mercy/compassion as an expression of God's being in revelation. This paper argues that Liberation Theology's (LT) account of compassion and the preferential option for the poor can benefit from an explicit account of compassion as a divine attribute. That is, LT's act of evoking of a theocentric and Christological account of human praxis in favor of the victims can benefit from an *explicit* theological ontology that grounds mercy in God. I propose here that the reformed theologian Karl Barth can assist LT by providing the necessary grounding. Furthermore, I propose that Barth's theology of divine compassion can benefit from LT's historically mediated vision of Jesus's identification with the suffering masses and compassion as a suffering virtue. I shall begin by providing an account of LT's theological principle of God's preferential option for the poor and how key liberationist thinkers elaborate on the virtues of compassion and mercy, as concomitant to the praxis of social transformation. Second, I will assess how Barth provides a Christological ontology of divine mercy that can be useful for LT's Christological focus. Finally, I offer a vista of the ecclesia as a com-passioned liberating community.

The Option for the Poor: A Theocentric Option

For the last five decades, LT has argued that Christianity's approach to the poor, the oppressed, and the marginalized should be more than charity-based (provisioned for temporary needs) or based on initiatives of acts of mercy or mercy ministries (alleviating social situations based on institutional presence).[7] The "option for the

---

7. See Jon Sobrino, *Jesus the Liberator: A Historical Theological Reading of Jesus of Nazareth*

poor" is a way to see the whole of Christian dogmatics, ethics, pastoral ministry, and mission from the perspective of the impoverished as agents whose destiny is implicated in the nature of Christian hope. The poor/impoverished/victims are in a privileged position in relation to the gospel, as the epistle of James claims: "Has not God chosen the poor in the world to be rich in faith and to be heirs of the kingdom that he has promised to those who love him? (Jas 2:5b).

The decision to center on the impoverished, those who tend to suffer the most injustice and violence, as privileged recipients of God's liberating acts, is an option rooted in life, as it is a way of choosing the God of life in historical experience. The concerns of liberation theologians are rooted in an unfaltering commitment to say "Amen!" to James' word, and most definitely in Jesus's self-declared prophetic mission "to bring good news to the poor" (Luke 4:18). Jesus's mission as liberator-savior is decisive for theological reflection.

Gustavo Gutiérrez explains the emergence of LT as grounded in the challenge that the suffering masses of the world pose to the public credibility of Christian hope.[8] The toughest test for the Christian faith arises from the marginalized sectors of society, specifically those not seen as fully human by dominant socio-political agents and structures. The challenge is not just about proclaiming God in a "world come of age" as Bonhoeffer stated,[9] but more critically, it is proclaiming God as Father in a world that dehumanizes people. As Gutierrez notes: "the question will not refer to the mode that must be used to talk about God in an adult world, but more so to the way that [God] has to be announced as a Father in a non-human world, [and] to the consequent implications of the fact of saying to the non-human that [he] is a child of God."[10] This perspective binds the telos of theologizing to the lived realities of the most vulnerable, highlighting the need for theologies to address their reality and affirm their inherent dignity as human beings as children of God.[11] The church's partiality for theologizing and acting in favor of the impoverished is rooted in the example set by it's Lord. "The option for the poor means, ultimately, an option for the God of the Kingdom that Jesus announces to us."[12]

(London: Bloomsbury Academic, 1994), 90–91. José María Vigil, "La Opción por los Pobres es Opción por la Justicia, y no es preferencial. Para un reencuadramiento teológico-sistemático de la OP," *RELAT* #371, https://servicioskoinonia.org/relat/371.htm.

8. For an elaboration of the following themes in this section see Jules A. Martinez-Olivieri, *A Visible Witness: Christology, Liberation, and Participation,* Emerging Scholars (Minneapolis: Fortress, 2016) 33–35.

9. Dietrich Bonhoeffer, *Letters and Papers from Prison*, ed. John W. de Gruchy, trans. Isabel Best, Dietrich Bonhoeffer Works 8 (Minneapolis: Fortress, 2010) 23–27.

10. Gustavo Gutiérrez, "Praxis de liberación: Teología y anuncio," *Concilium* 96 (1974) 366.

11. Gutiérrez, "Praxis de Liberación," 366.

12. Benedito Ferraro, "Jesucristo liberador: Cristología en América Latina y Caribe," in *Bajar de la*

Advocating for compassion and the option of the poor as theological imperatives also requires attention to the structures of oppression. Feminist theologians have added more specificity to the terms "poor" and "oppressed." Within the logic of oppression, women bear a disproportionate burden worldwide. Hence, they propose as a *locus theologicus* the experience of women as historically oppressed subjects, who suffer doubly according to their gender, class, or skin color.[13] Theologizing in the historical horizon of these realities is also at the core of intersectional theologies, recognizing "that each of us exists in differing relationships to power and hierarchy based on gender, race, class, nation, sexual identity, ability, age, and other forms of social difference."[14] The intersectionality of the option of the poor is an inclusive socio-political reality.

The concept of "liberation" has significant implication for the field of soteriology, especially within the context of liberation theologies, which seek to understand and convey the divine redemptive work of God through Jesus Christ. Gutiérrez identifies three primary levels of liberation, each encompassing a distinct aspect of freedom. The *socio-political* dimension of liberation pertains to freedom from systemic oppression imposed upon individuals and communities. The *anthropological* level of liberation relates to the nature of individual freedom and its flourishing. Finally, the *theological* level of liberation addresses issues such as freedom from sin, reconciliation, justice, and communion with God. Jesus's actions are redemptive, liberating, across all levels.[15] Witnessing this liberation, Gutiérrez states, is a "prophetic option we make, one which strikes its roots deep in the gratuity of God's love and is demanded by that love."[16] This love moves the church towards a culture of compassion. Gutiérrez maintains that the church's compassionate praxis originates in God's mercy. The foundation for the preference of the poor is not based "in the social analysis we employ, nor in the direct experience we may have of poverty, nor in our human compassion. It is a theocentric and prophetic option that is rooted in

---

cruz a los pobres: Cristología de la liberación, ed. José María (Mexico: Dabar, 2007) 107, my translation.

13. See Nancy Pineda-Madrid, "Feminist Theory and Latina Feminist/Mujerista Theologizing," in *The Wiley Blackwell Companion to Latino/a Theology*, ed. Orlando O. Espin, Wiley Blackwell Companions to Religion (Malden, MA: Wiley, 2015) 348–349.

14. Grace Ji-Sun Kim and Susan M. Shaw, *Intersectional Theology: An Introductory Guide* (Minneapolis: Fortress, 2018), 41—and they write further, at the same page: "We simultaneously experience advantage and disadvantage based on the intersections of these identities within interlocking systems of oppression, and these complex and nuanced distinctions play an important role in how each of us does theology. Our identities and experiences are never removed from the theologies we produce."

15. Gustavo Gutiérrez, *Teología de la Liberación : Perspectivas* (Salamanca: Sígueme, 1994) 91–92.

16. Gustavo Gutiérrez, "Pobres y Opción Fundamental", in *Mysterium Liberationis* I, ed. Ignacio Ellacuría and Jon Sobrino (Madrid: Trotta, 1990) 309. See also Jon Sobrino and Ignacio Ellacuría, eds., *Systematic Theology: Perspectives from Liberation Theology* (Maryknoll, NY: Orbis, 1996).

and required by the gratuitousness of God's love."[17] This is a theological and historically mediated conception of compassion that seeks to adequately locate theological praxis within the concreteness of suffering communities.

In the Beginning, the Merciful God

The biblical narrative illustrates God's steadfast love and compassion towards humanity.[18] In this line, Gutiérrez maintains that the church's compassionate transformational praxis originates in God's mercy for humanity: "the ultimate foundation for the preference of the poor is in God's mercy, and not in the social analysis, or in human compassion, no matter how relevant these things could be."[19] Gutiérrez provides us with a historically mediated conception of compassion and mercy that adequately locates them within the realism of a suffering world and its tragedy.

In this context, Jon Sobrino and Leonardo Boff provide further elaboration on the idea of compassion and mercy as integral to God's liberating acts toward the vulnerable. In his book, "The Principle of Mercy," Jon Sobrino provides a theological analysis of God's mercy as the foundation of salvific experience.[20] The passage in Exod 3:7–8 serves as a paradigmatic locus of divine compassion, where God's awareness and response to human suffering initiate the salvific experience. God responds to the suffering and hopelessness of the people of Israel and delivers them from genocide. The memorial of the exodus is sacred to Israel, and through it, they come to understand that the Lord's compassion for them will never falter, even after their breach of the covenant: "The LORD, the LORD, a God merciful and gracious, slow to anger, and abounding in steadfast love and faithfulness, keeping steadfast love for the thousandth generation, forgiving iniquity and transgression and sin," (Exod 34:6b–7a). The motif of the experienced divine mercy also shapes the liturgical life of

---

17. Gustavo Gutiérrez, "¿Dónde dormirán las pobres?" in *El rostro de Dios en la historia*, edited by Gustavo Gutiérrez et al., Centro de Estudios y Publicaciones 175 (Lima: CEP, 1996) 18.

18. Hebrew terms such as רחם (*rḥm*), חנן (*ḥnn*), and חסד (*ḥsd*) form our understanding of God's compassion and love. The semantic range of these terms overlap. Translated variously as "to be merciful" or "have compassion" (*rḥm*), "to show favor" or "to have mercy" (*ḥnn*), "loyal love" or "mercy" (*ḥsd*). In the New Testament, Greek terms like ἐλεέω (*eleeō*) and σπλαγχνίζομαι (*splagchnizomai*) further elucidate the concept of mercy and compassion. Particularly noteworthy is the way these virtues are exemplified in the life and ministry of Jesus Christ. For a summary discussion, see John Frederick, "Mercy and Compassion," in *Lexham Theological Wordbook*, ed. Douglas Mangum et al., Lexham Bible Reference Series (Bellingham, WA: Lexham, 2014).

19. Gustavo Gutiérrez, *Hablar de Dios desde el sufrimiento del inocente: Una reflexión sobre el libro de Job* (Salamanca: Sígueme, 1995) 16–17. See also Gustavo Gutiérrez, *La fuerza histórica de los pobres*, 2nd ed. (Salamanca: Sigueme, 1982) 26.

20. This is the English translation. Jon Sobrino, *Principle of Mercy: Taking the Crucified People from the Cross* (Maryknoll, NY: Orbis, 2015). In this paper I will use the original Spanish as the main source.

Israel, as seen in many psalms that exult God's covenantal faithfulness: "The LORD is merciful and gracious, slow to anger and abounding in steadfast love" (Ps 103:8); "As a father has compassion on his children, so the Lord has compassion on those who fear him" (Ps 103:13). And in Psalm 146:7, YHWH is one "who executes justice for the oppressed, who gives food to the hungry. The LORD sets the prisoners free." This theme is echoed by Jesus's own declaration of the nature of his vocation at the beginning of his public ministry (see Luke 4:16–19).

In these biblical texts, Sobrino sees paradigmatic patterns for the portrayal of God's mercy and compassion for Israel and the nations, grounding the primordial experience of God's relationship with the people. Indeed, conceptually, these depictions of divine action alleviating human suffering constitute, for Sobrino, the "structure of the liberative movement," that is, the ways in which God *enacts* or *effects* salvation.[21] If salvation is understood as liberation from sin and oppression, and liberation is an expression of divine love, it follows that mercy is the way through which God's love is experienced.

Mercy, Sobrino explain furthers, is a mode of being that reflects the assumption of others' suffering. It is the internalization of the suffering of the other that catalyzes the divine response.[22] Mercy is not a passive emotion, but a fully active expression of love, shaping the entirety of God's interaction with humanity.[23] Theology, then, not only concerns itself with mercy and compassion from a theocentric perspective but, most vitally, from a Christological perspective, is grounded in dependence on Jesus Christ. The compassion that Jesus demonstrated toward human suffering serves as a driving force behind his actions. The plight of the crowds moved him, and he was deeply affected by their harassment and helplessness, likening them to sheep without a shepherd (Matt 9:36). He preached about the covenantal care of God the Father, whose mercy extends to everyone, regardless of their status (Matt 5:45).

Jesus's mercy is love enacted by the sight of unjust suffering. It is a "praxic love" motivated by the mere existence of suffering without the need to be compelled by any other external cause or deontological commitment.[24] Sobrino illustrates this through the parable of the Good Samaritan, Jesus's healings, and God's welcome of the prodigal son, emphasizing that mercy is dramatically portrayed as an intrinsic attitude toward alleviating others' misery. The prevalence of compassionate acts by Jesus, in continuation with the testimony of the Hebrew scriptures, functions as a

---

21. Jon Sobrino, *El principio-misericordia: Bajar de la cruz a los pueblos crucificados* (Santander: Sal Terrae, 1992) 32–33.
22. Sobrino, *El principio-misericordia*, 33.
23. Sobrino, *El principio-misericordia*, 33.
24. Sobrino, *El principio-misericordia*, 35.

theological criterion. Sobrino calls it "the mercy-principle" (*principio-misericordia*). The conceptual labor of theological reflection (*intellectus fidei*) is vivified as a public witness when it is also an *intellectus amoris et misericordiae*, a mode of performative discourse grounded in love for the sake of compassionate praxis. Sobrino avers, "We hold that this principle of mercy is the basic principle of the activity of God and Jesus, and therefore, ought to be that of the activity of the church."[25]

Leonardo Boff's perspective on divine compassion and mercy encompasses an ecological care that extends from humanity to earth.[26] "Mercy is the great perfection of the maternal Father that Jesus asks us to imitate: 'Be merciful as your Father is merciful' (Luke 6: 36)."[27] Moreover, God's mercy expresses providential care for all creation and creatures. When humans actualize the telos of God's loving care in their essential care for one another, our humanity is realized.[28] In this experience, the option for the poor is not only an option for helping those who are impoverished, but as Boff states, an affirmation of the agency of the poor, oppressed and excluded to commit themselves, with their allies, to the faithful work and aspiration of "a new type of society in which the exploitation of human beings and the plundering of the Earth are overcome."[29] Hence, compassion, as an active relational emotion, is political in its expression because it anchors the ethical identification with the most vulnerable. This paradigm of care is a criterion for Christian praxis.

So far, we have seen how a theocentric and Christological historical vision of God's compassion can energize Christian theology and praxis in solidarity with the impoverished and oppressed. However, even though the theme of God's relation to the poor in history abounds in liberation thought, the theological elaboration of this relation in terms of recourse to the doctrine of God is still under development. One reason for this might be the strong concern and emphasis on God's historical immanence, which tends to constrain recourse to dogmatic accounts of God's immanent life, or to the Christ event's metaphysical and transcendent dimensions. However, in his *Trinity and Society*, Leonardo Boff worked on a dogmatic account of the Triune God, seeking to consolidate the methodology of liberation and apply it to the nature of God in relation to soteriology.[30] The main question Boff addresses is

---

25. Sobrino, *El principio-misericordia*, 33.

26. Leonardo Boff, *El cuidado esencial: Ética de lo humano, compasión por la tierra* (Madrid: Editorial Trotta, 2002), 103–105. For the English translation see Leonardo Boff, *Essential Care: An Ethics of Human Nature* (Waco, TX: Baylor University Press, 2008), 89–92.

27. Leonardo Boff, *Trinidad, sociedad y liberación* (Madrid: Ediciones Paulinas, 1987), 211.

28. Leonardo Boff, *El cuidado esencial*, 105.

29. Leonardo Boff, *El cuidado esencial*, 115.

30. See Leonardo Boff, *Trinity and Society*, trans. Paul Burns (1988; reprint, Eugene, OR: Wipf & Stock, 2005).

how God's nature and identity are good news for the poor and oppressed. Boff's answer is that God's salvific action in history, a revelation of the divine immanent and economic life, fundamentally consists of creating communion.[31] God's triune life is understood as communion, the co-eternal and mutually constituting unity of God, the Father, Son, and Spirit. Boff argues that this communion should be the theological and spiritual model of the church community in human society. However, Boff does not work to attend explicitly to divine ontology and attributes in relation to our concerns regarding mercy and compassion. For this purpose, we turn to the contributions of Karl Barth.

Retrieving Barth: God's Being in Mercy

In an analogous way to liberation theologians, who asked how we can announce a kingdom of life in a reality marred by poverty and death, Barth asked decades before them, in the middle of the twentieth century: how can we confess the preeminent God of grace before an enlightened and fascist Europe? Barth defended Christian socialism, advocated for the just treatment and compensation of the working class, and with the rise of the Nazis in Germany, crafted the Barmen Confession, a document of theological fidelity to Jesus Christ and resistance for a church pressured to offer allegiance to the Third Reich. Although Barth was not a political theologian *per se*, his centering on the revelation of God in Jesus Christ as determinative for Christian faith is undoubtedly theologically political.[32]

There are common themes and judgments between Karl Barth and liberation theologians. George Hussinger, one of the leading Barth commentators defined this relationship as a "political solidarity."[33] Barth's concerns for justice and the impoverished are analogous to those present in liberation theologies. For example, in his essay, "Poverty," which is part of his post-war writings, Barth discusses how economic and sociological poverty has been a persistent historical situation in Scripture.[34] He views the constant presence of material poverty and the dialectic of the poor and rich as a tragic human situation but under the purview of God's providence. Still,

---

31. Consider Boff's summary of his account of the doctrine of the Trinity in chapter 15 of *Trinity and Society*.

32. See Peter Scott and William T. Cavanaugh, eds., *The Blackwell Companion to Political Theology*, Blackwell Companions to Religion (Malden, MA: Blackwell, 2004) 126–127. Also note the discussion by Alberto Roldán, *Reino, política y misión: Sus relaciones en perspectiva Latinoamericana* (Lima: CENIP, 2011).

33. George Hunsinger, "Karl Barth and Liberation Theology," in *Karl Barth and Radical Politics*, ed. George Hunsinger, 2nd ed. (Eugene, OR: Cascade, 2017) 198.

34. Karl Barth, *Against the Stream: Shorter Post-War Writings* (New York: Philosophical Library, 1954) 243–46.

God is "on the side of the poor."³⁵ Similar to LT, Barth argues that there is "the unmistakable and definite sympathy towards poverty throughout the biblical testimony, a pattern of attention that regards the poor as recipients of God's love. Furthermore, God is favorable toward the poor and is "the upholder and avenger" of their rights.³⁶ Barth also discerns that the poor are recipients of divine blessing and grace and have priority as recipients of the gospel. This blessedness contrasts with the perils of the rich, who tend to be contraposed with the poor in pride and practice. The condition for liberation for the rich is freedom from material attachments. They are called to quit them and become like the poor.³⁷ In Barth's words: "the Bible is on the side of the poor, the impecunious and the destitute. He whom the Bible calls God is on the side of the poor."³⁸

Further, Barth observes that as Jesus Christ was poor, he is the companion of the poor of this world.³⁹ Jesus, in fact, is the "Christ of poverty for all who are poor, all who are truly destitute and suffer any privation: such a one is the conqueror, who makes all poor men rich, and only such a one!"⁴⁰ As Barth elaborates in *Church Dogmatics* II/2, Jesus's humanity and solidarity with humanity represent a merciful and compassionate identification that stems from God's being.⁴¹ Barth makes this claim about Jesus in light of his doctrine of election: God's decision to love humanity freely. For Barth, election is God's decision to elect Godself for fellowship with humanity and humanity for fellowship with God. In the history of Jesus Christ, the Logos incarnate is the one elected. In the Incarnation, God took on humanity and decided to be *for* humanity. Jesus is both the God who elects and the elected man. As the Son of God, Jesus Christ is the one who elects. As the Son of man, Jesus Christ is the one who is elected (Eph 1:4, "just as he chose us *in Christ* before the foundation of the world to be holy and blameless before him in love.".)

Jesus's solidarity is not only based on the ethical logic of acts of mercy as a faithful Jew in the prophetic tradition—a concern also shared by Sobrino and Boff.⁴²

---

35. Barth, *Against the Stream*, 44.

36. Barth, *Against the Stream*, 44. Barth does not pay critical attention to how the rich can be oppressors, but he admonishes them to be mindful of the poor's rights and use their wealth in their favor.

37. Barth, *Against the Stream*, 246.

38. Barth, *Against the Stream*, 245.

39. Barth, *Against the Stream*, 245.

40. Barth, *Against the Stream*, 245.

41. See Barth's discussion on the mercy and righteousness of God in: Karl Barth, *Church Dogmatics* II/1: *The Doctrine of God*, ed. G. W. Bromiley and T. F. Torrance, trans. T. H. L. Parker et al. (Edinburgh: T. & T. Clark, 1957), 368–406.

42. See Jon Sobrino, *Christ the Liberator: A View from the Victims*, trans. Paul Burns (Maryknoll, NY: Orbis, 2001), chap. 9; and Leonardo Boff, *Jesus Christ Liberator: A Critical Christology for Our Time*, trans. Patrick Hughes (Maryknoll, NY: Orbis, 1978) 82–83.

Barth grounds Jesus's compassion and mercy ontologically in God's eternal decision to be the human God in Jesus. He explains that, in Jesus's existence, there is no distance from the plight of humanity:

> For the community everything depends upon the readiness not to try to be anything more or better or surer than His people, His body, and to live and grow as such on earth.[43]

Hence, Jesus is necessarily the merciful savior. Humanity matters to Jesus because human relations are internal to the reality of his personhood in time. Like his liberationist successors (Sobrino and Boff), Barth pays attention to Jesus's relationality in the Gospels, and his response to the suffering masses at Galilee (Matt 9:36). As the crowds "were distressed" and "were scattered abroad, as sheep having no shepherd," Jesus felt compassion for them. Jesus takes on the suffering of others to himself due to an internal disposition. This mercy is part of Jesus's humanity, which is relational in its constitution. Thus, Jesus is not only a sympathetic participant in the angst of others, but also identifies with suffering humanity in the most extensive way possible.

Furthermore, Barth argues in *Church Dogmatics* II that God's will to be his people's life and righteousness is exceptionally seen in the way God is the savior, especially of the poor and defenseless.[44] Barth clearly argues that God's being is rooted in a love that is ultimately meant for all people.[45] This scriptural "political tendency" compels an ethical responsibility consistent with the message.

Also consider Barth's commentary on Matt 6:25–34, which is part of his exegesis of the beatitudes in *Church Dogmatics* IV/2. Discussing the concept of Mammon in Jesus's polemics against avarice, Barth reflects that in the longing for material possessions, there is a reality "opposed to the kingdom of God, the antithesis of the rich and the poor being adopted as a basic schema for all the blessedness or otherwise of man."[46] Hence, Jesus proposes a reorganization of human life based on freedom. Barth argues that this signifies a more provocative Christological reality: "the royal man Jesus penetrating to the very foundations of economic life in defiance of every reasonable and to that extent honorable objection."[47] Jesus, as the "royal man," not only confronts the socio-political order, but is the one whose very life opposes sinful humanity as the judge who will renew creation. Jesus's identification with humanity

---

43. Barth, *Church Dogmatics* IV/2: *Doctrine of Creation*, ed. G. W. Bromiley and T. F. Torrance; trans. Harold Knight et al. (Edinburgh: T. & T. Clark, 1960) 676.

44. In general, see Barth, *Church Dogmatics* II/2, 3–31.

45. Barth, *Church Dogmatics* II/1, 272–97.

46. Karl Barth, *Church Dogmatics* IV/2: *The Doctrine of Reconciliation*, ed. G. W. Bromiley and T. F. Torrance, trans. G. W. Bromiley (Edinburgh: T. & T. Clark, 1958) 178.

47. Barth, *Church Dogmatics* IV/2, 180.

is not a generic disposition against certain iconic ethical or political ideas. More specifically, Barth states, Jesus is the "poor man" who is himself a "partisan of the poor, and as this revolutionary."[48] He is the "revelation of the mercy of God, of His Gospel, His kingdom of peace, His atonement."[49] Jesus is the royal man who liberates and redeems.

Jesus attends to the blessed "poor, sad and meek" as the ones who suffer the most the miseries of the age.[50] They are blessed, so that the eschatological kingdom of God might be evident in all spheres of humanity.[51] Barth infers God's merciful partiality by stating that in contrast, "the fortunate of this world cannot help the fact that the cosmos is not revealed in them and the new thing of the kingdom of God does not shine in them."[52] Taking his cue from the parable of the rich man and Lazarus (Cf. Lk 16:19–31), the rich are to be "pitied because the kingdom of God, the presence of Jesus, cannot be seen in their lives."[53]

However, recipients of God's mercy in Jesus are not inherently privileged; rather, their life situations lead them to receive it as an expression of God's salvific love. Barth emphasizes that the poor are blessed due to the presence of divine grace in their misery, as indicated in Matt 11:5b: "The poor have good news brought to them." This qualification helps maintain God's freedom and the absolute gratuity of divine compassion. Furthermore, Barth notices that the blessed *poor* are accompanied by the blessed *persecuted*, who, by their active testimony and passive reception of hostility, participate in Christ's suffering.[54] Jesus grants the freedom to be recipients and participants of a blessed life as a providential act of eschatological mercy.

Mercy/Compassion for the Marginalized

Liberation theologians like Gutiérrez, Sobrino, and Boff agree with Barth that the love of God is God's relentless will to establish fellowship with humanity through the revelation of Godself in Christ.[55] This love is discernable as mercy and compassion. Because divine love consists in this inclination, Barth states, "God's loving is

---

48. Barth, *Church Dogmatics* IV/2, 181.
49. Barth, *Church Dogmatics* IV/2, 182.
50. Barth, *Church Dogmatics* IV/2, 191.
51. Barth, *Church Dogmatics* IV/2, 191.
52. Barth, *Church Dogmatics* IV/2, 191.
53. Barth, *Church Dogmatics* IV/2, 191.
54. Barth, *Church Dogmatics* IV/2, 191.
55. See for example Leonardo Boff, *Passion of Christ, Passion of the World* (Maryknoll, NY: Orbis, 1993) 110–111; Jon Sobrino, *Jesus the Liberator: A Historical Theological Reading of Jesus of Nazareth* (London: Bloomsbury, 1994) 230–31.

necessary, for it is the being, the essence and the nature of God."[56] Liberation theologians echo this confession and emphasize that God's primordial mercy is an experience of liberation in history. God's mercy is not only historicized in Jesus's message and praxis but is also a fundamental requirement for humans to be humane. Seeking this humanization is a special call for the people of God, as they seek to extend this mercy in *imitatio dei*.[57] In imitation of God, the church reiterates God's patterns of saving acts, affirmation of human dignity, and establishment of justice that are particularly directed to the most vulnerable. That is, the church in its missional praxis opts for mercy for the marginalized.

Barth's Christology and doctrine of God offer a way for liberation theologians to ground the preferential option for the poor in divine ontology. Mercy is a divine perfection, a mode of experiencing divine love.[58] It is God's being in communicative action. Such mercy is God's free revelation to take upon the removal of human misery.[59] For Barth, the proper way to recognize divine love as a divine attribute is through "the reflection of God in men unfolded by His Word."[60] The divine movement to relieve the creature's anguish is not an accidental or contingent mode of action dependent on some external state of affairs (history) but stems from God's life. When confronted with creatures' resistance to the majesty of God, God in Christ confronts their misery with compassion. God extends mercy—an expression of his eternal love—to the self-inflicted wounds of humanity, overcoming the omnidirectional solitude and injustice of their resistance.

Because mercy is an expression of divine love in freedom, it is a communicable attribute that humans can live by and extend to others. Since God's compassionate mercy logically precedes God's soteriological acts in the economy of redemption, it is the very condition upon which liberation is enacted. As a result, God's compassion for humanity, the church, emerges as a visible and social sign of divine mercy, a society characterized by a culture of compassion.

Ecclesia: A *Com-passioned* Public Witness

In liberation theology, the preferential option for the poor is a principle that holds political, ethical, and evangelical importance for the church. It is a political obligation for theologians to collaborate within social settings, where they must support

56. Barth, *Church Dogmatics*, II/1, 280.

57. Sobrino, *El principio de misericordia*, 33.

58. See Eric J. Titus, "The Perfections of God in the Theology of Karl Barth: A Consideration of the Formal Structure," *Evangelical Journal of Theology* 4.2 (2010) 210–211.

59. See Barth, *Church Dogmatics*, II/2, 283 -285.

60. Barth, *Church Dogmatics* II/1, 285.

those who are victimized by systemic oppression. It is also an ethical imperative to address the unjust reality of material and political suffering and the systems that perpetuate and exacerbate misery and exploitation. Additionally, it is an evangelical commitment grounded in eschatological promises in scripture regarding the destiny of the impoverished and captives.[61] Thus, theology must prioritize God who imparts life, protects, and redeems the destitute by placing them at the core of its focus. The universal proclamation of the gospel assumes significance when understood from the vantage point of marginalized people. As Sobrino indicates, "this means that no one should feel excluded from a church that adopts this perspective, yet no one can claim to be a part of the Church without embracing it."[62]

Compelled by her union with Christ through the Spirit, the ecclesia seeks to reproduce the praxis of Jesus, the compassionate in choosing the vulnerable, sick, and neglected—as a sign of God's reigning action. In opting for the poor, Jesus's voice becomes a doorway to the priorities of social witnesses:

> When you give a luncheon or a dinner, do not invite your friends or your brothers or your relatives or rich neighbors, in case they may invite you in return, and you would be repaid. 13 But when you give a banquet, invite the poor, the crippled, the lame, and the blind. 14 And you will be blessed, because they cannot repay you, for you will be repaid at the resurrection of the righteous. (Luke 14:12–14)

This evangelical scene is not only about feeding those who are starving; it involves true and performative spirituality, a walk of love that seeks justice with the other. The church confronts public evils of violence, corruption, ethno-nationalism, racialization, homophobia, white supremacy, xenophobia, gender violence, and ecological destruction by denouncing the anti-kingdom realities that promote or perpetuate these conditions. The kingdom is for the poor, and God has chosen the poor of the world to make them rich in faith and to be the heirs of his reign (Jas 2:5).

---

61. A popular approach to interpreting the Bible's references to the poor is to spiritualize their material impoverishment. However, this approach has its drawbacks, as it downplays the significance of the material aspects of poverty. While it is true that one can be spiritually impoverished, the primary reference to the poor in the Old Testament, the Gospels, and Epistles is to those who are materially impoverished. These individuals are often at risk of losing their lives and face various forms of oppression. However, the term "poor" in the New Testament can refer to more than just material poverty. It can also refer to those who are socially marginalized, such as sinners, prostitutes, the humble, the small ones, and those who practice despised professions. In this sense, the poor are those who are denied even minimal dignity and are sociologically poor. It is important to understand these various notions of poverty in the Gospels and not to overlook the centrality of the materially impoverished as Jesus's primary audience. See further, Jon Sobrino, *No Salvation Outside the Poor: Prophetic-Utopian Essays* (Maryknoll, NY: Orbis, 2008), chap. 2, "Depth and Urgency of the Option for the Poor."

62. J. Lois, "Opción por los pobres. Síntesis doctrinal," in *La opción por los pobres*, ed. J. M. Vigil (Santander: Sal Terrae, 1991) 5.

Liberation theology emphasizes the Christian's act of sacrificial love for others. It is an act that relocates the priority of commitment to following Jesus and his actions to the forefront of Christian spirituality.[63] The internalization of love and compassion precedes the formalization of discourse. Christology serves the church by commending "el seguimiento del Señor", a disposition of devotion to the practical commitments of Jesus and his vision of God's kingdom in history. Doctrine is no mere confession but a performative discourse; it prompts the church to move in the ways of compassion, in the path of orthopathy. As Sobrino describes it, orthopathy is "the correct way of letting ourselves be affected by the reality of Christ."[64] In other words, while orthodoxy (right doctrine) and orthopraxis (right practice) might serve as foundational reference points for the church's confessions and discipleship, orthopathy is a rightly ordered, passionate praxis that mirrors God's own redemptive acts. Christians live the gospel when they live the rightly passioned praxis that mirror God's redemptive pathos. As Pentecostal theologian Samuel Solivan states, orthopathos "looks to the manner in which human suffering can be transformed into a resource for liberation" in the community of believers as a visible witness to society.[65]

In choosing the impoverished, the ecclesia functions as a witness to God's presence, participating in speech and act in the magnification of the works of Christ. Our current sociopolitical struggles—which include a great majority of human beings still suffering from sickness, violence, lack of health and material goods—are an opportunity, as Nancy Bedford observes, for "an unexpected *kairos* where the 'social gospel' and the 'verbal gospel' can meet and overcome their absurd polarization."[66]

Conclusion

This paper has argued that while liberation theologians like Gutiérrez, Sobrino, and Boff rightly emphasize God's compassionate solidarity with the poor and oppressed, and the kind of praxis that emulates God's redemptive love, it can benefit from an explicit grounding of compassion in God's ontology. By engaging aspects of Barth's Christology and theological ontology, LT can strengthen the centrality of the preferential option for the poor and the vitality of compassioned praxis in God's merciful

---

63. Note Jon Sobrino, *Liberación con espíritu: Apuntes para una nueva espiritualidad* (Santander: Sal Terrae, 1985) 15–6. For the English translation, see Jon Sobrino, *Spirituality of Liberation: Toward Political Holiness* (Maryknoll, NY: Orbis, 2015).

64. Sobrino, *Christ the Liberator,* 210.

65. Samuel Solivan, *The Spirit, Pathos, and Liberation: Toward and Hispanic Pentecostal Theology* Journal of Pentecostal Theology Supplements 14 (Sheffield: Sheffield Academic, 1998) 61.

66. Nancy E. Bedford, "Teología de la misión integral y dicernimiento comunitario," in *La iglesia como agente de transformación,* ed. C. René Padilla and T. Yamamori (Buenos Aires: Kairós, 2005), 54.

nature. Barth's view of God's compassionate nature as revealed paradigmatically in the incarnation of the Son, the divine will to be for us and with us, is congruent with LT's call to align human praxis with God's liberating work among the marginalized. LT's Christological focus on Jesus's identification with the victims highlights compassion's costliness amidst systemic injustice. On the other hand, Barth's trinitarian perspective can be enriched by LT's focus on the historical-material dimension of human existence. LT can illuminate how the eternal compassionate God identifies with suffering humanity, enacting mercy through human agents in concrete sociopolitical contexts. Compassion is faith-seeking *pasionada participationis*. God's compassion for humanity in Jesus is more than a sympathetic posture of his love. God's compassion heals the creature's despair and energizes the praxis of those whom God freely determines will have the ministry of reconciliation: the church.

RESPONSE TO MARTINEZ

Rose Lee-Norman

Prior to May 25, 2020, as a pastor I made a delineation between acts of compassion and acts of justice as it pertained to the vocation of the church as disciples of Jesus. I delineated these two because I saw compassion as a program of charity and justice as the work of societal transformation. While there may be some truth in that at times, the murder of Mr. George Floyd problematized that for me. In reading Dr. Jules Martinez's paper, his scholarly and passion-filled presentation reinvigorated questions I held that summer while serving at Sanctuary Covenant Church as a white female associate pastor in a black-led, black-centered urban multiethnic church situated in Minneapolis, Minnesota. In this response to Dr. Martinez's work, as a practitioner I hope to provide questions of praxis that enliven my vocational calling toward seeking the peace and liberation of the city (Jeremiah 29:7) through the prioritization of the marginalized. I believe Dr. Martinez's paper provides substantive reflections for Christ-followers gathered as the Church.

In my previous delineation between acts of compassion and justice, our senior pastor and I would regularly remind our congregation that acts of compassion were necessary in meeting the tangible needs of our community, but they differed from acts of justice that interrogated and disrupted the system that required acts of charity in the first place. There is truth to that delineation between charity and justice, especially in a capitalist society. However, living through the summer of 2020 in Minneapolis as our city grieved the murder of Mr. Floyd at the hands of white supremacy, the relationship between compassion and justice collided. This collision took place for me in our church parking lot.

As grief and pain seized our city, we all witnessed the array of emotions erupt on our streets and out our front doors. A few days following Mr. Floyd's murder, our main neighborhood grocery store was damaged and subsequently closed. Living in a food desert already and lacking other accessible grocery stores in the area, our church, which was located across the street from the grocery store, became a makeshift food distribution site almost overnight. We were immediately flooded with an outpouring of food, supplies, and monetary donations to support our community. In those days and weeks following we handed out 42,000 rolls of toilet paper (no small feat during the COVID-19 pandemic in 2020) and 10,500 bags of food. Three thousand three hundred volunteers partnered with us to provide a safe, equitable, and compassionate space for tangible resources to 1,500 households in our neighborhood. These numbers represent tangible acts of compassion.

What complicated my previous delineation between compassion and justice happened over the many weeks of building relationship with neighbors through our food distribution program. In hearing stories of our neighbors' lives and sharing my own, grieving over the sin and destruction of racism that was not only impacting our city in that moment but has created generational harm in our neighborhood, and imagining a transformed city block on our church property, the work of justice infiltrated and became enmeshed in those acts of compassion. In building deeper relationships with our neighbors, we gained a keener sense of justice-centered transformation for our block, undergirded by presenting charitable acts of compassion. The two were no longer separated.

From this experience and reflecting on Dr. Martinez's work, deeper questions of vocation, situated in our call to compassion and justice, developed. Questions such as, how are Minneapolitan Christians to pursue in tandem justice and compassion for our city? What is the influence of justice and where is the ministry of compassion, given the egregious exploitations of power in our city? And the question that became most prevalent for me as a pastor and resident in Minneapolis was, what is the relationship between compassion and justice?

I ask this seemingly simple question because, through my personal experience in pastoring our congregation through the uprising in Minneapolis that sparked world-wide calls for justice, our pastoral team intentionally delineated for our congregation acts of compassion that were charitable in nature from acts of justice that were transformative in nature. However, Dr. Martinez's submission has caused me to rethink and wonder about the relationship between the two. Is compassion a facet of the broader vocation of justice? Are they distinct? If so, how? Is there a point at which justice and compassion conflict or are they always congruous? Finally, has compassion been too stringently delineated from justice so it is only seen as charity and therefore has been wrongfully simplified as such? The words of Zechariah 7:9 provide helpful guidance: "Render just judgments, show kindness and mercy to one another."

It is clearly the vocation of the Christian to engage in both and from Dr. Martinez's work, they are interrelated in deeper ways than I had previously seen. Particularly his treatment of the church as "a *com-passioned* political witness" expressed this interconnected relationship for me that I experienced in the summer of 2020. In times of great need and societal suffering, the church seeks both to enact the compassion of Jesus as well as "a walk of love that seeks justice with the other." Because of the compassionate nature of God, Dr. Martinez is correct in stating our work as Christians in the society is to denounce "the anti-kingdom realities that promote or perpetuate [unjust] conditions." In reading Dr. Martinez's work and through the experience of loving our neighbors and working toward justice in the summer of 2020 in Minneapolis, Minnesota, I realized I had diluted compassion strictly to charitable acts instead of a more robust understanding of the work of compassion toward justice. In our conversation during the symposium, Dr. Martinez engaged my question regarding the relationship of compassion and justice. And in his response, he stated that justice without compassion is mechanical. It made me wonder then if compassion is a means of agency for the most vulnerable in enacting and leading the work of justice with their own voice and authority? This shift is what enriches the interconnectedness of compassion and justice toward liberation. And the interconnectedness of compassion and justice is expressed by biblical studies and restorative justice scholar Christopher D. Marshall when he states, "Compassion is the key ingredient that inspires and enables justice to be done."[1]

Through his authoritative and thorough reflection, I am grateful to learn from Dr. Martinez and his careful presentation of the theo-politics of compassion expressed by Karl Barth in assistance to Liberation Theology. It has confirmed my practical experience in enacting Jesus's mission statement in Luke 4:14–21—to tangibly prioritize the oppressed, transform oppressive structures for a redemptive Kingdom, and work toward the liberation of all of society.

---

1. Christopher D. Marshall, *Compassionate Justice: An Interdisciplinary Dialogue with Two Gospel Parables on Law, Crime, and Restorative Justice,* Theopolitical Visions 15 (Eugene, OR: Cascade, 2012), 10.

SOME TEXTS AND OUR POLITICS

Vincent Bacote

Almost everyone has an opinion about politics. For Christians, views extend from "avoid politics at all costs" to "it is our job to build the kingdom." There are numerous texts that inform and guide the various perspectives on politics taken by Christians. I am taking this opportunity to reflect on eleven texts (NIV), not primarily to adjudicate between correct interpretation and application but more as an acknowledgement of some of the ways encounters with the Scriptures have informed a range of responses. This is not at all an exhaustive survey; not only is this a small sample of texts, but I also highlight a single trajectory of political response to each one.

But first, a necessary disclaimer: my approach to faith and politics is in the domain of the Reformed tradition, particularly informed by prominent elements from the Dutch theologian and statesman Abraham Kuyper. In particular, Kuyper's doctrine of common grace is central for me; this doctrine emphasizes God's active preservation of the creation and thus makes possible constructive participation in the world, including politics. Common grace, for me, has played an important role in providing theological permission for cultural engagement in general and political action in particular. To be clear, I have deliberately chosen to use the language of "neo-Kuyperian"[1] to describe my own approach, not only because the stewardship of theological legacies includes an ongoing refinement process but also because there are versions of political theology with connections to the Reformed tradition (e.g., Christian Reconstructionism, Dominion Theology, Theonomy, and others) that I find problematic in their triumphalism.

Though this is my perspective and factors into the perspective expressed in the Genesis text below, for the most part my aim here is to consider views in addition to my own. By the end of this journey with selections from the Bible, I will offer a way forward to what I hope will be a generous view of Christian faith and political engagement. Rather than a thematic approach, I will proceed in accordance with the order of the canon (of course, there will not be sixty-six different texts!).

---

1. See Vincent Bacote, *The Spirit in Public Theology: Appropriating the Legacy of Abraham Kuyper* (2005; reprint, Eugene: Wipf & Stock, 2010), 155–56.

Genesis 1:26–28

> Then God said, "Let us make mankind in our image, in our likeness, so that they may rule over the fish in the sea and the birds in the sky, over the livestock and all the wild animals, and over all the creatures that move along the ground." So God created mankind in his own image, in the image of God he created them; male and female he created them. God blessed them and said to them, "Be fruitful and increase in number; fill the earth and subdue it. Rule over the fish in the sea and the birds in the sky and over every living creature that moves on the ground."

This text contains what some call "the creation mandate" or "cultural mandate." Many have interpreted this text to mean that management of the creation is a central dimension of God's purpose for human beings. This management includes political life and is one dimension of the rule given to human beings in the declaration in verse 26, and the blessing/command given in verse 28. This text is echoed in Psalm 8, most relevantly in verse 6: "You made them rulers over the works of your hands; you put everything under their feet." Some translations use the word "dominion" instead of "rule," either of which has been a source of concern because of the potential implications of exploitative and destructive practices. Two of the most prominent questions that emerge when connecting this text to politics concern whether politics would be necessary in a pre-fall created order and whether the language of rule too easily encourages destructive zeal.

On the first question, it is important to note the view of those who argue that the need for government only emerges after the fall and the "new normal" of discord between humans. Those who argue in favor a pre-fall politics (at least in terms of potentiality) would respond that politics is not defined exclusively by the need for the sword of justice that protects or for sociopolitical guardrails that provide a form of social and political restraint. Instead, an argument is made that first thinks of political life as management of our life together. In this sense, even if there were no fall, there would remain the need for humans to discern life together beyond family units.

On the second question, while there are surely those Christians who have interpreted "dominion" language as a green light for selfish domination of the created order, the language is better understood as a weighty exercise of stewardship. It is stewardship because the creation belongs to God and not humans, thus the rule or dominion granted to humans is not a playground for folly but a responsibility for which one must give account. From this perspective, the various dimensions of creation stewardship (from agriculture to politics) have a level of gravity that can impede tendencies toward selfish exploitation.

This approach to the text in Genesis is a foundation for political engagement, while not providing specificity regarding any specific approach to politics itself. It presents us with an open vista of possibility with considerable responsibility.

Exodus 5:1

> Afterward Moses and Aaron went to Pharaoh and said, "This is what the LORD, the God of Israel, says: 'Let my people go, so that they may hold a festival to me in the wilderness.'"

This text presents the first encounter between Moses and Aaron before Pharaoh where they bring a proclamation from God that commands freedom for the enslaved Hebrew people. This confrontation is repeated six times in chapters 7–10 (7:6, 8:1, 20, 9:1, 13, and 10:3). In these texts, God sends his messenger with a demand for deliverance and warnings of the consequences for refusal. It is the demand for freedom that we see articulated by some Christians as part of their approach to politics. How does this work, given the distinctive circumstances we find in Exodus?

The phrase "Let my people go" is used by some Christians who are seeking contemporary forms of sociopolitical freedom. This use of the text regards the confrontation between Moses (with Aaron) and Pharaoh as pattern to be repeated in the face of great challenges for groups of people, such as we find in the African American experience. It is a liberation motif where a person or corporate/institutional entity is analogous to Pharaoh and those who suffer oppression are analogous to the Israelites. The figure of Moses (with Aaron) is not necessarily a singular person (though we can see this in *Go and Tell Pharaoh*, the memoir of Al Sharpton, and in the ways some regard figures like Frederick Douglass and Martin Luther King Jr.) but could also be any group of persons. A recent example of this can be found in Raphael G. Warnock's *Harvard Divinity Bulletin* article "Let My People Go: The Scandal of Mass Incarceration in the Land of the Free." His use of the phrase:

> People of faith and moral courage should lead the charge and embrace the challenge of saying to a failed system, "Let my people go." That is what God told Moses to tell Pharaoh. "Let my people go that they may worship me." Liberate them from human bondage so that they might blossom and live lives of human flourishing, lives that give glory to God rather than to human systems. Moses had a speech impediment, yet God picked him. Moses had a record. Yet, God picked him in spite of his record. Or, maybe God picked him *because* he had a record. In my tradition, God has a record of using people with

a record: Moses had a record. He slew an Egyptian. He killed a man. God had more in store for him . . . [2]

Warnock not only emphasizes the prophetic challenge to the system but also the character of Moses (and he goes on in sermonic fashion to identify others "with a record") as someone God would use in spite of some characteristic that would be held against them, as would often be the case of those incarcerated. In the use of this liberation motif, we see attention to patterns that can inform Christian political practice. It is one used that also takes the larger narrative into account, because the subsequent liberation of the Israelites took place; the path to freedom included the confrontation of Pharaoh prior to God's deliverance.

Amos 5:24

But let justice roll on like a river,
    righteousness like a never-failing stream!

This phrase appears amid God's confrontation with Israel (the Northern kingdom) and his warning of the impending exile. This is one of many texts where God makes clear his disinterest in formal ritual obedience amid practices of idolatrous infidelity that violate the covenant between the LORD and his people. The language for justice strongly suggests that God desires his people to perform acts of social righteousness. The implications for politics are explicit; the one true God wants his people to be practitioners and emissaries of justice, at the very least within their own faith community and at most in society at large. The language of a rolling river indicates that attention to justice is not a matter for special occasions. One might say that the practice of justice should be so characteristic of the community that they are known as justice people. John Perkins's *Let Justice Roll Down*, one of his first books, takes its title from this text.

Micah 6:8

He has shown you, O mortal, what is good.
And what does the LORD require of you?
To act justly and to love mercy and to walk humbly with your God.

---

2. Raphael G. Warnock, "Let My People Go: The Scandal of Mass Incarceration in the Land of the Free," *Harvard Divinity Bulletin*, Autumn/Winter 2020, https://bulletin.hds.harvard.edu/let-my-people-go/.

This text has similar resonance with Amos 5:24 and is also set in the context of God's critiques and warnings to his people (the Southern kingdom). In contrast to the prior verse, which poses the question about what God truly desires in terms of voluminous and costly sacrifice, God makes clear that he wants each of his people to be characterized by the practice of justice along with a merciful character and humble walk with him. Just as with the Northern Kingdom, God desires a people who are practitioners of justice. It is important that this practice is pursued amid the other two characteristics, as the practice of justice can be selfish and distorted otherwise. This text was recited by Jimmy Carter at his inauguration in 1976, and Christians of various traditions will quote this text as a guiding principle in their political pursuits.

Perhaps the most important aspect to consider here is that an emphasis on justice in both Amos and Micah indicates that Christians cannot make this aspect of politics optional. While the command to practice justice is clear, the specific contemporary implications remain an open question. The challenge is to consider what justice should look like in our contemporary sociopolitical settings, and there is no consensus among Christians as to the top priorities for justice that stem from a well-known text such as this.

Matthew 5:13-14

> You're the salt of the earth. But if the salt loses its saltiness, how can it be made salty again? It is no longer good for anything, except to be thrown out and trampled underfoot. You are the light of the world. A city on a hill cannot be hidden. Neither do people light a lamp and put it under a bowl. Instead they put it on its stand, and it gives light to everyone in the house. In the same way, let your light shine before others, that they may see your good deeds and glorify your Father in heaven.

These words from the Sermon on the Mount emphasize influence that has an effect on contexts local to global. While there are a range of views on the political implications of these verses, here I highlight the prominent and controversial Seven Mountains perspective (also referred to as the Seven Mountain Mandate or Seven Mountain Prophecy). This view emerged in 1975 when Bill Bright (founder of Campus Crusade for Christ) and Loren Cunningham (founder of Youth with a Mission) both shared with each that they had a dream from God about the need for Christians to influence and transform cultural and religious institutions to bring change to the nations. The seven mountains are media, government, education, economy, family, religion, and celebration (arts/entertainment). This view is present primarily in some Pentecostal and charismatic settings and is a version of what some call Dominion theology.

In the Seven Mountains view, Jesus's command that we are to be salt and light is understood to encourage strategies of permeating the places of greatest influence, including politics. The result of being the light of the world is not only the witness of good deeds but also the transformative effects on persons and institutions, including governments. Eschatologically this view appears to be a kind of postmillennialism, though that is not the prominent terminology. While controversial and arguably not on the radar of other Protestants, it is important to note this example of interpretation given the continued growth of Pentecostal and charismatic movements.

Luke 20:25

> He said to them, "Then give back to Caesar what is Caesar's, and to God what is God's."

In response to an effort to trap Jesus with a seemingly lose-lose scenario about whether to pay taxes (If he says "no," then he is a traitor to the empire, and if he says "yes" he is a traitor to his own people who bristle under Roman rule), Jesus confounds his opponents. He gives an answer that acknowledges a place for paying taxes and for having complete fidelity to God. The political implications of the text could be seen to suggest that the realm of earthly government has its designated domain and that the church is a separate domain. This view could lead to an approach to Christian politics that allows participation in government but with a distinct barrier that keeps it separate from the church; this would reflect the aim of avoiding confusion between the church and political/governmental realms.

Another view could begin with an emphasis on Jesus's identity as divine and human, which would then have the potential implication that his response acknowledges government but places it under the domain of the one who is the creator and ruler of the universe. Understood in this way, political engagement would be given an identity distinct from the church but without the implication that direct Christian influence is problematic. Rather, Christian influence (here I assume a context different from the Roman empire where great influence would be less likely pre-Constantine) that does not attempt to remake the government in the image of the church is possible and to be encouraged.

Romans 13:1-2

> Let everyone be subject to the governing authorities, for there is no authority except that which God has established. The authorities that exist have been established by God. Consequently, whoever rebels against the authority is rebelling against what God has instituted, and those who do so will bring judgment on themselves. For rulers hold no terror for those who do right, but for those who do wrong. Do you want to be free from fear of the one in authority? Then do what is right and you will be commended.

We now come to a text that has been the source of much intrigue. Does it tell Christians simply to obey those in governmental authority regardless of circumstance? In context, perhaps a better view is to understand this text as normative guidance in circumstances where rulers tend to approximate God's standard for justice in society. In the immediate context of Romans, Christians are living in the Roman Empire, arguably sometime in the AD late-fifties during the time of Nero (prior to persecutions in the AD mid-sixties) when law and order had been established throughout the provinces. In part, this reading of the text takes into account the larger canonical witness where unjust rulers are opposed by God and occasionally opposed by the people of God (situations such as Moses before Pharaoh as mentioned above). A more important dimension here may be the fact that the text gives recognition to the place of government and rulers. Even with Christ's advent, the arrival of the Messiah is not reason for God's people to become the next group who seek an overthrow of government, particularly in situations where a rebellion is likely a suicide mission. Government has its place until Christ returns to put everything under his feet. Put another way, politics is not antithetical to the ways of God.

Philippians 3:20

> But our citizenship is in heaven . . .

Paul makes a contrast between the Christians in Philippi and their fellow members of the Roman Empire, making clear the primary political identity. They do not cease to be citizens of Rome, but they are to conduct their lives in accordance with Christ who has come and will return and not only reign but renew the bodies of his people at the resurrection. This text provides the opportunity to highlight an Anabaptist approach to politics. The Schleitheim Confession (1527) is one of the earliest Anabaptist statements. Under the section that addresses the use of the sword, this Philippians text is used as part of the answer given to the question of whether a Christian should be a magistrate (government official):

> . . . one can see in the following points that it does not befit a Christian to be a magistrate: the rule of the government is according to the flesh, that of the Christians according to the Spirit. Their houses and dwelling remain in this world, that of the Christians is in heaven. Their citizenship is in this world, that of the Christians is in heaven. The weapons of their battle and warfare are carnal and only against the flesh, but the weapons of Christians are spiritual, against the fortification of the devil. The worldly are armed with steel and iron, but Christians are armed with the armor of God, with truth, righteousness, peace, faith, salvation, and with the Word of God. In sum: as Christ our Head is minded, so also must be minded the members of the body of Christ through Him, so that there be no division in the body, through which it would be destroyed.[3]

Fidelity to Christ and the integrity of the body of Christ are primary reasons for a Christian to refrain from participation in government and to refrain from violence. The Anabaptist tradition conveys a stark and convicted awareness of the pitfalls of participation in government. The contrast emphasized in the above quote does not lead to the conclusion that the Anabaptist tradition is apolitical. It is more accurate to regard the tradition as committed to an alternative politics that is modeled within the life of the community. Here it is important to note that there are many contemporary Christians who are not part of Anabaptist denominations or communities, but who find the emphasis on an alternative politics as helpful or strongly compelling. With an Anabaptist disposition, the Christian identity as citizens of another kingdom prompts political practice with a strong focus on the integrity of the church.

1 Peter 2:2–17

> Live such good lives among the pagans that, though they accuse you of doing wrong, they may see your good deeds and glorify God on the day he visits us. Submit yourselves for the Lord's sake to every human authority: whether to the emperor, as the supreme authority, or to governors, who are sent by him to punish those who do wrong and to commend those who do right. For it is God's will that by doing good you should silence the ignorant talk of foolish people. Live as free people, but do not use your freedom as a cover-up for evil; live as God's slaves. Show proper respect to everyone, love the family of believers, fear God, honor the emperor.

At first glance this text may appear to be making an argument identical to Romans 13, but there is a significant contextual difference. The context of 1 Peter is Christians

---

3. Schleitheim Confession, https://www.anabaptistwiki.org/mediawiki/index.php/Schleitheim_Confession_(source).

who are in an exilic situation, scattered across the Roman Empire. They are people with little or no social or political capital, regarded with suspicion and under threat of persecution. Thus, the emphasis on living lives of moral excellence "among the pagans." The political guidance here is to live as those who are the best possible citizens, rather than people whose behavior displays or implies antagonism toward governing authorities. They are encouraged to live as free people, but not as an excuse to live a wild or politically revolutionary life. Though they may have minimal political influence, they are to inhabit their political context as those who aspire to be blameless citizens (as long as they are not asked to oppose their faith). This is political practice that will be in some ways common but also distinctive, because the personal morality of Christians will be in stark contrast. They will perform good deeds that may only be misinterpreted by those who oppose them and refuse to see any possibility of good citizenship when Jesus is Lord instead of Caesar. It is a kind of faithful politics while one is perpetually aware of their status as foreigners.

Revelation 7:9

> After this I looked, and there before me was a great multitude that no one could count, from every nation, tribe, people and language, standing before the throne and before the Lamb. They were wearing white robes and were holding palm branches in their hands. And they cried out in a loud voice:
>
> "Salvation belongs to our God,
> who sits on the throne,
> and to the Lamb."

This vision of the great multitude worshipping God may seem apolitical and mainly a worship-oriented text, but it contains an important element that informs the political commitments of some Christians. This crowd beyond number is a multi-ethnic people giving praise and honor to God. Their ethnic diversity displays a fulfillment of God's promise to Abram in Gen 12:3 that all the nations would be blessed, a blessing whereby people from every *kind* of people will be able to have life with God through Christ.

While the vision is future, some perceive important political implications for the present. Given the post-fall new normal of enmity between human beings, inter-ethnic/inter-racial conflict has been typical. The good news of the gospel is for people from all ethnicities, and this new people are a single people of God, without the obliteration of their ethnic particularity. The visible unity of this people need not be reserved for the future; it is a present possibility for the people of God as they walk the path of sanctification together. The accomplishment of this visible unity may often require addressing the ways political life has inflamed ethnic loyalties and divisions, thus Christians who are captured by the eschatological vision in this text may be catalyzed to engage the political process. This is not participation in the political process merely to facilitate the visible unity of God's people, but also the expression of a commitment to justice in the world, which includes seeking the good of all people (not only those in the church). While it is not a naïve pursuit of perfect unity prior to the eschaton, it can be a patient commitment to pursuing signposts of the kingdom. This might be considered as one aspect of the persistent practice and pursuit of sanctification. This would be a path toward holiness that involves pursuing and facilitating the development of societies where public policies and the culture encourage not only the flourishing of all ethnic groups but also respectful unity across differences. Ideally this would be most evident among Christians but would have the type of public influence where it is seen also to some degree among those outside the church.

Revelation 21:9-10

> One of the seven angels who had the seven bowls full of the seven last plagues came and said to me, "Come, I will show you the bride, the wife of the Lamb." And he carried me away in the Spirit to a mountain great and high, and showed me the Holy City, Jerusalem, coming down out of heaven from God.

The bride coming from heaven is the Holy City. The church is the bride of Christ. While the text is often read as depicting the future, Peter Leithart reads this in a different way. He argues that the holy city is already present:

> The city of God exists *now*, in the present, as a real-life society among the societies of men. This real-world, visible community is the family of the Father, the body of the Son, the temple of the Spirit. It exists to transform and renew human societies, inside and out, top to bottom. As God's city, the church's carries out a global mission of urban renewal."[4]

Unlike the Seven Mountains vision above, Leithart does not see this mission with the same strategy or with the same view of victory. The primary work is worship and opposition is to be expected:

> The world is always hostile to the church, but some worlds are more hostile than others. Our world is more hostile than most, since it's built on an explicit rejection of Christian faith. Our world is also fracturing and decaying.

---

4. Peter Leithart, "The Theopolitan Vision," https://theopolisinstitute.com/leithart_post/the-theopolitan-vision/.

Politically, geopolitically, economically, culturally, the world is crumbling. That only makes it more vicious: A cornered bear is a dangerous bear . . .

Death isn't a defeat. Far from it. We share in Christ's dying so that we can share in His abundant life and glory. When we share in Christ's death, when we are like the early martyrs who did not "love life even to death" (Rev 12), we become a world-changing force. Courageous witness shatters old worlds and lays the foundations for new ones. It's through the cross that God's city renews the cities of men.[5]

This is a politics that emphasizes formation via the liturgy of the church, which then spills into confrontation with society at all levels. This is another kind of alternative politics where martyrdom is to be expected on the path to renewal.

Now What?

What is the path for Christians toward winsome politics? Which texts should be foundational for our understanding of political life? What helps us to navigate our time of intense political polarization? Do we start with creation? Do we start with our identity as citizens of heaven? Do prophetic motifs provide a standard for public rhetoric and activism? Does acknowledgment of government's role incline us toward strategies of quiet compliance? These are some of the questions that arise for the church as we navigate the terrain of politics.

What is not immediately obvious is that many of these questions and others arise not as matters of theoretical reflection, but often as the result of vexing challenges amid the pursuit of fidelity to God. The different types of questions can lead us to begin with different texts. To use a personal example, my primary question was *whether* Christians could or should participate in politics, particularly when I heard warnings about being "too worldly." This led me toward the question of a Christian foundation for politics and to texts like Genesis 1 and Psalm 8. As some of the examples above make clear, questions about the identity and nature of the church or the legitimacy of government can lead to starting with other texts. While many of us may have well considered perspectives on the interface of our faith and politics and may have had spirited disagreements with others, each of us should consider what catalyzed our engagement with political life and how our questions led us to particular texts.

It is with this kind of consideration in mind that I thought to look at the ways different texts may lead to different points of emphasis. While there is a place for making a case for what I call my neo-Kuyperian approach, here I am more inclined

---

5. Leithart, "The Theopolitan Vision."

to consider how to cultivate a greater attention to the factors that lead us toward our engagements with Scripture and resultant framing of Christian political engagement.

Here is another way to put it: context matters not only for our understanding of the biblical text but also for our approaches to politics. All or most at this symposium are from the United States, a country where there is considerable possibility for political participation. This level of political participation is foreign to the world of the Bible and offers both political opportunity and hazards. In contrast, a Christian who lives in a country like North Korea or Saudi Arabia finds themselves in places where political agency beyond their Christian communities is minimal or nonexistent; they will only have the most local of political actions. This question of context is one of the most important to consider as we think about what is genuinely possible. If we have considerable agency, we might find ourselves inclined to think about political actions when we ask how we are to facilitate human flourishing and may go to the Genesis text or even to the Exodus text because of the possibilities for formation of policy and free speech. If we are in contexts of minimal agency, we will more readily identify with texts such as 1 Peter because of what will seem more like an exilic experience. Part of what this tells us is that even if we have an ideal view of Christian political involvement, the sociopolitical context presents opportunities and limitations; those of us whose views incline us toward participation in the political structures of society may find ourselves to be practical Anabaptists in settings where access to the political process is walled off.

As we consider how Scripture can guide our political engagement, another important question to ask is what might be constant elements that are less limited by context. Of the texts briefly mentioned here, the identity of the church is a constant. Wherever Christians are, they remain the church whether or not there are possibilities for activities such as voting, holding office, or advocating for public policy. The church always has opportunity within itself for confessing and practicing a political reality where the citizens of heaven continually seek to order their lives in accordance with Christ their king. Within the community, the citizens of heaven cannot escape the obligation to be a people characterized by the consistent practice of justice. Indeed, one of the opportunities of the church as an alternative witness (in any society) is the pursuit of justice within the community, perhaps especially on questions of race, gender, and class. Hearkening to the language in Micah, the practice of justice requires the guardrails of lovingkindness and a humble walk with God. Our identity as God's people and the requirement of justice are constant and inescapable.

At this point I introduce another text, one that I haven't given much attention in the past when thinking about Christian political engagement. That Scripture is 1 Sam 8:4–8:

> So all the elders of Israel gathered together and came to Samuel at Ramah. They said to him, "You are old, and your sons do not follow your ways; now appoint a king to lead us, such as all the other nations have."
>
> But when they said, "Give us a king to lead us," this displeased Samuel; so he prayed to the LORD. And the LORD told him: "Listen to all that the people are saying to you; it is not you they have rejected, but they have rejected me as their king. As they have done from the day I brought them up out of Egypt until this day, forsaking me and serving other gods, so they are doing to you."

The Israelites came to Samuel and asked for a king "as all the other nations have," and in response to Samuel's prayer God tells him that the people are rejecting him as king. What occurs in this text is a cautionary tale as Christians consider political engagement. It was an old pattern for the Israelites to state fidelity to God, only to look around at other nations and follow their gods and their ways. As we consider political engagement, a good practice may be to consistently ask whether our approaches to politics are (wittingly or unwittingly) derived from looking around at what seems good to those who are outside the church and then seeking the same things or simply trying to put a Christian veneer on "what the others have." An important qualification: I am not saying there is nothing Christians can learn from those outside the church; natural law and common grace are legitimate ways of discerning truth outside of special revelation. Rather, I am considering 1 Samuel 8 and prompting myself (and hopefully others) to consider whether there are things we take for granted that may seem good to us but if examined more closely these things are perhaps not as helpful for political life as they first appear. I am just beginning to consider this question in a way I have not in the past.

This does not mean I am about to join "team Anabaptist," but it is helping me to further sharpen my understanding of the ways our politics are at best penultimate strategies for bringing good to society. I am still inclined toward my modified view of a Kuyperian approach to a politics that emerges out of the cultural mandate in Genesis 1, though the exercise of engaging these different texts inclines me to hold my position in a way that is more welcoming of infusions and seasoning from other perspectives.

I will briefly consider a final question as I close: what are we to do amid our intense polarization and concerns about Christian nationalism and lingering challenges of race? One answer is that if we take into consideration the opportunities of political agency in places like the United States, we have possibilities for at least considering how to orient Christian communities to be models of fidelity to Christ over flag and to the search for strategies that will help us learn how to better practice unity within the church. We have a long way to go on this, but the opportunity remains even when fellow believers are resistant, hesitant, or jaded about such possibilities. If, as stated above, politics and the pursuit of justice are not optional, then it falls to churches to seek counsel from their King, asking him to give them courage, patience, and a strategic imagination that will lead to a catechesis of Christian politics that will display at least a slight glimpse of the joyful unity that is ahead for God's people. We can both lament in our realism as we face this challenging moment as well as move forward in hope toward the future that will one day be our eternal present.

RESPONSE TO BACOTE

Jonathan Wilson

I am honored to be a respondent to Dr. Bacote. I appreciate the framework that he has set forward for the follower of Jesus to engage in the public sphere. In this article, and in his 2015 volume *The Political Disciple*, Dr. Bacote shows that the individual believer may ground one's engagement with the public sphere in one's whole-life discipleship to Christ.

I treated this theme in an historical manner and from a Pietistic rather than a Reformed perspective in my 2019 volume, *God on Three Sides: German Pietists at War in Eighteenth America* (Eugene, OR: Pickwick). In its conclusion I set forth that while individual Christian laypeople have and do act on political convictions as part of their exercise of faith, as it concerns clergy a traditional Lutheran constraint of pastoral neutrality might still be preferred.

I do not see my conclusions as a counter-thesis, but as a means of bringing into focus a dialogue on the extent to which Dr. Bacote's framework applies to the church, especially the local congregation where the politically active lay-person is a member. In my present role as a church pastor, I have shared, at the time of this conference (2021), in the experience of many pastors in local churches who are feeling more vocational stress over public issues than before. This may have been part of discerning the timeliness of *Politics* as the topic for this year's symposium. My two main questions are these: To what degree is Dr. Bacote's model useful for the local church acting *as a unity* of Christ's body, and, to what degree can any model for public engagement be employed by pastors without deepening partisan fractures in their churches? Putting this second question another way, can the statement attributed to the pagan philosopher Hippocrates, "First, do no harm," be a guiding political value for pastors of local churches?

Dr. Bacote bases his model on a fresh reading and application of the Dutch theologian and politician Abraham Kuyper. Through Kuyper we are pulled into the world of nineteenth-century Protestant and evangelical optimism, when many assumed that the power of government ought to be leveraged by godly law-makers to address social ills in a redemptive manner. This was characteristic of many of Kuyper's contemporaries. For example, in Sweden Paul Peter Waldenstrom, the editor of a theological magazine which catalyzed the formation of new denominations, resigned as a priest of the Church of Sweden and then served for over twenty years in the lower house of Sweden's national assembly, the *Riksdag*.

In the nineteenth century many preachers took up socially progressive causes: abolition, emancipation, suffrage, temperance, work-place safety, labor laws, child protection, and Sunday sabbath. Meanwhile, the industry and might of the Atlantic World was being visited around the globe, and the benefits of Christian civilization, so it was presumed, were being exported to so-called heathen lands. For many of these visionaries, God's Kingdom, as it rode the crest of colonialism, seemed to be imminent in arrival and inevitable in triumph.

Competing visions opposed to this evangelical optimism also emerged. Some economic philosophers saw the industrial age as the harbinger of a godless eschatology, where history must end with the emancipation of the laborer from all external exploitation and all internal envy. These godless movements also gained momentum in the public sphere and in partisan politics. Abraham Kuyper's stance on what ought to be done about them was abundantly clear when he helped to found the "Anti-Revolutionary Party."

Part of me wishes that the causes of the nineteenth century were still before us, although shed of their ugly, unreflected assumptions regarding peoples of color and indigenous cultures. But as it concerns human trafficking and enslavement, free and available primary education, emancipation and suffrage for women, and the impact of addictions on homes and societies, these nineteenth-century issues continue to urgently require redemptive, public solutions.

Yet public discourse has largely moved on to other concerns that are mind-boggling in number and ethical complexity: creation care and energy consumption, student loan forgiveness, gun ownership and violence, ballot access, Deferred Action for Childhood Arrivals[1] pathways, racial inequities in incarceration rates, affirmation of life, affirmation of body sovereignty, the resort to lethal force upon the unarmed. Throw in an attempted coup on the nation's capital building, stir up vaccine mandates, bring to a boil. Many pastors have found this to be a recipe for disaster for the *koinonia* of their churches.

This is the world of the twenty-first century into which Dr. Bacote's disciple of Jesus journeys into the public sphere. It is not Kuyper's world, but Kuyper is appropriated. Most important to Dr. Bacote's neo-Kuyperian framework is Kuyper's premise that the public, political sphere is part of the unfallen Created Order.

---

1. Also known as DACA. See https://www.uscis.gov/DACA.

Christ-followers not only may but ought to engage in politics as part of their obedient discipleship as new creations in Christ.

Dr. Bacote focuses on treating eleven passages of Scripture. This is ample evidence that his neo-Kuyperian hermeneutic is companion to, and founded on, Scripture in its plain sense. To be clear, one might begin with Kuyperian political theology and then read the Bible as a means of confirmation bias, but that is not true of Dr. Bacote's journey, as he describes in his 2015 volume. Dr. Bacote drew conclusions from faithfully reading and exegeting Scripture, and did not discover Kuyper until later, when he found in Kuyper someone who was articulating conclusions similar to those he had arrived at already.

I found that my resonance with Dr. Bacote's reading for plain sense had me tracking along with his conclusions for the most part, but that there were two texts, appearing successively, where the treatment gave me pause. These were Luke 20:25, rendering to Caesar, followed immediately by Romans 13, obeying government. In treating the Luke passage, Dr. Bacote makes a passing reference to Constantine and leaves it at that. When it comes to the issue about Christians and public, political involvement and the exercise of worldly power, for many Christians in many traditions, Constantine is the elephant in the porcelain shop. As my response must be limited, I leave it with this: I encourage Dr. Bacote to do future work in how a neo-Kuyperian framework addresses and obviates the darker legacies of Constantine.

As it concerns the treatment of Romans 13, where government officials are to be honored and obeyed, Dr. Bacote states, "In context, a better view is to understand this text as normative guidance in circumstances where rulers tend to approximate God's standard for justice in society." I do not think I am being nit-picky when I raise, in this "context," the specter of Emperor Nero. Having risen to power in AD 54, it is quite likely that he was emperor when Paul wrote to the Romans. Even if the emperor were Claudius by then, this statement remains problematic. In any case, to speak of the context of a passage suggests here the context for Paul and his readers. I disagree that we can assume a context of secular leaders who approximate God's standard, when such leaders were almost completely unknown in Paul's day, despite the author Luke's effort to cast them in as positive light as possible.

There are other treatments of Scripture where I shout amen with Dr. Bacote, one of those being that ethnic distinctions are preserved, not erased, in the resurrected humanity. The "glory of the nations" will enter the city. We will be identifiable as coming from north, south, east, west. When I hear the U-2 lead Bono sing, "I believe in the Kingdom Come, when all the colors bleed into One," I always think to myself, "I would phrase that differently."[2]

---

2. U2, "I Still Haven't Found What I'm Looking For," *The Joshua Tree,* Island Records, 1987.

Perhaps it is assumed that these eleven texts have obvious applications to the faith community, but I am not persuaded that the applications are along the lines of the neo-Kuyperian framework for partisan alignments in public action. One of the most resonant themes in Dr. Bacote's 2015 volume *The Political Disciple* was that engagement in the public square would mean suffering. In light of 2021's trends towards toxicity and alienation, that might have been a helpful theme to develop in this paper, applied to both layperson and clergy. Public engagement, even when pastors have tried to stay non-partisan, has been the occasion for much suffering in the clergy. Many local churches, in the years since *The Public Disciple* was published in 2015, have become significantly weaker in the ability to present a unified public witness. Partisan polarization at the national level has translated into alienation and division in the local church.

Even a Christ-follower's private actions or statements that have public implication are given highly partisan, highly confrontational, highly alienating scrutiny. Some things as simple and personal as wearing a mask in a closed space, and receiving vaccines, are seen as charged partisan actions with divisive consequences. Churches that set policies on public matters of health have alienated whole factions that have realigned around this issue like few others in recent memory; pastors that have encouraged a Romans 13 abidance with local government guidelines and best medical practice have been pilloried by congregants, and some have already lost pulpits and calls for issues like following masking guidelines.

These issues are *much less substantive than*, for example, the use of excessive force on the unarmed, or the culture of incarceration, or fair and equal ballot access for all constituents across all precincts, etc., all of which demand the public, prophetic input of followers of Jesus. In the United States in 2021 it is not the world powers, it is the churches, that are crucifying pastors. At times the demand on the pastor to be a prophet must yield to the need for the pastor to be a shepherd. As Jesus avoided being thrown off the cliff outside Nazareth (Luke 4), knowing his death was to come outside Jerusalem, so pastors must discern the hills where God requires us to die, and those hills on which we are not asked to die, to commit vocational suicide.

Here are my two main questions, now restated in several of their aspects: Is a neo-Kuyperian framework for political involvement right for the layperson, but not for the pastor or church? On these matters of public conscience and prophetic witness, ought this distinction between pastor and layperson to be made? Is it legitimate for the individual believer to engage political issues as a matter of discipleship, yet to do so without expecting any support, even emotionally, from the church where one belongs?

Perhaps the calling of a pastor or church to engage in or desist from partisan political involvement is tied to a discernment of times and seasons, where every purpose has its time under heaven (Eccl 3:1). Perhaps this outlook is best summed up in this expression of the common grace that was upon pagans: "First, do no harm." Meanwhile the individual believer does well, does right, to pursue public life as a facet of obedient discipleship. With his neo-Kuyperian outlook and his plain reading of Scripture, Dr. Bacote has presented a helpful framework for discerning how the believer may obey Christ in the public sphere.

LOVE'S DOMAIN OR WHITE CHRISTIANS' DOMINION? A MISSIOLOGICAL RESPONSE TO THE AMERICAN CULTURE WARS

Janel Kragt Bakker

In the wake of the January 6, 2021 storming of the U.S. Capitol, in which a mob of supporters of then-president Donald Trump attempted to overturn his defeat in the 2020 presidential election, the image of Senator Josh Hawley's raised fist in solidarity with the rioters became ubiquitous. Hawley—who contested Congress' certification of the Electoral College's vote on the election results even after insurrectionists had harmed law enforcement officers, looted the Capitol, and put the lives of his colleagues in imminent danger—was heralded by many on the right as a champion of principled populism, while being decried by many on the left as a Trumpian sell-out or a brazen white Christian nationalist.

A devout evangelical, Hawley was certainly not the first high-profile white Christian figure in the U.S. to transgress traditional norms in support of Trump's leadership. From Trump's candidacy announcement in 2015 through his post-presidency, scores of conservative white Christian leaders have downplayed or even defended Trump's evidential sexual misconduct, frequent bullying of opponents, chauvinistic and xenophobic language, widespread misrepresentation of the truth, and challenge of democratic norms—not to mention the corruption scandals and inhumane policies that marked his administration. Rank and file white evangelicals followed suit, with roughly eight in ten voting for Trump in both the 2016 and 2020 elections.[1] White evangelicals were also strongly represented among those who disputed the 2020 election results, with evangelical messaging prominently featured in the attempts to overturn the election, and 75 percent of white evangelical Christian Republicans maintaining that Biden was not legitimately elected.[2]

1. Jessica Martinez and Gregory A. Smith, "How the Faithful Voted: A Preliminary 2016 Analysis," Pew Research Center, November 9, 2016; Elana Schor and David Crary, "AP VoteCast: Trump Wins White Evangelicals, Catholics Split," Associated Press, November 6, 2020.

2. Matthew Avery Sutton, "The Capitol Riot Revealed the Darkest Nightmares of White Evangelical

In the midst of a dizzying array of explanations among scholars and pundits for how white American evangelicalism came to be emblematized by ardent support for Donald Trump, it is clear that white evangelicalism in the U.S. is facing a missiological crisis. Adopting Carlos Cardoza-Orlandi's definition of mission as "the participation of the people of God in God's action in the world,"[3] in this paper I'll address the missiological implications of the political projects of white Christian nationalists and other white Christian conservatives. I'll also propose an alternative approach to Christian political engagement that is based neither on self-preservation nor on conquest, conversion, or control of perceived enemies. Rather, this vision is based on the call for Christian disciples to enter the realm of God's justice and receive the domain of God's love.

Practical theology, a discipline which seeks to bring theological and social theory and the practice of religious life into alignment, supplies my methodology. Practical theology often proceeds in four moments or tasks, as articulated by Richard Osmer.[4] The first task Osmer calls the descriptive-empirical task. The key question for this first task is, "What is going on?" I will begin this paper by probing this question in the context of the hardening of the culture wars and the ascendency of white Christian nationalism in the United States. Practical theology's second task is the interpretive task, with the corresponding question, "Why is this going on?" As part of this task, I will draw on social theory to help elucidate the contemporary missiological crisis among white Christians. The third task, the normative task, seeks to answer the question, "What ought to be going on?" Relying on New Testament depictions of the *basileia tou theou* ("kingdom of God", see Matt 12:28, for instance), I will present a missiological vision for Christian public engagement by bringing into focus the vocation of Christians to bear witness to God's rule of love and justice in our world. Finally, the fourth, or pragmatic task, addresses the question, "How should we respond?" I'll suggest ideas for responding to the call to mission set before Christians in this time and place in history. I focus on white American evangelicals not to center whiteness nor to dismiss the experiences of other demographics, but to reckon with the harmful legacy of my own background, and to highlight the urgency of the contemporary missiological crisis created by the missteps of white evangelical actors.

America," *The New Republic*, January 14, 2021; Daniel A. Cox, "Rise of Conspiracies Reveals an Evangelical Divide in the GOP," Survey Center on American Life, February 12, 2021.

3. Carlos Cardoza-Orlandi, *Mission: An Essential Guide* (Nashville: Abingdon, 2002), 15.
4. See Richard Osmer, *Practical Theology: An Introduction* (Grand Rapids: Eerdmans, 2008), 4.

Not Your Parents' Culture Wars: New Battle Lines for a New Generation

While the long distances that white evangelicals have been willing to travel in support of Donald Trump have come as a surprise to some, the alliance of white evangelicalism and political conservatism in the United States has significant precedence in what has come to be known as the "culture wars." This thesis maintains that the American cultural landscape has been marked by two opposing constituencies for decades. In one camp are religious, cultural, and political liberals and in the other are various stripes of conservatives. Traditionalists and progressives are not only ideologically distinct but are actively fighting against each other for influence in society.

The two-party thesis was first articulated by Martin Marty in 1970 in his book, *Righteous Empire*.[5] Marty argued that since the late nineteenth century, two Protestant parties, a "public party" and a "private party," have dominated the American religious landscape. Modernity played a key role in creating this division by pushing people to the poles, forcing them to choose between authority and experience, revelation and science, propositional truth and self- expression.[6] Birthed in the modernist/fundamentalist controversy engulfing American Protestantism at the turn of the twentieth century, the left/right divide has only expanded since then.

Building on Marty's work, sociologists James Davison Hunter and Robert Wuthnow were prominent advocates of the bi-polar thesis in the 1980s and 1990s. Wuthnow maintained that following World War II, American believers became increasingly polarized along the left-right continuum, regardless of religious tradition or ecclesiastical affiliation. Through the middle of the twentieth century, broad religious traditions like Protestantism, Catholicism, and Judaism had provided the salient categories of American cultural life, with each tradition presenting a particular way to be American.[7] But as communities became more religiously diverse and interfaith cooperation become more common in the decades following World War II, this sorting by religious tradition became less meaningful.[8] A new cleavage developed in the context of the social upheaval of the 1960s. Emerging on one side of the divide were those who stressed the importance of right belief and individual

---

5. Martin E. Marty, *Righteous Empire: The Protestant Experience in America* (New York: Dial, 1970).

6. See Nancey Murphy, *Beyond Liberalism and Fundamentalism: How Modern and Postmodern Philosophy Set the Theological Agenda* (Harrisburg, PA: Trinity, 1996).

7. See Will Herberg, *Protestant, Catholic, Jew* (Chicago: University of Chicago Press, 1965).

8. Robert Wuthnow, "Old Fissures and New Fractures in American Religious Life," in *Religion and American Culture*, ed. David G. Hackett (New York: Routledge, 1995), 378. See also Wuthnow, *The Restructuring of American Religion: Society and Faith since World War II* (Princeton: Princeton University Press, 1988).

responsibility; on the other were those who stressed the relativity of belief and the need to reform social institutions and systems.[9] The division between conservative and liberal Christians, residual from the modernist/fundamentalist controversy, became paramount in the 1960s and decades following. While the divide was most prominent among the white Protestant majority, it also came to be mirrored among other demographics. Conservative Catholics, Jews, and Muslims often found more in common with Protestant conservatives than with liberals in their own faith communities. Likewise, religious progressives identified more with secularists, humanists, and other cultural liberals than they did with traditionalists in their own religious families. Though many non-white Americans did not find their perspectives represented by either camp, they were increasingly pushed to the poles as well. Wuthnow pointed to a deep hostility between the two camps, each side struggling to trust or even coexist with the other.

Sociologist James Davison Hunter homed in on this hostility in his 1991 book, *Culture Wars*, which popularized the term.[10] Hunter acknowledged that points of contention always existed in American religious life. However, while differences in the past were largely political, ethnic, and ecclesiastical, they had become cosmological in the present. The principle disagreements "no longer revolve around specific doctrinal issues or styles of religious practice and organization but rather around fundamental assumptions about values, purpose, truth, freedom, and collective identity," said Hunter.[11] Hunter labeled the poles of this cultural/religious axis "orthodoxy" and "progressivism." Hunter described the culture war between these two groups as ubiquitous in American life, with battles being waged in voting booths, school board meetings, Sunday school classes, and newspaper columns.

Arguably, American society has only become more bifurcated over the last generation, as neighborhoods, educational institutions, churches, and social media spaces have increasingly become "echo chambers" in which dissent from the ideological party line is forbidden and even punished. A 2017 Pew poll found that over 80 percent of both Republicans and Democrats have unfavorable views of the other party; also, shares in both parties of people with very unfavorable opinions of the other party has more than doubled since 1994.[12] Nearly half of Americans say they disagree not just with their opponents' political views but with their values

---

9. Wuthnow, "Old Fissures and New Fractures," 379.

10. James Davison Hunter, *Culture Wars: The Struggle to Define America* (New York: Basic Books, 1991).

11. James Davison Hunter, "Sorting out the Present, Looking to the Future," *Believable Futures of American Protestantism* (Grand Rapids: Eerdmans, 1988) 22.

12. "The Partisan Divide on Political Values Grows Even Wider," Pew Research Center, October 5, 2017.

and goals beyond politics as well.[13] This divide has becoming increasingly clear in the COVID-19 pandemic, as even medical science and epidemiology have become highly politicized.[14] In this bitterly divided environment, politics itself has become a zero-sum game, with gridlock and antagonism the norm and rollback of the opposing party's gains a central goal of each party.

Intensifying polarization notwithstanding, traditional cultural war theorizing is insufficient to interpret the Trump era, especially when it comes to the role of religion. Religion has factored prominently in analysis positing a bi-party system in American life, not just as a category of belonging but as a source of moral reasoning. At both poles, so the argument goes, are people who rely on religious convictions to determine their positions on contested issues. In Hunter's analysis, both sides of the culture wars are defined primarily by religious worldview rather than identity markers such as ethnicity, class, religious affiliation, or political party. But in the contemporary context, particularly with regard to white evangelicals' ardent loyalty to President Trump, this reasoning does not hold. In the contemporary culture wars, the power of social identity prevails. Religious reasoning still features prominently in the rhetorical weaponry of the culture wars, but often as cover to promote identity politics or to elevate interest groups. Americans bring their deepest values to the public square, but even among many religious conservatives, those deepest values are largely political.

While the religious right has harnessed religion for political ends since at least the 1970s, in the Trump era the religious right increasingly abandoned hopes of producing their version of a godlier society in favor of agitating to protect their own perceived interests. Trump won a staggering level of support among white evangelicals not by a "traditional values" campaign but rather a campaign based on "America first" protectionism, reverence for market capitalism, and pledges to protect white Christian cultural dominance. Trump capitalized on the fear and nostalgia of social conservatives with slogans like "Make America Great Again" and promises to "bring back Christmas" and build a wall between the United States and Mexico. As president, he continued to exploit this anxiety and glorification of the past with such actions as instituting a ban on immigration from various Muslim-majority countries, attempting to prevent transgender people from serving in the military, crafting hardline policies to quell migrant crossings from Mexico to the U.S., defending white nationalists who marched in Charlottesville, and banning the promotion of critical race theory among public institutions.

13. Andrew Sullivan, "America Wasn't Built for Humans," *New York Magazine*, September 2017.
14. Giovanni Russonello, "The Rising Politicization of Covid Vaccines," *The New York Times*, April 6, 2021. https://www.nytimes.com/2021/04/06/us/politics/covid-vaccine-skepticism.html/.

Various white Christian supporters of President Trump have been transparent about the self-interested nature of their support. Some evangelicals looked to Trump to hasten the return of Christ and the end of the world, in which evangelical Christians will be taken to heaven while the rest of humanity will face destruction. In this schema, political action is relevant only insofar as it advances literalist readings of biblical prophesies. Backed by a premillennial dispensationalist interpretation of biblical texts, some fundamentalists maintained that a unified Israel with control over Jerusalem would build a new temple and set the groundwork for the end times. For this group, Trump's recognition of Jerusalem as the capital of Israel was a watershed moment in the unfolding of God's plan for history.[15] Some in this camp reasoned that in keeping with Old Testament tradition, God selected an unlikely, even flawed instrument to carry out God's will.

Others went further, claiming Trump as a righteous man of God, anointed for the role of American president. For them, the unlikeliness of the Trump presidency itself was proof that it was the will of God. Shortly after the 2016 election, Stephen Strang, an influential Pentecostal figure, published *God and Donald Trump*, explaining that Donald Trump was God's choice to restore American greatness and reestablish the country's Christian identity. Former Arkansas governor Mike Huckabee wrote the forward to the book, and it received endorsements from figures such as Michelle Bachmann, a former congresswoman, and Robert Jeffress, a prominent Baptist megachurch pastor. A growing body of literature followed suit. For example, take *The Faith of Donald Trump, Jr.: A Spiritual Biography*, published in 2018 by David Brody, a Christian Broadcasting Network correspondent, and Scott Lamb, a *Washington Times* columnist. Endorsed by Fox News pundit Sean Hannity and writer Eric Metaxas, the book argued that Trump, set apart and chosen by God for greatness, is the "one guiding figure who can return us to the traditional values . . . and truly make America great again in all ways."[16]

Perhaps most jarring among white evangelical justifications for supporting President Trump is the political theology of figures like Senator Josh Hawley. Known for much of his career as a well-educated, thoughtful, rule-following conservative, Hawley made headlines for increasingly embracing Trumpism in the name of faith-based populism—most notably with his refusal to concede the 2020 election and his support for the January 2021 insurrection at the Capitol. A devout member of the Presbyterian Church of America, a denomination in the Reformed and evangelical

---

15. Cristina Maza, "Trump Will Start the End of the World, Claim Evangelicals Who Support Him," *Newsweek*, January 12, 2018.

16. David Brody and Scott Lamb, *The Faith of Donald J. Trump: A Spiritual Biography* (New York: Broadside, 2018), back cover.

traditions, Hawley has agued that the role of Christians in politics should be to "advance the kingdom of God."[17] Hawley's version of "kingdom politics" centers on "rebuilding" a culture that protects the way of life of the "great American middle."[18] Fashioning himself as a Christian populist, Hawley has defended his support for President Trump, including his challenge to the election, in populist terms. "I will never apologize for giving voice to the millions of Missourians and Americans who have concerns about the integrity of our elections," Hawley said in a statement justifying his disruption of the Electoral College vote. "That's my job, and I will keep doing it."[19]

While Hawley's political vision is not as overtly theocratic as the approach of many fellow white evangelicals, it shares in common a bid to restore the power and influence of white Christians in the United States. Hawley's populism gives voice not to "millions of Missourians and Americans" across a broad demographic swath, but rather to an overwhelmingly white, heterosexual, male-dominated, conservative, and Christian population. The efforts of Hawley and other white evangelical kingmakers in the Trump area point to the rising influence of white Christian nationalism in American public life. As sociologists Andrew Whitehead and Samuel Perry describe it, Christian nationalism is a cultural framework that idealizes and advocates a fusion of Christianity with American civic life. Most, though not all Christian nationalists, are white evangelicals. And large numbers of white evangelicals are Christian nationalists. Christian nationalists seek to preserve a social order in which everyone recognizes their "proper" place in society. As Whitehead and Perry show, this social order is based on nativist, patriarchal, heteronormative, and white supremacist assumptions, alongside divine sanction for authoritarianism and militarism.[20]

Contending that America has been and should always be a distinctively Christian country, Christian nationalists in the Trump era were increasingly emboldened to use any means necessary to promote their interests. Seeing in Trump a champion of their cultural dominance, many white evangelicals rode the waves of his favor as they legitimized his power. Looking to examples such as Trump's appointments of Neil Gorsuch, Brett Kavanaugh, and Amy Coney Barrett to the Supreme Court, his defense of "religious freedom" in promoting the right of businesses to refuse to

---

17. Joshua Hawley, "A Christian Vision for Kingdom Politics: Immanentize the Eschaton!" *Patheos*, October 26, 2012.

18. Joshua Hawley, "The Age of Pelagius," *Christianity Today*, June 4, 2019.

19. Quoted by Catie Edmonson, "Hawley Faces Blowback for Role in Challenging Election Results," *The New York Times*, January 8, 2021.

20. Andrew L. Whitehead and Samuel L. Perry, *Taking America Back for God: Christian Nationalism in the United States* (New York: Oxford University Press, 2020), 10.

hire gay people, and his iron-fisted policies on crime and immigration, many white evangelicals gave Trump their unquestioning loyalty in return. According to religion scholar Robert Jones, "The Trump era has effectively turned white-evangelical political ethics on its head. Rather than standing on principle and letting the chips fall where they may, white evangelicals have now fully embraced a consequentialist ethics that works backward from predetermined political ends, refashioning or even discarding principles as needed to achieve a desired outcome."[21] Considering themselves a persecuted minority whose very way of life is under threat, many of Trump's evangelical supporters are willing to abandon values once thought to be central to the evangelical movement in order to promote their own perceived self-interest. Sociologist Nathan Glazer has labeled this strategy "defensive offensiveness."[22] Many white evangelicals have used this self-perception of victimhood as a defense for Machiavellian politics.

As the Trump era elucidates, white Christian nationalism is primarily an ethnic and political movement rather than a religious one. Christians who have fallen prey to this ideology have effectively secularized their public life by using faith as a political tool rather than letting Christianity speak on its own terms. White Christian nationalism illustrates what Italian political theorist Emilio Gentile identifies as the "sacralization of politics" accompanying the modern era. The "sacralization of politics," he says, is in part an affirmation of state sovereignty in relation to the church, and in part a glorification of the nation as the supreme entity to which citizens owe devotion.[23] While white Christian nationalists seek to promote their vision of the social order in both the church and the state, their agenda is principally political.

---

21. Robert P. Jones, "Donald Trump and the Transformation of White Evangelicals," *Time*, November 19, 2016.

22. Nathan Glazer, "Fundamentalism: A Defensive Offensive," in *Piety or Politics: Evangelicals and Fundamentalists Confront the World*, ed. Richard John Neuhaus and Michael Cromartie (Washington, DC: Ethics and Public Policy Center, 1987) 250–51. In a 2017 poll conducted by the Public Religion Research Institute, 57 percent of white evangelical Protestants said that there is a lot of discrimination against Christianity in the U.S. today, whereas only 44 percent said that Muslims face a lot of discrimination. White evangelicals were the only religious group more likely to believe Christians face discrimination compared to Muslims, with 66 percent of all Americans surveyed identifying discrimination against Muslims compared to 33 percent of all Americans identifying discrimination against Christians. See Robert P. Jones, "The Collapse of American Identity," *New York Times*, May 2, 2017.

23. Emilio Gentile, *Politics as Religion* (Princeton: Princeton University Press, 2006). See also Tamir Bar-On, "The Front National and the 'Religion' of Ethnic Nationalism," *Sightings*, April 20, 2017.

White Christian Nationalism: Religious in Name but Secular in Orientation

The growth of white Christian nationalism in the Trump era in the United States illustrates not just a secularization beyond religious traditions and institutions, but also a secularization from within. Secularization theory emerged in the nineteenth century as a lens for understanding the impact of modernity on religion, primarily in the West. In its original iterations, secularization theory held that alongside the growing influence of science, the reliance on the bureaucratic state, and the rise of capitalism, urbanization, and industrialization, religion was expelled from public life and relegated to the private domain in the modern period. Early secularization theorists also maintained that corresponding with modernity's ascent, religion lost its explanatory power and ability to determine personal and group identities. Founding figures of sociology of religion took for granted that religion was in decline, and many predicted that it would completely disappear. As the twentieth century progressed and religious faith lived on, social theorists began to rethink this logic. For instance, Thomas Luckmann circumscribed secularization not as the decline of religion *carte blanche*, but rather as the decline of religious authority at the societal level. In this process, religious institutions have foundered, while religious beliefs and practices have remained vital—if dispersed, individualized, and idiosyncratic.[24]

Clearly, religious institutions in the United States have borne out this decline. Americans have fled from organized religion in staggering numbers over the last generation. Those who classify themselves as "spiritual but not religious" and "secular" are growing subsets of the American population, and the institutional strength of many mainstream religious entities is at an all-time low. The religiously unaffiliated have skyrocketed to nearly one quarter of the population.[25] Declines have been

---

24. Thomas Luckmann, *The Invisible Religion: The Problem of Religion in Modern Society* (New York: MacMillan, 1967).

25. "The 2020 Census of American Religion," PRRI, July 2021. The institutional decline of religion has been most precipitous among white Christians, the overwhelming majority of the American population through the turn of the twenty-first century, who now compose only 44 percent of the American population. The Catholic Church in the U.S., seeing a mass exodus of white parishioners, has maintained its share in the country's religious distribution only because of growing numbers of Hispanic immigrants in the church. White Protestants, who alone constituted a majority of Americans until twenty years ago, are now down to 30 percent of the population. The decline of mainline Protestantism is by now a familiar story, with shares dropping from 24 percent of the population in 1988 to 16 percent of the population today. White evangelicals, largely thought to have bucked the trend in disaffiliation by holding constant at 22 percent of the population from 1988 to 2008, have now fallen to 14 percent of the population. African American Protestantism has largely held steady over the last generation at 7 to 8 percent of the population, though African American Protestants, too, have seen an aging of their coreligionists. Christians in denominations across the board are on average older than they were in previous decades, and over one third of Millennials are now religiously unaffiliated. See also Daniel Cox and Robert P. Jones, "America's Changing Religious Identity," *PRRI*, September 6,

especially precipitous among white Christians, with the exit of younger generations resulting in an aging population of white Christian adherents.[26]

This facet of secularization certainly plays into the American culture wars. Institutional decline has led to fear, anxiety, and nostalgia among members, producing a temptation to grasp at legitimacy, no matter the cost, in a bid for self-preservation. Tainted by exposed sins both active and passive, religious institutions themselves have lost credibility among the general public and become easy targets of attack. Religious institutions have often been reified by the right and caricatured by the left.

But another mode of secularization is perhaps even more influential in the contemporary culture wars. This mode of secularization is what Catholic philosopher Charles Taylor calls the "immanent frame." In his pivotal 2007 book, *A Secular Age*, Taylor draws attention not to the decline in religious institutions nor the decline in religious beliefs and practices, but instead to the cultural conditions that make religion optional, even irrelevant.

In the contemporary West, religious postures are "reflective," says Taylor. The universe has become disenchanted as contemporaries have looked to scientific explanations for natural events and human explanations for cultural events. As people interact with others who see the world differently, they are implicitly aware that their own beliefs are mutable and conditioned by factors outside of religion itself. The "conditions of belief" have changed such that Westerners are now unable to believe without reservations, without uneasily "looking over their shoulders." Many people are disconnected or only loosely connected to religious traditions, and those who are firmly invested in religious institutions find themselves feeling pressure to justify their devotion.

Taylor argues that it was Protestantism itself that produced the immanent frame. Early modern Reform movements delinked salvation from human flourishing in history, instead envisioning salvation as a transaction that determined one's destiny after death. In this move, salvation became largely tangential to life. Protestant theology also extracted individuals from society and society from the cosmos, promoting an anthropomorphism that was only one step away from humanism. Christianity became increasingly identified with bourgeois moral codes, rather than sacred power. The Enlightenment narrative supposed that people needed only their innate reason and benevolence to bring about progress, thus rendering God extraneous. Even when the Enlightenment project came crashing to the ground in the wake of two world wars and exposure of the underbelly of colonialism, it remained

---

2017; Jones, *The End of White Christian America* (New York: Simon & Schuster, 2016), 51.

26. Robert Putnam and David Campbell, *American Grace: How Religion Divides and Unites Us* (New York: Simon & Schuster, 2010).

possible, even probable, for people to experience the world as entirely immanent.[27] The 1960s ushered in a culture of expressive individualism, in which each person's path of realizing authenticity is unique.[28] As people have come to accept only what they personally believe rings true, the link between religion and widely accepted civilizational order has been all but severed, says Taylor.

Early secularization theorists' prediction that religion would disappear in industrialized societies has been false. Even though religious practices are often undertaken outside of formal religious structures, they remain an important part of American life. The decline of traditional religious institutions has not resulted in widespread unbelief but rather in religious experimentation, hybridity, and innovation. Religion and spirituality have evolved more than disappeared—they are increasingly diffuse, individualized, and therapeutic rather than institutionalized and socially cohesive.

Some scholars predicted that Americans' increasing distance from religious institutions would dissolve the culture wars in favor of a widespread "live and let live" ethos. But that has not been the case either. Far from settling into a comfortable irreligiosity, our society is deeply cross-pressured.[29] The ubiquity of the immanent frame has not resulted in a social consensus and a shared sense of meaning. The culture wars have arguably only become more vitriolic. Rather than disappearing, lines between "us" and "them" have darkened, and alliances have become even more prejudicial.

In the immanent frame, religion is not dead, but its curtailed social influence leaves a vacuum of collective meaning. The public square, rather than a being a colony of secular orthodoxy, is contested territory. The immanent frame has produced not cosmopolitanism but tribalism. Instead of a contest of competing religious worldviews or a battle between monism and multiculturalism, today's culture wars are better understood as a conflict between and among social groups.[30]

In this context, religion is often selectively appropriated on the basis of a group or individual's social location.[31] Americans who are active in religious institutions are increasingly concentrated on the political right. In the evolving landscape of religious authority, religious institutions themselves are often perceived to be vested in conservative politics. Additionally, as sociologists Mark Chaves and Michele

27. Charles Taylor, *A Secular Age* (Cambridge: Harvard University Press, 2007), 376.
28. Taylor, *A Secular Age*, 475.
29. Taylor, *A Secular Age*, 727.
30. For a discussion of the monism versus multiculturalism framing device, see Putnam and Campbell, *American Grace*.
31. Penny Edgell, "An Agenda for Research on American Religion in Light of the 2016 Election," *Sociology of Religion* 78.1 (2017) 1–8.

Margolis have demonstrated, many Americans are now determining their religious identities based on their politics.[32] By making political issues central to their identity, religious groups have effectively encouraged people to use religion to sort themselves politically.[33]

Both sides of the culture wars often fall prey to a *de facto* secularism; identity sectarianism is evident on both the left and the right, extending beyond allegiance to one's group to demonization of those outside of it.[34] The contemporary culture wars, while ostensibly fueled by religious and ideological reasoning, are to a greater extent powered by identity markers such as ethnicity, class, religious affiliation, and political party. In the culture wars, religion is used as a means to an end rather than speaking on its own terms.

The Missiological Crisis of Sacralized Politics

The sacralization of politics and the preeminence of the culture wars point to a missiological crisis in American Christianity, especially among white evangelicals. "When politics trumps faith, the prophetic voice is silenced," writes historian Kristin Kobes Du Mez. "And without the prophetic, religion itself becomes something else entirely."[35] Charles Taylor's assertion that modernity created a public space circumscribed by the "immanent frame" is not the end of his argument. This cultural space pushes all of us, whether religious or not, to account for our world outside of religious reasoning. But Taylor also identifies the hollowness of such a world—wherein people have difficulty producing meaning, accounting for suffering, or finding motivation for protecting the wellbeing of all.

In his *magnus opus* exploring various paradigms in Christian mission throughout history, South African missiologist David Bosch identifies a tendency among Christians in positions of power to embrace the values of the world and baptize them with Christian religion. He labels this tendency the "secularist temptation." Privileged Christians' attempts to recreate a mythic past or realize a utopian future, while seemingly driven by Christian spirituality, are expressions of the ethos of imperialism. A Christian vision of cultural engagement that seeks to control or dominate others is a vision rooted in idolatry, argues Bosch. The church, or the "Christian

---

32. Michele Margolis, *From Politics to the Pew: How Partisanship and the Political Environment Shape Religious Identity* (Chicago: University of Chicago Press, 2018).

33. Mark Chaves, *American Religion: Contemporary Trends*, 2nd ed (Princeton: Princeton University Press, 2017).

34. Sullivan, "America Wasn't Built for Humans."

35. Kristin Kobes du Mez, "Democrats Have a Religion Problem: But They're Not the Only Ones." *Patheos*, June 29, 2017.

worldview," or the "Judeo-Christian heritage" becomes the object of worship, and the spirit of God is denied any activity in the world outside of what Christians in positions of power are doing. The church sees itself as exclusively containing, and even controlling, God.[36]

This was the logic of Christendom, which confined the work of God to a particular territory and people group, and which married the church to political power. As the history of European and American colonialism in the modern period illustrate, the project of advancing Christendom led to exploitation of people, land, and resources on an unprecedented scale. Christian mission and colonialism were intertwined in a complicated relationship, with European and Euro-American missionaries more often supporting than undermining colonizing projects. To the extent that some Christians attempted to buck religious, cultural, or political imperialism by standing in solidarity with local people in colonized territories around the globe, they did so from the margins rather than the centers of political power.

The "kingdom politics" of Senator Josh Hawley and other white evangelicals who believe themselves to be ambassadors of God's kingdom on earth is a poignant example of the secularist temptation and the impulse of Christendom. Hawley provided clues regarding his motivation for propping up Trumpism in writings and speeches published both prior to and during his tenure as senator, presented in a distinctly theological tenor. In a 2012 *Patheos* piece, written when he was a law professor at the University of Missouri, Hawley laid out his vision for "kingdom politics." In contrast to what he called the "conversionist approach" of evangelicals in the 1980s and 1990s, in which evangelicals sought to resurrect America's Christian identity and reassert Christianity's privileged place in American culture, Hawley advocated for an evangelical approach to politics based on the New Testament metaphor of the "kingdom of God." According to Hawley, "Scripture teaches that political government is mandated by God for his service and is one means by which the enthroned Christ carries out his rule." Thus, Christians' purpose in politics should be to advance the kingdom of God, or "to immanentize the eschaton." Giving up on trying to create a theocracy, this approach acknowledges that the state's purpose is to preserve order and promote justice rather than to convert non-Christians, said Hawley. Providing examples of political agenda inspired by Christ's kingship, Hawley pointed to efforts to broaden the private economy in order to strengthen the labor market, expand educational opportunities, and protect women's roles as mothers.[37]

---

36. David Bosch, *Transforming Mission: Paradigm Shifts in Theology of Mission* (Maryknoll, NY: Orbis, 1991).

37. Hawley, "A Christian Vision for Kingdom Politics."

A second elucidation of Hawley's political theology comes from a 2017 speech he gave to the American Renewal Project after being elected as Attorney General of Missouri. Emphasizing the "lordship of Christ" over all aspects of human life, Hawley invoked a famous quote by Dutch theologian and politician, Abraham Kuyper, voiced in a speech to open the Free University of Amsterdam in 1880: "There's not a square inch in the whole domain of human existence over which Christ, who is Lord over all, does not exclaim, 'Mine'!" "We are called to take that message into every sphere of life that we touch, including the political realm," Hawley reflected. "That is our charge. To take the Lordship of Christ, that message, into the public realm, and to seek the obedience of the nations. Of our nation!"[38]

Thirdly, in a 2018 piece published by *Christianity Today*, Hawley argued that contemporary American society has fallen prey to the widespread belief that "liberty is the right to choose your own meaning" and that freedom means emancipating oneself "not just from God but from society, family, and tradition." This philosophy has made American society more hierarchical and elitist, in Hawley's estimation. Hawley's proposed solution was to rebuild a culture that protects the way of life of the American middle. "We must rebuild a democracy run not by the elites, but by the great middle of America, a democracy that allows the working man and woman to realize their God-given ability to govern themselves and help manage the life of his nation."[39]

Hawley has made clear in his actions as senator that the "American middle" whose interests he works to advance is white, Christian, and conservative. Rather than providing a theological backing for public service oriented around promoting the common good and standing with those who are marginalized, Hawley's "kingdom politics" justifies the privileged position of white Christians. In Hawley's political vision, Christ is a supreme ruler bent on "lordship" and "obedience." Christians are given authority to "advance the kingdom of God" and "take the Lordship of Christ . . . into the public realm." Hawley's vision assumes that Christians—especially those who enjoy influence in society—are given special access to the kingdom of God and that the kingdom of God is theirs to advance. Moreover, by maintaining that the state's God-given role is to preserve order, Hawley suggests that protecting the power structure in the United States that privileges white Christians is a worthy goal. Many American Christians who share Hawley's Reformed and evangelical tradition define Christianity as a propositional belief system, such that the label "Christian" excludes

---

38. Joshua Hawley, untitled speech, American Renewal Project, December 7, 2017. https://youtube/rw4BxVdrUnc.

39. Joshua Hawley, "The Age of Pelagius."

people who are not white evangelicals.[40] With this move, adherence to a particular faith statement becomes a license to pursue power over others, since only Christians, narrowly defined, are divinely authorized to represent God's rule on earth. Hawley's neo-Kuyperian political vision, while not overtly theocratic, is a form of Christian triumphalism that provides cover for white nationalism. Hawley's supposed populism is a populism of white Christian conservatives who are called to advance their version of the kingdom of God. His political vision looks to Christianity to shore up crumbling power structures of White Anglo-Saxon Protestant America by legitimizing its institutions and leaders. As a justification for preserving the power and expanding the influence of white Christian conservatives, Hawley's "kingdom politics" is ultimately a secular endeavor.

Trumpism has also been propped up by another embodiment of the secularist temptation, sometimes labeled "prosperity theology" or the "gospel of health and wealth." David Brody and Scott Lamb's argument in *The Faith of Donald Trump, Jr.* that Trump's economic success proved his favored status in the eyes of God reflects this gospel. Based on the notion that health and wealth are measures of a successful life and are determined by individual choices rather than social factors, numerous other white evangelical supporters of Trump also reproduced this argument.[41] Adherents of prosperity theology embrace a worldview that is highly supernatural, even magical. Yet, the aim of their religiosity is the same as market capitalism: for humans to be successful. Even though prosperity-minded American Christians view God's actions in the world in an almost transactional way, their picture of the world is similar to that of other Americans who are captivated by the promise of material comfort. Prosperity theologies excuse social inequality as divinely sanctioned, and baptize wealth and power reflecting divine favor. Various evangelical supporters of Trump embraced the gospel of health and wealth as they looked to Trump's economic and political success as evidence of his virtue, and approached the crumbling social order with nostalgia. The slogan "Make America Great Again" served as both a recognition of the loss of white Christian dominance as well as a promise to restore that dominance. Anxious about the old order passing away and a new order emerging, some white evangelicals found in Trump not just someone who promised to restore their lost influence but also someone who demonstrated that such influence is their birthright.

While white Christian conservatives' capitulation to the secularist temptation has been egregious, it is not just Christians on the right who have succumbed to

---

40. See Jemar Tisby, *The Color of Compromise* (Grand Rapids: Eerdmans, 2019).

41. See Amy Sullivan, "Millions of Americans Believe God Made Trump President: A Surprisingly Fascinating Book Explains Why," *Politico*, January 27, 2018.

this impulse. Some progressive Christians have also subsumed their faith into their politics. Historian Gary Dorrien points out that liberal Christians have tended to make modern culture their ultimate authority, rendering their public witness tepid and unremarkable.[42] Even while preaching racial justice, mainline Protestantism has alienated many non-white Christians and has failed to reflect the ethnic and racial diversity of America. Some progressive Christians disregard divine agency altogether, while others embrace a spirituality that is solely individual and therapeutic. Raphael Warnock, a theologian, pastor, and senator, identifies a crisis in the mission of the black church as well. In *The Divided Mind of the Black Church*, Warnock argues that the black church is increasingly swayed by prosperity theologies and biblical fundamentalism, eclipsing its historic emphasis on the power of Christian faith to address racism and other forms of oppression.[43]

In their capitulation to the norms of empire, whether in acquiescing to the status quo or in attempting to supplant the status quo with an alternative empire, Christians who have fallen prey to the secularist temptation become embroiled in a power struggle and preoccupied with their own success. Alternatively, some Christians have advocated for a retreat from the public square as they have come to realize that winning the culture wars is either an unholy quest or a lost cause. Appearing in various iterations, Christian separatism focuses on building robust Christian communities that are set apart from the ways of the world.[44] Yet, such efforts to shore up Christian enclaves can serve as another form of empire building. Even if circumscribed in territory, the call to preserve what is ostensibly in danger of being lost is also a call to protect existing power relations. Additionally, a focus on self-preservation is a sign of what missiologist Eleazer Fernandez calls "goal displacement." Goal displacement confuses "self-preservation with life, growth with vitality . . . techniques with sound theology . . . fellowship with hospitality."[45] In short, the church forgets its reason for being and instead becomes preoccupied with itself. When survival is paramount, says missiologist Donald Messer, John Wesley's famous dictum "the world is our parish" becomes "the parish is our world."[46] David

---

42. Gary Dorrien, *The Making of American Liberal Theology: Crisis, Irony and Postmodernity, 1950–2005* (Louisville: Westminster John Knox, 2006).

43. Raphael Warnock, *The Divided Mind of the Black Church: Theology, Piety, and Public Witness* (New York: New York University Press, 2013).

44. See, for example, Stanley Hauerwas and William Willimon, *Resident Aliens: Life in the Christian Colony* (Nashville: Abingdon, 1989); Rod Dreher, *The Benedict Option: A Strategy for Christians in a Post-Christian Nation* (New York: Sentinel, 2017).

45. Eleazar Fernandez, *Burning Center, Porous Borders: The Church in a Globalized World* (Eugene, OR: Wipf & Stock, 2011).

46. Donald Messer, *A Conspiracy of Goodness: Contemporary Images of Mission* (Nashville: Abingdon, 1992) 22.

Bosch labels this strategy of withdrawing from public life altogether in the name of purity the "otherworldly temptation." This separatist strategy, he notes, tends toward dualism. Life is divided into sacred and secular activities, and salvation is reduced to an individual's fate after death. The separatist strategy fails to acknowledge that God is always and everywhere at work, both in the church and in the world.[47]

The *basileia tou theou* as a Vision for Christian Public Engagement

Strategies of culture war promote over-identification with a logic of empire, and strategies of cultural retreat promote under-identification with a Christian call to public witness. If staking out political territory and, conversely, retreating from the public square are both disastrous strategies for Christian cultural engagement, where does that leave Christians who seek to be faithful in the public realm? Reaching beyond the immanent frame, Christians are called to enact their Christian identity as a call to self-transcendence—a call to love God and neighbor, and to practice the work of seeking justice and peace. Charles Taylor closes his discussion of "a secular age" by proposing a reorientation of the Christian faith around "the practical primacy of life" and the radical experience of agape love. Taylor maintains that humans' experience of the world is not primarily a theoretical stance but rather a relationship of involvement and concern. Our loves exercise greater power than our ideas. We are drawn to communion with God not by following rules, believing in propositions, or affiliating with labels of identity, but rather by transformative experiences of value and beauty. Vibrant Christianity is a way of being in the world that embodies an experience of divine love. Christianity at its best, says Taylor, speaks to human longings for fullness by directing us to the wellspring of God's love and inviting us to share out of the abundance that we have received.[48]

To shine a light on this way of being and alternative path of Christian public engagement, I turn to the same metaphor that Josh Hawley has used to justify his version of white Christian triumphalism, the *basileia tou theou* (or "the kingdom of God" in Hawley's verbiage). Appearing more than 100 times in the Gospel accounts, usually in the words of Jesus, the *basileia tou theou* refers to the domain of God's love and justice.[49] While it is ironic that this metaphor has often been used to justify Christian dominance over others, the *basileia tou theou* is a theological treasure

---

47. Cardoza-Orlandi, *Mission: An Essential Guide*, 37.

48. Taylor, *A Secular Age*, 728–72.

49. Richard Chilson, C.S.P., proposed this translation, noting that the *basileia* is the dominion wherein the God of love rules. See Chilson, *Yeshua of Nazareth: Spiritual Master* (Notre Dame, IN: Sorin, 2001).

trove for helping us move beyond the tyranny of the immanent frame, the carnage of the culture wars, and the irrelevance of cultural retreat.

In the Gospels' accounts, Jesus often invoked this metaphor to demonstrate patterns of faithful responses to God's desire for justice, healing, and the flourishing of all creation. In the *basileia tou theou*, the blind see, the lame walk, the captives are freed, the sinners are forgiven, and the lost are found.[50] In referencing the *basileia tou theou*, Jesus pointed to what Desmond Tutu calls "God's dream" for human societies.[51]

The term *basileia tou theou* from the Greek New Testament (which itself is translated from Hebrew and Aramaic) is often rendered in English as "kingdom of God" or "reign of God," though these translations have problematic hierarchical, gendered, territorial, and imperial connotations that are not warranted by the New Testament texts. Sensitive to these misleading connotations, other theologians have translated *basileia tou theou* as "kingdom" or "commonwealth," noting that the *basileia tou theou* is marked by social harmony, mutuality, and inclusion.[52]

Not only is the *basileia tou theou* difficult to translate, it is also difficult to define. Gospel depictions of the *basileia tou theou* are wide-ranging and evocative, often rendered in stories or word pictures. As Jesus depicts the *basileia tou theou* in the Gospel accounts, he paints a vivid portrait of the domain of God's rule of love, peace, and justice that will be fully realized in the future but is also in the process of breaking into the present. In the Gospels' telling, the *basileia tou theou* signifies God's intervention in human history through the person of Jesus. The *basileia tou theou* is at hand, yet impossible to grasp.[53] Contrary to the view of Josh Hawley and many other Christians invested in the logic of Christendom, Jesus did not instruct his followers to *build* or *advance* the *basileia tou theou*. Rather, he invited his disciples to *enter* the domain of God's love by doing God's will, *receive* the domain of God's love by assuming the posture of a child, and *find* the domain of God's love by having faith, even as small as a mustard seed.[54]

The domain of God's love is radically different from the empires of this world. Liberation theologians have pointed out that Jesus's depiction of the *basileia tou theou* was a deliberate, if indirect, criticism of the Roman system of domination. For Jesus, the *basileia* includes, and even honors, the poor, the outcasts, the sick,

---

50. See Luke 4:18–19.

51. Desmond Tutu, *God Has a Dream: A Vision of Hope for Our Time* (New York: Doubleday, 2004).

52. See David Ray Griffin, et al., *The American Empire and the Commonwealth of God: A Political, Economic, Religious Statement* (Louisville: Westminster John Knox, 2006).

53. See Matt 3:2; Mark 1:15; Luke 17:21.

54. See Matt 13:44–46; 17:20; 18:3; 19:14; Mark 10:15; Luke 18:17.

and the persecuted.[55] The *basileia tou theou* is a domain unlike any other, based not on domination but on self-emptying love. Jesus himself explicitly rejected the title "king,"[56] preferring instead "the human one."[57] The *basileia tou theou* is a realm of radical action that Jesus demonstrated through welcoming social outcasts, healing those who were sick, forgiving sinners, loving his enemies, and living joyfully in God's presence. Biblical writers maintained that unlike political regimes, the realm of God's love and justice will never pass away.[58]

The *basileia tou theou* stands in stark opposition to the politics of scarcity and the zero-sum economy featuring winners versus losers. In contemporary American culture, the pursuit of profit, the quest for power over others, and the appetite for personal fulfillment capture the imaginations of many. But in the *basileia tou theou*, the goal of accumulating wealth and power is replaced with a concern for the wellbeing of those at the margins of society. In this sense, the *basileia tou theou* is a subversion of the status quo and a threat to the logic of empire. In the moral economy of the *basileia tou theou* the first shall be last and the last shall be first, and the greatest among us are the ones who serve others.[59]

To avoid over-identifying or under-identifying the work of redemption with human efforts, it is important for Christians who seek to orient their public engagement around the *basileia tou theou* to acknowledge that God is the architect and chief actor in this domain. Moreover, it is not the powerful but the poor and oppressed who are in the best position to welcome the *basileia tou theou*.[60] Christians who view themselves as kingdom builders easily fall prey to triumphalism, self-righteousness, and judgmentalism. Christians who conscribe their faith only to personal devotionalism, on the other hand, fail to challenge injustice and miss opportunities to join God in God's work of redemption and renewal, justice and peacemaking. Instead of envisioning the *basileia tou theou* as a project to accomplish or a phenomenon to passively behold, followers of Jesus are invited to see the *basileia tou theou* as Jesus depicts it: as a gift to receive and a realm to enter. Just as Jesus's ministry was oriented around the *basileia tou theou* so too Christian mission should be centered on participating in and proclaiming the ultimacy of the domain of God's love. Rather than

---

55. See Glen Stassen and David Gushee, *Kingdom Ethics: Following Jesus in Contemporary Context*, 2nd ed. (Grand Rapids: Eerdmans, 2016).

56. See John 18:37.

57. The Common English Bible uses this translation for the term used to describe Jesus sixty-nine times in the Synoptic Gospels and twelve times in the Gospel of John, mostly by Jesus himself. Most other translations render the English as "the Son of Man."

58. See Daniel 2; Daniel 7; Rev 11:15–18.

59. See Matt 20:16; Mark 9:35.

60. See Luke 16:19–31; Luke 12:13–21.

possessing or controlling the *basileia tou theou* Christians stand under its scrutiny. Christians are called to respond to God's invitation to join the work that God is doing in the world, partnering with anyone who shares a commitment to common good. We must recognize that our motives are seldom pure and our efforts are often limited. Even so, we are invited to pray for the *basileia tou theou* to be realized, and to participate in that prayer with our actions.[61]

Cultural engagement oriented around the *basileia tou theou* promotes both a critical posture toward society's norms and positive participation in the life of society. Christians enter the *basileia tou theou* as they love neighbor and enemy alike, stand against oppression, and work for justice and peace. The breadth and depth of the *basileia tou theou* is limitless. Rather than delineating "sacred" and "secular" spaces, the good news of God's *basileia tou theou* is as broad as human life, found in the heart of all reality.[62]

Christians embrace the call to receive and enter the *basileia tou theou* through practices of faithfulness. These practices are myriad in number and wide-ranging in scope, from the personal, to the communal, to the political. We receive and enter the *basileia tou theou* by honoring the strangers, the outcasts, and the marginalized among us. We receive and enter the *basileia tou theou* by promoting the healing of human individuals and communities, as well as the earth itself. We receive and enter the *basiliea tou theou* by protecting the dignity of all people, regardless of their identities or affiliations.

All Christians are called to practices of justice and peacemaking with the *basileia tou theou* in view. But each particular path of Christian discipleship is informed by variables such as one's giftedness, social location, and life circumstances. Given the legacy of white Christian nationalism and other oppressive forms of public engagement that have been enacted by white American Christians, those of us who fall within this demographic in particular are called to welcome the *basileia tou theou* by acknowledging and repenting of wrong-doing committed by our communities. We are called to seek to repair harm caused by white Christian legacies of religious, cultural, and political imperialism—both on an interpersonal and a societal level. Recognizing that the political projects of white Christians in the United States have often coopted Christianity for self-interested, and even totalitarian ends, white Christians are invited to reject the secularizing impulse of political engagement oriented around white Christian identity.

---

61. See Matt 6:10.

62. See Michael Goheen, *Introducing Christian Mission Today: Scripture, History and Issues* (Downers Grove, IL: InterVarsity, 2014), 210–15.

Responding to the missiological crisis perpetuated by Christian efforts to "win" the American culture wars, all Christians in our context can look to the domain of God's justice and love to propel social and political engagement. In the contemporary cultural context in the United States—in which distrust, deceit, oppression, demonization, and despair are rampant—practices such as lament, repentance, and hospitality offer faithful alternatives to these disturbing patterns. These practices encourage us to put down weapons of war and recognize our common humanity. They reveal the strategies of drugging ourselves with nostalgia, bullying others with the Bible, taking refuge in our tribalism, and basing our success on other people's losses to be hollow and counter-productive. They move us beyond the immanent to transcendent meaning; beyond self-interest to the common good; beyond Christianity as a belief system, moral code, or constituency, to Christianity as a path of transformative love.

RESPONSE TO BAKKER

Christopher W. Skinner

Introduction

I am grateful for the privilege of participating in this symposium and for the opportunity to respond to such a substantive and thought-provoking paper. As a white male who was raised and educated in evangelical spaces in the American south and is still connected to many family members and friends from that world, I regard Dr. Bakker's critique as fair and accurate throughout. Numerous times I reacted to one of her insights by writing "yes!" in the margin of her manuscript, though I must admit that my more consistent reaction while reading was one of depressed resignation. The polarization she identifies is as depressing as its underlying motivations are pernicious. Systemic racism—which, by definition, is discrimination embedded within our systems, laws, and institutions—has enabled a number of identifiable phenomena here in the United States. First, it has allowed for unwitting participation in discriminatory acts by a populace that is largely oblivious. Second, it has further relegated those who are already on the margins, and in a way that renders its mechanisms for marginalization nearly invisible. Third, it has engendered a debate among Americans as to what constitutes racism and activated a uniquely American mantra which objects by proclaiming, "I'm not racist." Considering the *subtle* ways racism can be enacted in our culture, it is jarring then to see how *openly racist* and how *unapologetically rooted in white supremacy* significant pockets of American evangelicalism have become in the Trump era. Dr. Bakker gets at the heart of why the so-called "culture wars" have become the perfect vehicle for ushering in such an era and how it is possible for those who profess to be followers of Jesus to fall under the spell of those who look and sound nothing like him. In what follows, I want to amplify a few insights from Dr. Bakker's paper, while also offering a brief critique of her treatment of the *basileia tou theou* ("kingdom of God").

America, the New Israel?

First, in the section of her paper entitled, "Not Your Parents' Culture Wars," Dr. Bakker does an admirable job of situating our current political crises in their immediate and proximate historical contexts. However, I wonder if we might also extend our reflections on this problem to a period a bit earlier in the American experiment. In particular, I am led to reflect on the idea of our "Manifest Destiny," and its rootedness in the assertion that America is somehow the new Israel, or God's new chosen nation.[1] Manifest Destiny is that doctrine that promoted the inevitability of westward expansion accompanied by the belief that this dominion/domination had been prepared or even ordained by God. The belief that America was a new Israel was foundational to early American expansion and there is no doubt that this sort of rhetoric continues today, even if only under the surface. Further, this mentality is largely unquestioned within some displays of American civil religion. To have this confirmed, one need only attend church service on a July Fourth Sunday, hear the pastor speak of "praying for *our* troops," (as if the church had troops) and then witness the congregation launch into a rousing rendition of "The Battle Hymn of the Republic"—a hymn which boldly proclaims God's goodness in "civilizing the savages" as we march ever westward:

> Mine eyes have seen the glory of the coming of the Lord
> He is trampling out the vintage where the grapes of wrath are stored
> He hath loosed the fateful lightning of his terrible swift sword
> His truth is marching on.

As an aside, I submit that if these words were attributed to a national hymn written within an Islamic context, they might quickly be denounced and likely even labeled as Jihadist by many here in the United States.

As a New Testament scholar who reflects often on Israel and its centuries-long history of subjugation, it is hard for me to deny that the United States has historically behaved much more like Rome during the time of Jesus and Paul, or Babylon under the reign of Nebuchadnezzar II.[2] America is not now, nor has it ever been God's new

---

1. "The belief that America has been providentially chosen for a special destiny has deep roots in the American past, and it is a belief that still finds expression in our so-called 'secular age.' It has resided at the heart of the attempt by Americans to understand their nation's responsibility at home and abroad. It is a conviction that has manifested itself most vividly in occasions of public worship when American citizens have met to share common religious sentiments," see "Introduction," *God's New Israel: Religious Interpretations of American Destiny*, ed. Conrad Cherry, rev. ed. (Chapel Hill: University of North Carolina Press, 1998), 1.

2. After the northern kingdom (Israel) was overtaken by Assyria in 722 BCE, the southern kingdom (Judah) was conquered by Babylon in 605 BCE. Babylonian rule (605–539 BCE) gave way to Persian rule (539–331 BCE) which then gave way to Hellenistic rule (331–143 BCE). The Maccabean

Israel.³ However, as long as American Christians (in general) and white evangelicals (in particular) are tempted to see themselves as the recipients of God's holy promises and as the object of God's divine affection, they will have little problem advancing their own ends in the political realm. I am convinced that this way of thinking—which is deeply embedded in the American psyche at both the secular and sacred levels—needs to be challenged every bit as much as some of the more recent political motivations Dr. Bakker identifies.

She closes this section of her paper by noting: "While white Christian nationalists seek to promote *their vision* of the social order in both the church and state, their agenda is principally political (emphasis added)." All this leads me to wonder: How much of this *vision* is determined by a desire to adhere to things Jesus is known for saying and how much of it is driven simply by the desire for power and influence? If one of the primary goals of the "culture wars" is to gain control of our narratives and our civic institutions, then evangelical zeal to win these wars is simply misplaced. If we examine the pursuit of power and influence through New Testament lenses, we will undoubtedly discover that its teachings are at odds with the aims of many white American evangelicals.⁴

The "Kingdom" through Various Lenses

The final section of Dr. Bakker's paper is entitled, "The *Basileia tou theou* as a Vision for Christian Public Engagement." Here she discusses New Testament language related to the "kingdom of God" and examines its implications for how the church should function in the world. Since her reading of the kingdom is an attempt to challenge the egregious misreading of New Testament kingdom language on the part of influential public figures such as Senator Josh Hawley and others, it seems prudent to spend a little time here. While surveying a handful of gospel quotations attributed to Jesus, Dr. Bakker emphasizes the centrality of the ethic we see repeated throughout the Hebrew Bible, and manifested in depictions of Jesus's ministry in the New Testament: caring for the poor, the widow, the stranger, and the outcast, and

---

revolt resulted in an 80-year period of "home rule," where the Judeans had religious and political autonomy for the first time in nearly six centuries (143–63 BCE). However, in 63 BCE, the Roman general Pompey sieged Jerusalem during his eastward military campaigns, and this resulted in Roman rule over Palestine, which lasted until 192 CE. If we are going to think honestly about Israel's historical legacy, it is mostly one of being dominated, and only rarely one of exerting power over others.

3. At one level, the idea that America is the new Israel seems rooted in supersessionism, but it also makes evangelical support for the modern state of Israel seem quite ironic.

4. In John 18:36, Jesus himself acknowledges: "My kingdom is not of this world. If my kingdom were of this world, my followers would be fighting so that I might not be handed over . . . But as it is, my kingdom is not from here" (author's translation).

protecting the dignity of all people.[5] She notes, "Appearing more than 100 times in the Gospel accounts, usually in the words of Jesus, the *basileia tou theou* refers to the domain of God's love and justice." Like many theologians and ethicists I have read on the subject, Dr. Bakker treats these texts, at least in places, as if they speak with univocality on the kingdom of God, but the truth is a bit more complicated than that. To be sure, there are areas of overlap, but each gospel also has its own distinctive take on the kingdom.

Scholars largely agree that the kingdom of God was central to Jesus's teaching and is one of the more historically secure elements of his ministry.[6] However, they are also careful to note that these texts are not in complete agreement with one another about the nature of the kingdom. Jesus never offers a definition or explanation of his particular understanding of the kingdom of God in any gospel text, and as a concept, it appears to be quite malleable. When we speak of the kingdom, are we looking forward to something concrete that will emerge in a future eschatological moment? Or is the kingdom here, right now? Should we think of the kingdom as a realm or domain in which to enter? Or should we think of something that resides within us? Is the kingdom a mindset, or an ethical agenda? If we consider the words of Jesus in the various gospel narratives, each one of these seems to be a possibility.

Let us first consider the Gospel of Mark, which likely emerged around the year 70 CE, just after the destruction of the Second Temple. The "kingdom of God" in the preaching and ministry of Mark's Jesus differs significantly from notions of the kingdom present elsewhere within Second Temple Judaism. The picture here is not of the establishment of an actual, literal kingdom where God rules as king on earth and subjugates all enemies under his feet. Rather, the "kingdom" or "reign" of God in the Gospel of Mark is more akin to the in-breaking rule of God in the here-and-now.[7] In the early chapters, Jesus preaches, heals, and casts out unclean spirits (e.g., 1:21–45; 2:1–12; 3:1–11, among others). By means of these paradigmatic behaviors,[8] God's reign enters the human realm decisively and with immediacy. This is likely

---

5. Since many theologians and ethicists look to Matthew 5–7, the "Sermon on the Mount," as a basis for determining an ethics of Jesus, it was surprising to me that of the nineteen biblical texts cited in Dr. Bakker's paper, only one of them (Matt 6:10) is from that discourse.

6. On this claim, see John Meier, *A Marginal Jew: Rethinking the Historical Jesus*, vol. 2., Anchor Bible Reference Library (New York: Doubleday, 1994) 237–43.

7. In Mark 1:15, Jesus proclaims that the kingdom of God is "at hand" (Greek: *ēggiken*). Adela Yarbro Collins notes that this verse, "implies that the prophecies of scripture and the hopes of the people are in the process of being fulfilled" (*Mark: A Commentary*, Hermeneia [Minneapolis: Fortress, 2007] 154).

8. These specific behaviors—proclaiming, healing, and casting out unclean spirits—not only define Jesus's ministry in the early chapters, but these are the very acts for which he commissions (3:13–15) and sends out (6:7–13) his disciples.

one reason for Mark's continued use of the term "immediately," especially throughout the early chapters of the gospel.[9]

We do not have space here to rehearse the distinctive features of each gospel's take on the kingdom, but a few cursory comments are in order. First, except for four instances,[10] Matthew's Gospel (ca. 75–80 CE) famously prefers the more mysterious, and potentially more confusing phrase, "kingdom of heaven."[11] When I survey students in my own classes, the vast majority indicate that they think immediately of "heaven" when they hear the term "kingdom" used in a Christian context. I suspect that Matthew's Gospel is at least one reason for this. Noting that Matthew's differences from the other two Synoptics extend beyond simply the choice to substitute "heaven" for "God" in this critical phrase, Jonathan Pennington writes:

> The answer is found in recognizing that Matthew's "kingdom of heaven" language is but one part of an elaborate theme of "heaven and earth" woven all throughout the First Gospel. Recognizing this theme sheds light on Matthew's choice to speak of the kingdom in this unique way, and it also reveals a deep and powerful theological point—the apocalyptic and eschatological contrast between heaven and earth.[12]

While Matthew's presentation of the kingdom is similar to Mark in some ways, he also departs from Mark in other significant ways.

Luke's Gospel (ca. 80–85 CE), while overlapping with the other two Synoptics and clearly reliant on Mark for both structure and content, includes a passage elsewhere unattested in the New Testament, where Jesus proclaims: "the *kingdom of God is within you*" (Luke 17:21, my translation). While this is only one part of Luke's larger presentation of the kingdom, it is certainly noteworthy for its difference.[13] Finally, the Gospel of John (ca. 95–100 CE), easily our most enigmatic gospel narrative, differs markedly from the other three. The phrase, "kingdom of God" appears

---

9. The Greek term *euthus* ("immediately," "at once") appears in all but three chapters of Mark's gospel, with its strongest concentration in chapters 1 and 4—both of which feature a great deal of ministerial activity. See Mark 1:10, 12, 18, 20, 21, 23, 28, 29, 30, 42, 43; 2:8, 12; 3:6; 4:5, 15, 16, 17, 29; 5:2, 29, 30, 42; 6:25, 27, 45, 50, 54; 7:25; 8:10; 9:15, 20, 24; 10:52; 11:2, 3; 14:43, 45, 72; 15:1.

10. The phrase, "kingdom of God" appears in Matt 12:28; 19:24; 21:31, 43. Otherwise, Matthew prefers "kingdom of heaven."

11. Scholars recognize that this is a Semitism but debate whether there is a qualitative difference between the phrases "kingdom of God" and the "kingdom of heaven" in Matthew's understanding. For an authoritative treatment of why Matthew prefers this title, see Jonathan Pennington, *Heaven and Earth in the Gospel of Matthew*, NovTSup 126 (Leiden: Brill, 2007).

12. Jonathan Pennington, "The Kingdom of Heaven in the Gospel of Matthew," *Southern Baptist Journal of Theology* 12.1 (2008) 46.

13. For a full treatment of the theme in Luke's Gospel, see Karl Allen Kuhn, *The Kingdom according to Luke and Acts: A Social, Literary, and Theological Introduction* (Grand Rapids: Baker Academic, 2015).

only two times in the entire text—both in the infamous conversation with Nicodemus (John 3:3, 5), and both appear to suggest that the kingdom is a realm or sphere to be entered, not unlike heaven. In fact, there does not appear to be any ethical element to the kingdom of God in the Fourth Gospel whatsoever.[14] Noting these minor differences is only scratching the surface of a much larger discussion, though these differences should suffice to demonstrate that the presentation of the "kingdom" across the four canonical gospels is complex and variegated and should be handled with care.

Conclusion

Dr. Bakker has helpfully highlighted some of the important political motivations of contemporary white evangelicals. She has also identified some contours of the various NT presentations of the *basileia tou theou*, though I believe there is still room for additional nuance on this question. Against that backdrop, I would like to conclude by calling for each of us to engage the biblical text with greater care on issues of politics and kingdom. I am convinced that an approach to Bible reading that lacks nuance is one of the factors contributing to the political and religious polarization Dr. Bakker has so ably described in her paper.

---

14. In addition to the question of the role of the "kingdom" in John, scholars have long debated the very presence of ethics in the Fourth Gospel. On this question, see the various chapters in Sherri Brown and Christopher W. Skinner, eds., *Johannine Ethics: The Moral World of the Gospel and Epistles of John* (Minneapolis: Fortress, 2017).

WHAT'S IN A NAME? IDEOLOGY AND NAMING

Kay Higuera Smith

"I'm not a Christian; I'm a Catholic!" I hear these words every semester as Catholic students identify themselves in my World Religions class. By the same token, Protestant, mostly evangelical, students announce proudly, "I'm a Christian!" What's in a name and how can naming be political? What social norms have been so prevalent that they have caused Catholics to name themselves as "not-Christian" and evangelical Protestants to assume that their branch of Christianity identifies and sets the standard for all forms of Christianity? Both of these narratives exemplify the social power of naming and its political force in setting and regulating norms.

By the twenty-first century, White evangelicals have co-opted the name "Christian" and have successfully employed it politically to reinscribe a racialized, gendered, anti-Jewish hierarchy on their form of Christianity while fostering ignorance among their congregants of the contingent and limited nature of their form of Christianity, on the one hand, and of its hierarchical genealogy, on the other. They have done so by redefining the name while asserting that their definition is comprehensive for all Christianities. They have been equally adept at masking the racialized, anti-Jewish, and gendered nature of the hierarchies they put forth. These developments have now crystalized into a movement whose social violence and, at times, physical threats of violence, can be well documented.

Naming is a fundamentally political act. María S. Rivera Maulucci and Felicia Moore Mensah explain: "We recognize naming as a political act of ascribing identities to ourselves and others in ways that may liberate, maintain, or dehumanize."[1] Therefore, it is appropriate to examine those who claim the authority to name themselves and their adherents as "Christian" without any adjectives or qualifying and to analyze whether such naming functions politically in the ways described by Rivera Maulucci and Moore Mensah. In this case, I will argue that such naming functions

---

1. María S. Rivera Maulucci and Felicia Moore Mensah, "Editorial: Naming Ourselves and Others," *Journal of Research in Science Teaching* 52 (2015) 2.

not to liberate but to dehumanize, and that other forms of Christianity must call White evangelicals to account for the contingent nature of these claims and resist their efforts to universalize their naming of what is a "Christian" while cloaking its oppressive epistemologies.

In the twenty-first century, White evangelicalism came into its own politically.[2] This increase in political power has come at a cost, though. People are leaving politically conservative churches in high numbers and have been disaffected by the social hierarchies inscribed in its practices. Sadly, however, they seem to believe they have nowhere else to go. In 2020, White evangelical Protestant Christians made up only 7 percent of the 18–29 age demographic in the U.S.[3] It is likely this number will continue to decline. During the Trump era, White evangelicalism, which had been enjoying steady increases at the expenses of White mainline churches, lost members while White mainline and White Catholic churches gained.[4] We can deduce from this that the claims of White evangelicalism to the privilege of naming and determining the definition of what a Christian is are being challenged by others. This loss of membership has not stopped White evangelical elites from asserting their claims all the more vociferously, however. Some are even threatening violence. Recently, Sean Feucht, a White evangelical worship leader at Bethel Church in Redding, California, tweeted about a worship rally he held in Portland, Oregon, railing against what he called an Antifa attack on a prayer rally the previous day. Posting a picture of himself flanked by a large number of men in military uniform, Feucht tweeted,

> THANK YOU to our security team (half pictured) tonight in Portland (flag emoji, flexed arm emoji). These are all ex-military, ex-police, private security & most importantly LOVERS OF JESUS & freedom. If you mess with them or our 1st amendment right to worship God—you'll meet Jesus one way or another.[5]

---

2. Ruth Braunstein and Malaena Taylor, "Is the Tea Party a 'Religious' Movement? Religiosity in the Tea Party vs. the Religious Right," *Sociology of Religion* 78.1 (2017) 33–59. See also Anthea Butler, *White Evangelical Racism: The Politics of Morality in America* (Chapel Hill: University of North Carolina Press, 2021) 122.

3. Public Religion Research Institute Staff, "The 2020 Census of American Religion," *Public Religion Research Institute,* July 8, 2021, https://www.prri.org/research/2020-census-of-american-religion/#page-section-1/.

4. "In U.S., Decline of Christianity Continues at Rapid Pace," *Pew Research Center,* October 17, 2019; https://www.pewforum.org/2019/10/17/in-u-s-decline-of-christianity-continues-at-rapid-pace/; Public Religion Research Institute Staff, "The 2020 Census of American Religion," *Public Religion Research Institute,* July 8, 2021; https://www.prri.org/research/2020-census-of-american-religion/#page-section-1/.

5. Sean Feucht, twitter.com/seanfeucht?s=11/.

To be sure, Feucht's threats of violence represent an extreme form of attempting to name and define what it is to be "LOVERS OF JESUS"; however, he is not alone in asserting his definition without irony or apology.

The power to name is the power to assert the norms, and social and political identifying factors of a social group. What appears to be innocent, however, becomes coercive in asserting those norms through various regulatory means. Perhaps one of the most effective forms of coercive action is the masking and cloaking of political acts as personal. Since the 1970s, as the religious right has emerged, their advocates have focused on "a personal relationship with Jesus Christ," implying that they had no political motives while, at the same time, advancing a very tightly woven political set of goals that responded to the urgent questions of White U.S. residents rather than taking into account the needs and aspirations of Black, Indigenous, and People of Color (hereafter BIPOC) populations as well as new immigrants and people from international cultures. All of these norms of the religious right, who are the most likely to name themselves and their way of life as "Christian," without any clarifying adjective, have resulted in a populace that is overwhelmingly White, concerned to maintain the economic status quo, often with no respect for the goals and desires of Christian BIPOC populations, and willing to justify ongoing social hierarchies.

There are other effects of the dominant culture's power to define the name "Christian." As a particular social group gains the social power to dictate the norms and salient values of a name, the process also results in the silencing of the myths, stories, and salient norms and values that the dominant group does not share, despite the possibility that such norms and values represent long-standing traditions elsewhere among those who have shared that name. Given that we are dealing with the name "Christian," we can find myriad examples. One example is the racialized nature of Christian identity. Diana Orcés has documented how Black Christians who identify as "born-again":

> are twice as likely as all Americans (33%) and three more times as likely as white evangelicals (20%) to identify as Democrats, while only eight percent of Black evangelicals identify as Republicans (compared to 51% of white evangelicals) . . . Only 22% of Black evangelicals reported a favorable opinion of former President Trump, while 80% favored President Joe Biden.

These differences translate to different perspectives on race relations, police department funding, social services, and immigration.[6] What these demographic distinctions translate to is that preachers in White and Black churches, respectively,

---

6. Diana Orcés, "Black, White, and Born Again: How Race Affects Opinions among Evangelicals," *Public Religion Research Institute*, February 17, 2021, https://www.prri.org/spotlight/black-white-and-born-again-how-race-affects-opinions-among-evangelicals/.

bring to the fore the issues with which their congregants resonate and are silent on those which fail to respond to salient norms.

In the case of Black churches, they do so while acknowledging that their social locations are in Black communities and that the needs of those communities shape the issues they address. However, it is rare to hear a preacher in a White church acknowledge the limited, contingent nature of the issues brought forth in sermons and in the identities of the church populace. John Piper, for example, a noted preacher and author who often represents White evangelical Christianity as simply "Christianity," with no qualifier, has argued that the New Testament supports a good kind of slavery. He writes in 2021 that the New Testament affirmed slavery but that, if it was to be followed, such slavery would have been transformed.[7] In publishing such a claim, Piper appears ignorant of, and makes no attempt to cite, alternate interpretations of slavery in the New Testament put forth by Black Christian scholars.[8] For those who listen to Piper, the perspectives of other forms of Christianity, even "born-again" Christianities in churches of BIPOC, are silenced. Piper's "Christianity" is one in which his racialized assumptions go unremarked and unnoticed by his followers.

In the same way that coopting the name "Christian" can be coercive and can silence many Christians, so it also constructs people in certain groups as deviant. In the contemporary U.S., 51 percent of White evangelicals identify as Republican and 81 percent favored President Trump. At the same time, 62 percent of Black "born-again" Christians identify as Democrat and 80 percent favored President Biden.[9] In White evangelical spaces, if church attendees find that their core convictions do not align with those conveyed by the majority of the church community, they will experience themselves as deviant and peripheralized, which in itself is a kind of social violence, resulting in the attendees either leaving (self-selecting out of the group) or staying and being forced to self-censor and face microaggressions and silencing and policing from the dominant group.

Another social violence that occurs in such environments in which the name "Christian" is widely assumed to define a contingent social group's absolutized definition is that those members who want to be Christian but do not align with the salient norms of the group tend to be rendered invisible. This occurs because the social

---

7. John Piper, "How Could Jonathan Edwards Own Slaves? Wrestling with the History of a Hero," DesiringGod.org, August 10, 2021; https://www.desiringgod.org/articles/how-could-jonathan-edwards-own-slaves/.

8. See, for instance, Clarice Martin, "The *Haustalfen* (Household Codes) in African American Biblical Interpretation: 'Free Slaves' and 'Subordinate Women,'" in *Stony the Road We Trod*, ed. Cain Hope Felder (Minneapolis: Fortress, 1991), 206–31.

9. Orcés, "Black, White, and Born Again."

group has not been fully successful in convincing some BIPOC or women members about the legitimacy of its racialized, anti-Semitic, gendered norms. In some cases, peripheralized members internalize these assumptions and deny the urgent questions of their own social or ethnic group to which they belong or in which they were raised. We see this often among women who internalize biological determinism, accepting their purportedly subservient "roles" as divinely ordained and thus not appropriate for leadership or agency, or Jewish converts who reject any claims to the Jewish people as a theological category in itself.[10]

It is crucial for an absolutizing form of Christianity to base its claims of being the normative form of Christianity upon mystified concepts. This is accomplished through both social memory and deliberate social ignorance. The group's elites reinforce certain social memories. For instance, John Piper, mentioned above, retains his admiration for Jonathan Edwards by knowingly constructing a romanticized social memory of the slave-owning Edwards. Piper himself acknowledges that he may have been engaging in wishful thinking, what we might call willful social ignorance. Growing up as a White Protestant in the Jim Crow South, Piper was educated in environments that suppressed and collectively "forgot" the inhumanities and injustices of slavery. Piper acknowledges that he had read Edwards's works for twenty years, including "all of his major works and many sermons and smaller treatises and letters, plus at least three biographies," before he saw a problem. He states, "I had never heard that Edwards owned slaves, nor that he pushed back against those who opposed slave ownership."[11] Piper demonstrates here, without irony or question, that the social world that marked his own development engaged in a collective forgetting not only of Jonathan Edwards's slaveholding history but of the injustices of slaveholding at large. Charles Mills defines this phenomenon as "systemic misperception." Mills explains: "What I want to pin down, then, is the idea of an ignorance, a non-knowing, that is not contingent, but in which race¾white racism and/or white racial domination and their ramifications¾plays a causal role . . . To begin with, *white ignorance* as a cognitive phenomenon has to be clearly historicized" (emphasis mine).[12] Mills, an epistemologist, has argued that White ignorance is a form of active resistance against justices sought by BIPOC. It is a conscious forgetting in order to contribute to the mystification of social spaces in which White norms dominate.

---

10. See Beth Allison Barr, *The Making of Biblical Womanhood: How the Subjugation of Women Became Gospel Truth* (Grand Rapids: Brazos, 2021); on Jewish self-abnegation, see J. Kameron Carter, *Race: A Theological Account* (Oxford: Oxford University Press, 2008).

11. Piper, "How Could Jonathan Edwards Own Slaves."

12. Charles Mills, "White Ignorance," in *Race and Epistemologies of Ignorance,* ed. Shannon Sullivan and Nancy Tuana, SUNY Series: Philosophy and Race (Albany: State University of New York Press, 2007) 20.

A significant strategy supporting this process is collective memory and collective forgetting. These acts have a moral component, as they result in the various forms of social violence hitherto discussed herein.[13]

Social memory and social forgetting are parts of what Mills calls "flawed processes" of cognition, and they result in real-world moral damage to the peripheralized other.[14] He acknowledges that there are all sorts of ignorances beyond just White ignorance. There is gender ignorance, anti-Jewish ignorance, ignorance of the violence done in the name of settler colonialism and against those living with disabilities, etc. All of these forms of ignorance work to mystify the socially violent acts of silencing, naming the social/cultural Other as deviant, invisible, and biologically ordained to be subject to other humans, at best, and oppression and genocide, at worst, while at the same time legitimizing the dominant group's claim to be operating as unqualifiedly "Christian."

All of these regulatory norms also underwrite authoritarian regimes, which in turn mystify and divinize rigid hierarchies. Relationships based on domination and subordination are central to the regulating norms of the hierarchy. Those who question or challenge are quickly silenced, peripheralized, and rendered invisible. The social hierarchy is reinforced not only by mystifying hierarchies as divinely ordained but also as biologically inevitable. Social hierarchies based on biological determinism ensure that only males serve as leaders and that the interests of males outweigh the interests of women and intersex or queer church members. More subtle social hierarchies may appear to welcome BIPOC, but such people are noticeably absent from the highest forms of leadership in the social structures. These kinds of determinism are portrayed as not only established in nature but also by divine decree. Owen Strachan, for instance, writes that Christianity

> does indeed offer us models for manhood and womanhood, scripts for how we should live out our days to the glory of God in our sex, our gender. Men must not shun the work of provision for their wives and children; this role is given them of God. Women must not demean home-making and child-raising; such is their inheritance from the Lord.[15]

Strachan's efforts at mystification occur not only through selective memory and forgetting but through a selective hermeneutic that ignores much of Scripture while portraying certain favored passages of Scriptures through a highly edited lens. Strachan offers his hierarchical hermeneutic as unqualifiedly "Christian": "Christianity,"

---

13. See Mills, "White Ignorance," 22.
14. Mills, "White Ignorance," 23.
15. Owen Strachan, "Of 'Dad Moms' and 'Man Fails': An Essay on Men and Awesomeness," *Journal for Biblical Manhood and Womanhood* 17.1 (2012) 26.

he asserts, does "not offer captivity, but freedom."[16] Here we have an example in which the unqualified naming of a contingent and socially-bound form of Christianity is mystified as "Christianity" writ large, both reinforcing and cloaking a hierarchy based on biological determinism in order to legitimize its own norms and asserted virtues.

It is not just gendered hierarchies that get reinforced in the "naming" of Christianity by White evangelicals. Hierarchies based on Western vs. non-Western, White vs. BIPOC, Insider vs. Outsider, Christian vs. non-Christian all reinforce social structures in which members of the dominant group discursively produce the subordinate group as inherently unsuited to lead for a variety of reasons, some based on biological determinism, some on the Western myth of manifest destiny, and some on racialized or ethnic "Ignorance," as defined by Mills. In all cases, the Other is produced by the discourse of the dominant group, which maintains its power to name what is normative "Christianity."

Finally, the power to name becomes mystified throughout history by elites redefining the term to adjust to new social realities. The most overt example of this is the redefinition of patriarchy as "complementarianism." Patriarchy sounds just too hierarchical to twenty-first-century ears and thus requires a euphemism to maintain its hold. "Complementarianism" sounds softer and more enfranchising. It is not. Nevertheless, by changing the terminology and shifting the epistemology to adapt to new epistemic spaces, the hierarchy continues to be underwritten through mystification. This phenomenon occurs in all long-lasting hierarchies. If we are to analyze the strategies of mystification that underwrite the power to name, this strategy is one of the most urgent.

Because social identity is fluid, it requires constant vigilance by White evangelical elites to police and regulate the group's boundaries. Employing the unqualified name "Christian" is an effective form of camouflage that reinforces the mystification needed to police and regulate. Shifting other definitions, such as redefining patriarchy as "complementarianism" or anti-Jewishness as Dispensationalist Christian Zionism, or anti-Black racism as opposition to rioters and anarchism serves to maintain the mystification underwriting a certain form of oppressive, White supremacist Christianity as normative. Here is the irony. On the one hand, the name "Christian" indeed has been marked by racialized, anti-Jewish, and gendered discourse since its inception. In that sense, to name a group that legitimizes racialized, anti-Jewish, and gendered discourse as "Christian" is, to be sure, an act that lines up with history. But at the same time the name "Christian," because it has such a long history and global reach, can also resist such normalizing efforts. Hence, we see the uptick in

---

16. Strachan, "Of 'Dad Moms' and 'Man Fails,'" 26.

membership at mainline churches at the expense of White evangelical churches.[17] Naming also serves as a form of resistance and as a political force for recreating new or hybrid social identities. Nevertheless, in order to understand and document the power of naming to create normative environments that underwrite hierarchies and commit social violence, it is worthwhile to examine the intellectual history of similar efforts in history to employ the name "Christian" as a political tool meant to construct socially or martially violent hierarchies.

Reinforcing the Ideology: Race, Anti-Judaism, Gender

Scholars of race, gender, and Christian-Jewish relations have all noted a common epistemic development in Christian hierarchies attempting to reinforce their regulatory norms in the face of shifting social and cultural developments while legitimizing their power to name. What I will demonstrate, in the limited space allotted, is that in each case—that of race, anti-Judaism/anti-Semitism, and gender—the hierarchy was established, but it anchored itself to shifting ideological commitments over time. At the same time, it cloaked and masked those shifts, claiming that the social hierarchies it affirmed were timeless. This is an example of the attempt to mystify. That is, in Christian history, we have good evidence that in the case of these three social hierarchies, the elites in each case claimed that their hierarchy was timeless and inscribed in Christian tradition, and for that reason, divinely ordained and hence virtuous and moral.[18] The reality, however, is that the ideological justification for each hierarchy shifted over time. What this demonstrates is that the hierarchies under examination here are not based on timeless truths but get resignified and realigned as the churches experience epistemic shifts over time, making the underlying justifications unsupportable. The justifications that are being made even today to support certain forms of these hierarchies are based on contemporary ideological commitments rather than traditional ones, showing that, far from being ancient traditions, these traditions, as they are being manifested in the twenty-first century, are innovations structured to take advantage of contemporary ideological commitments. This occurs, despite the claims by the adherents that their hierarchy is somehow traditional and hence divinely ordained.

---

17. "In U.S., Decline of Christianity Continues at Rapid Pace," *Pew Research Center*, October 17, 2019. https://www.pewforum.org/2019/10/17/in-u-s-decline-of-christianity-continues-at-rapid-pace/.

18. I limit myself to these three hierarchies because of lack of space. Anti-immigrant, anti-Indigenous, and hierarchies that peripherize people based on age, class, and ability also undergo these various shifts while the elites insist on universal justification for the hierarchy.

Race

In the case of race, scholars are in agreement that "race," as it is understood since the time of modernity, did not exist in antiquity as a social organizing construct. Most writers who discuss forms of social organizing in antiquity prefer the word "ethnicity," as we do not see arguments for social hierarchies based singularly on skin color. Because social identity is always fluid and being reconceptualized over time, there can be no fixed notion of race. Denise Kimber Buell describes social identity during the Roman period, for instance, stating, "Romans give little attention to common ancestry or language in defining Romanness in the imperial period, favoring instead factors such as education, observance of Roman laws, morality, piety, and citizenship."[19] When language about race was used, it was as often as not used to describe religious groups as any other criterion.[20] Buell cites Aristides, *Apology* (2nd C.), in the Greek version, which uses the word γένος (typically translated as "race") to refer to different religious groups, writing, "For it is clear that there are three kinds (*genē*) of humans in this world: worshippers of so-called gods, Jews, and Christians (*Apol.* 2.2)."[21] Nevertheless, Buell still wants to use the term "race" to refer to constructions of Otherness based on skin color; however, she urges that we maintain the notion of "inexactness" when we use it.[22]

Language about ethnicity in antiquity, however, does show some consistency in construing the social/cultural Other in negative terms, including those whose phenotypes differ from the majority of Greeks or Romans. Moreover, given the long history of whiteness as being associated with purity and goodness (e.g., Isa 1:18) and blackness being associated with darkness and the absence of light, early Christian writers transferred the light/dark imagery to the imagery of the black Ethiopian (Isa 50:3; Job 3:5). Athanasius, writing in the mid-fourth century, writes of the Egyptian monk Anthony, in the *Vita S. Antoni*, and his temptations meant to detract him from the ascetic life. The devil, furious that Anthony will not succumb to his temptations, responds, Athanasius writes: "Gnashing his teeth as it is written, and as it were beside himself, he appeared to Antony like a black boy, taking a visible shape in accordance with the colour of his mind."[23] Here, the evil of the devil's mind is conceptualized

---

19. Denise Kimber Buell, *Why This New Race: Ethnic Reasoning in Early Christianity* (New York: Columbia University Press, 2005) 40.

20. Buell, *Why This New Race*, 35.

21. Buell, *Why This New Race*, 36.

22. Buell, *Why This New Race*, 14.

23. Athanasius, *Vita S. Antoni* 6.1, in *Select Works and Letters,* Vol IV, *Nicene and Post-Nicene Fathers,* Series II, ed. Philip Schaff and Henry Wace, trans. H. Ellershaw (New York, 1924, repr. 1957); https://sourcebooks.fordham.edu/basis/vita-antony.asp/; cf. David Brakke, "Ethiopian Demons: Male Sexuality, the Black-Skinned Other, and the Monastic Self," *Journal of the History of Sexuality* 10

as black, like the skin of a black child. Anthony responds to the devil, "Thou art very despicable then, for thou art black-hearted and weak as a child."[24] This narrative shows how the Ethiopians' black skin was construed as associated with evil as opposed to the purity of whiteness.

Nevertheless, references to demons appearing in the form of Black humans are rare among the desert mystics. These references do not reflect a systematic notion employed to describe Black people in general. Moreover, the notion of race (*genos*) could include religion, culture, and ethnicity as well. Such examples, while significant for recognizing that Blackness was indeed used as a tool to reinforce stereotypes, show no evidence of a pervasive racism based on skin color. The ancients indeed employed anti-Blackness in their social hierarchies, but they did not do so exclusively. Anti-Jewishness and other forms of xenophobia based on geographic distance served just as easily to underwrite hierarchical language. In other words, in antiquity, other justifications for social hierarchies existed. Aristotle put forward an anthropology that imagined the Greek or Roman males as at the top of the social hierarchy because of their purported greater rationality. At the lower ends of the hierarchy were women, slaves, and males and females from non-Greek social groups. The Aristotelian social hierarchy then would have viewed Ethiopians and sub-Saharan Africans as not capable of rationality, but no more than women, white slaves, or others Aristotle deemed "barbarian." That is, in the Aristotelian anthropology, which church elites adopted, skin color did not calculate uniquely into the equation. In antiquity, then, the Greek word *genos*, "race," was used to refer to ethnic groups, regional affiliations, and groups distinguished, not exclusively, by education, class, morality, and religious affiliation.[25]

This would shift over time, first with the Spanish Inquisition and then with the Enlightenment. In the case of the Spanish Inquisition, the word *genos*, now translated into the Spanish *raza*, "race," was used to refer to former Jews and Moors. Either they or their forebears had converted to Christianity during the Inquisition, but their conversions had become suspect. This is where we also get the term *limpieza de sangre* ("purity of blood"), to associate race with blood purity. As the post-Reformation period dawned in the Americas and the African slave trade grew exponentially, we see race being used by Christians in this new way, as a biological category used to refer to people of a particular skin color. This innovation, in turn, supported older hierarchies while basing itself on new, modernist epistemologies

---

(2001) 509.

24. Athanasius, *Vita S. Antoni* 6.4.

25. Buell, *Why This New Race*, 40–41; Buell (1) notes, "*Genos* is a term widely used for Greeks, Egyptians, Romans, and *Ioudaioi*—groups often interpreted as ethnic groups or their ancient equivalents."

based not on Aristotelian natural order but on a notion of natural order that ensured an ordered society. Thus, points out Ibram X. Kendi,

> Throughout the social tumult of the 1690s, [Cotton] Mather obsessed over maintaining the social hierarchies by convincing the lowly that God and nature had put them there, whether it applied to women, children, enslaved Africans, or poor people. In *A Good Master Well Served* (1696), he presumed that nature had created "a conjugal society" between husband and wife; a "Parental Society" between parent and child; and, "lowest of all," a "herile society" between master and servant.[26]

In this construction, "servants" were assumed to be either natives indigenous to the Americas or African slaves. The development is worth noting. In antiquity, skin color may have played a role to support a racial hierarchy, but it did not do so uniquely. The word *genos* might just as easily be applied to structure populations on moral, geographic, religious, or ideological grounds. If blackness was presented in a negative light, it was not because of any widespread ideology about skin color. Rather, it drew metaphorically from the biblical notions of darkness and light. In the Aristotelian anthropology, the distinction was not based on skin color but on social groups identified as women, slaves, or barbarians—non-Greeks. While skin color sometimes was a factor in antiquity for defining different *genē*, such distinctions just as easily were based on other criteria. In the American colonies, race continued to be a factor in justifying social hierarchy, and the Christian beneficiaries of racialized hierarchies did so by reconceptualizing race epistemically. It is yet another example of the ways in which European or White Christian elites throughout history have asserted the power to name and have done so by shifting the definitions that underwrite unjust social hierarchies, cloaking and mystifying those hierarchies, and engaging in social forgetting in order to buttress their authoritative claims to define "Christianity."

To give credence to these underlying justifications, the academic guilds of modernity, influenced also by Romanticism, provided Christian elites racist theories based in the science of the era. This was the *Wissenschaft* period in German scholarship and a time when social/cultural/racial "essences" were being identified, taxonomized, and hierarchized.[27] In the Jim Crow era, racism had to cloak and mask itself anew, because previous laws supporting racial hierarchies were being struck down. It did so through enhancing and advancing prison policies already well established

---

26. Ibram X. Kendi, *Stamped from the Beginning: The Definitive History of Racist Ideas in America* (New York: Nation, 2016) 63.

27. On the development of scientific racism, see Kendi, *Stamped*, 44–46. On racism and the *Wissenschaft* tradition, see Shawn Kelley, *Racializing Jesus: Race, Ideology and the Formation of Modern Biblical Scholarship* (New York: Routledge, 2002).

in the South, based on the loophole in the Thirteenth Amendment that allowed for involuntary servitude in the case of punishment for crimes. At the same time, segregation became the rallying cry for maintaining a racialized hierarchy, based on the ideology of "separate but equal." Christians were at the forefront of supporting new assumptions based on these epistemic shifts and the Christian private school and home school movements arose under the same leadership as the segregationists.[28] The Jim Crow laws were voided by the Supreme Court in 1965 and new scientific discoveries in human evolution, health care, and criminal law emerged.[29] Racist ideologues were forced to put forth new justifications for their hierarchies. Under President Reagan, new drug laws developed that targeted Black and Latinx people while limiting liability for Whites and constructing and stigmatizing an image of the Black welfare queen.[30] Bill Clinton reinforced the ideology by doubling down on the "welfare queen" myth and by attacking and distorting anti-racist claims.[31] George H.W. Bush won his presidency based on his exploitation of the myth of the dangerous Black man.[32] During President Obama's terms in office, Birtherism—the claim that Obama could not have been born in the U.S.—justified racial animus. Nevertheless, no recent President has used such overtly racialized rhetoric as did President Trump, who rekindled myths of exploitative welfare queens, dangerous violent black men, and birtherism. During all these periods, racialized hierarchies have been reinforced, resulting in infant mortality, among other maladies, being significantly higher among Black populations than White, Asian, or Hispanic.[33] As the Black Lives Matter movement developed in response to the unjust killings of Trayvon Martin, Mike Brown, and others, a new rhetorical tool is being employed currently to argue that those who advocate for equal justice for Black lives are cloaking those claims to hide their desire to riot and destroy the country, also drawing on myths of Blacks as insurrectionists and seditionists.[34] This language is prevalent

---

28. Tal Levy, "Homeschooling and Racism," *Journal of Black Studies* 39.6 (2009) 905–23.

29. Regarding genetic advances, see R. C. Lewontin, "The Apportionment of Human Diversity," in *Evolutionary Biology*, ed. T. Dobzhansky et al. (New York: Springer, 1972); https://doi.org/10.1007/978-1-4684-9063-3_14; Ning Yu et al., "Larger Genetic Differences Within Africans Than Between Africans and Eurasians," *Genetics* 161.1 (2002) 269–74; https://www.genetics.org/content/161/1/269.

30. Kendi, *Stamped*, 433–37.

31. Kendi, *Stamped*, 451–52.

32. Kendi, *Stamped*, 441–42.

33. "Infant Mortality," *Centers for Disease Control and Prevention*; https://www.cdc.gov/reproductivehealth/maternalinfanthealth/infantmortality.htm.

34. During the slavery era, there is a long history of White racialized activism based on an assumption about Black men as "hypersexual Black-faced animals that, if freed, would ravage the exemplars of human purity and beauty [White women]." On this see Kendi, *Stamped*, 177, 451.

in White evangelical churches. Even in the contemporary scene, then, racial hierarchies are maintained while the ideologies that justify them shift and morph to adapt to changing norms.

In all cases, White church elites have been at the forefront of postulating the justifications for such new epistemic shifts. Several presidents of major seminaries in the Southern Baptist Convention, one of the largest denominations in the U.S., have recently forbidden that critical race theory be taught in their seminaries, launching an emotional and often irrational public discourse attacking the use of critical race theory, an interpretive approach which, at its core, is merely a tool to unmask those social institutions who have mystified and cloaked their racialized ideological assumptions.[35] In all of these various manifestations, powerful and socially significant churches have followed the ideological shifts of their racist forerunners in academia and politics. Their claims to be "color blind" and to reject racism mask the continuation of racialized hierarchies being perpetuated in their midst.[36]

Anti-Judaism

The shifts in anti-Jewish rhetoric in the church and in the larger society mirror the shifts in race throughout each era. During the pre-modern era, Christian anti-Jewish rhetoric shows up as early as the second century in the *Epistle of Barnabas*:[37]

> Ye ought therefore to understand. And this also I further beg of you . . . to take heed now to yourselves, and not to be like some, adding largely to your sins, and saying, "The covenant is both theirs and ours. But they thus finally lost it, after Moses had already received it. For the Scripture saith, "And Moses . . . received the covenant from the Lord . . . "; but turning away to idols, they lost it.[38]

---

35. See Yonat Shimron, "Southern Baptist Seminary Presidents Nix Critical Race Theory," *Religion News Service,* December 1, 2020; https://religionnews.com/2020/12/01/southern-baptist-seminary-presidents-nix-critical-race-theory/; see also Gary Peller, "Opinion: I've Been a Critical Race Theorist for Thirty Years. Our Opponents Are Just Proving Our Point for Us," *Politico*, June 30, 2021, https://www.politico.com/news/magazine/2021/06/30/critical-race-theory-lightning-rod-opinion-497046?fbclid=IwAR0aUuFwPtUMNAe9vG9O3i2XTJYDwXH_n0ggEzBeY0XHAEF0jvXWQxvq0Ps.

36. Kendi, *Stamped*, 467–68.

37. Many scholars identify overt anti-Jewish rhetoric to the New Testament itself. See, for instance, the various essays in Paula Fredriksen and Adele Reinhartz, eds., *Jesus, Judaism & Christian Anti-Judaism: Reading the New Testament after the Holocaust* (Louisville: Westminster John Knox, 2002). I read the NT texts as Jewish non-elites vilifying what they perceive as elites. However, in either case, certainly by the second century, this kind of rhetoric has been taken up by an emerging power base of Christians as a tool to oppress and delegitimize emerging rabbinic Judaism. This becomes a much clearer case of oppression once Christianity becomes the religion of the Roman Empire.

38. *Epistle of Barnabas* 4, trans. Roberts-Donaldson, *Early Christian Writings,* http://www.early-christianwritings.com/text/barnabas-roberts.html.

Just as anti-Black sentiment in the church reinforced social hierarchies that peripherized Blacks, Indigenous, and other people of color, so Christian anti-Jewishness also worked to suppress and ultimately to destroy any collective Jewish presence in the church while Christian elites were asserting the justice of their approach. Furthermore, just as church elites reformulated anti-Black rhetoric as epistemic shifts occurred in society, so anti-Jewish rhetoric based itself on shifting epistemologies to ensure that Jews remain oppressed and subordinated.

Jewish subordination was reinforced in the fourth century CE by Augustine with his doctrine of the Jews as Cain, in which he argued that just as God imposed on Cain a punishment to be an eternal fugitive, wandering the earth (Gen 4:11–16), so it was incumbent upon Christendom to ensure a similar fate for the Jewish people:

> Then God says to Cain: "You are cursed from the earth, which has opened its mouth to receive your brother's blood at your hand." . . . So the unbelieving people of the Jews is cursed from the earth, that is, from the Church, which in the confession of sins has opened its mouth to receive the blood shed for the remission of sins by the hand of the people that would not be under grace, but under the law. And this murderer is cursed by the Church.[39]

Gavin Langmuir has argued that the Augustinian conviction that it was incumbent upon Christians to oppress Jews in obedience to enforcing the curse of Cain, gave way to a new notion of Judaism in Medieval Europe as *chimera*, a mythical creature, almost monster-like, which has no grounding in reality, underwriting charges against Jews of ritual murders and blood libels.[40] Peter Schäfer, however, argues that associating mythic and misanthropic characteristics to Jews permeated ancient Roman society as well. He prefers the term "Judeophobia."[41]

In either case, as the Spanish Inquisition ramped up, "race"/*raza* took on new meaning as a category describing both Jews, Moors, and even their Christian descendants, with the Spanish Inquisition's concerns about purity of blood, as discussed above regarding race and skin color. While, to be sure, the Jewish people were marked as a race in antiquity, it was not a uniquely biological category. Now Jewishness flowed in the veins and was considered a biological reality which could not be escaped, even through conversion. Cecil Roth notes that, during the Inquisition in Portugal,

---

39. Augustine, *Contra Faustum* 12.11; http://www.newadvent.org/fathers/140612.htm.

40. Gavin I. Langmuir, *Toward a Definition of Antisemitism* (Berkeley: University of California Press, 1990) 61.

41. Peter Schäfer, *Judeophobia: Attitudes toward the Jews in the Ancient World* (Cambridge: Harvard University Press, 1997), 210.

anti-Semitic works, which refused to differentiate between *converso* [converts to Christianity] and Jew, poured from the presses in a steady stream. In 1562, the Portuguese bishops presented a petition requesting that the New Christians should be compelled to wear special badges, and to be segregated in Ghettos, just as their unconverted ancestors had been.[42]

Here we have an epistemic innovation that now conceptualized Jewishness in the blood and in biology. The interests of Christian elites in Spain required new categories to rid them of those *conversos* in their midst whom they suspected—often wrongly—of maintaining Jewish ritual practice. Anti-Jewishness or Judeophobia had taken on new ideological underpinnings in order to justify continued social hierarchies within the church which ensured that Jews, and even their converted descendants, remain at the periphery of the European and New World society.

During the Enlightenment period in Europe, as in the case of race, we see another shift, which at first was welcomed by the Jews, who called it the *Haskala*, or Emancipation. Jews now could see themselves as individuals who were entitled to the same individual civil rights as all citizens of the emerging nation-states. But it was not long before many Jews' refusal to assimilate culturally gave rise to an even more virulent form of blood and soil anti-Semitism than was seen earlier. Building on the blood-based anti-Jewishness of the Spanish Inquisition, European elites began to write of Jews as innately and constitutively unable to assimilate, thus justifying the need either to punish them, at best, or eliminate them, at worst. As before, Christian church elites in Europe propounded and enforced this Enlightenment-based anti-Semitism. Immanuel Kant is striking in this regard. Drawing on ancient Christian and Roman notions of the Jews, Kant argued that Jewish particularity must fade away in the face of universal Christian morality.[43] What began as a welcome movement among Jews quickly morphed into a new epistemology that justified anti-Jewish policies, both in the emerging secular nation-states and in the churches.

Finally, in the twentieth century, American anti-Semitism continued largely unchecked. Even in our era, old notions of Jews drawing on phenotypical stereotypes and calls for genocide persist.[44] One might argue that the contemporary movement of Christian Zionism marks a shift away from anti-Semitism; however, it appears to be another manifestation of a cult of masculinity that finds a romanticized but objectified icon in the intrepid Israeli.[45] Equally telling is that for Christian Zionists, who

---

42. Cecil Roth, *A History of the Marranos* (New York: Jewish Publication Society, 1932), 76.

43. See Wojciech Kozyra, "Kant on the Jews and Their Religion," *Diametros* 17 (2020) 37, https://diametros.uj.edu.pl/diametros/article/view/1540/1427/.

44. See Robert Michael, *A Concise History of American Antisemitism* (New York: Roman & Littlefield, 2005).

45. On the cult of masculinity in contemporary evangelical Christian discourse, see Kristin Kobes

draw on the nineteenth century doctrine of Dispensationalism, Jews will almost all be annihilated in the eschaton in order for Christ to return. Here again, Jews are a stereotyped Other, whose own goals and aspirations are reconceptualized in light of Christian Zionists' own interests and biblical interpretations. This objectification of real Jews is even more marked and more violent in contemporary Christian Zionists' objectification of contemporary Palestinians and their plight under occupied Israel. Throughout Christian history, then, animus toward Jewish people has been consistent while the ideological and epistemic justifications for it have shifted. In every era, Christian elites justified their unjust treatment of Jews by mystifying their constructed social hierarchy while claiming the right to define their form of Christianity as normative. The efforts of contemporary, White evangelical Christians to mask their own continued construction of Jews as outgroup using claims of love and support, while funding efforts that could easily lead to war and destruction of both Jewish and Palestinian lives, is but one more manifestation of this change. As did their forebears, White evangelical Christians, while claiming the epistemic authority to define the name "Christian" without qualifier, reinforce the discourse by cloaking and masking the anti-Jewishness and anti-Semitism that has marked their own construction of Jews and Palestinians. In such a context, they are indeed "Christian," in that they are maintaining Christian hierarchies that peripherize Jews in the social imaginary and that structure Jews as outgroup. On the other hand, they are masking those discursive efforts in an attempt to claim their contingent Christianity accessible to contemporary audiences while insisting that their norms are universal.

Women

Finally, it should come as no surprise that contemporary White evangelical Christianity has followed its forebears in performing the same discursive moves when it comes to women.[46] As in the case of race and anti-Semitism, the justification for gender hierarchy within the church, with women at the bottom of the hierarchy, shifts over time in order to justify its perpetuation.[47] This shift follows the same pattern. Churches make universalizing epistemic claims and justify oppressive social hierarchies in light of those claims. As epistemologies shift or arise from new

---

Du Mez, *Jesus and John Wayne: How White Evangelicals Corrupted a Faith and Fractured a Nation* (New York: Liveright, 2020).

46. Time does not allow a discussion of gender at large; however, the same case easily could be made, especially in light of contemporary research in biology on intersex. See, for instance, Megan K. DeFranza, *Sex Difference in Christian Theology: Male, Female, and Intersex in the Image of God* (Grand Rapids: Eerdmans, 2015).

47. Barr, *The Making of Biblical Womanhood*.

knowledge that is produced, churches adapt the new epistemologies and found their hierarchical claims anew. They do this all the while insisting that their hierarchies are eternal and God-ordained. So, in Christian antiquity, many gender norms were based on Aristotelian notions of females, slaves, and barbarians as ordained by nature to be ruled by freeborn Greek males.[48] Clarice Martin has shown how the New Testament household codes are structured according to Aristotelian household codes, grounding their patriarchal systems in the normative epistemologies of ancient Greco-Roman social imaginaries.[49] Additionally, Greco-Roman ideologies of public and private spheres shaped early Christianity. Christian women in the pre-modern period got around these codes and norms by advocating virginity and celibacy, which would allow a woman to preach and teach Christ without requiring the legal authority of a male.[50] For proponents of the Protestant Reformation, however, virginity could not be sustained as a value in the church. Here again, we see that this response, which claimed to be a traditional approach to gender, in fact drew from post-Reformation economic and political interests. Arguing for the "eternal" value of marriage, post-Reformation Protestants reconceptualized social identity by engaging in a social "forgetting" of the active, single, and celibate women who had furthered the work of the church.[51] What resulted were gender hierarchies in the church that became even more rigid and impermeable.

In the contemporary era, patriarchy persists, especially among large swaths of White evangelicals. As a response to the gains of feminism within Christian churches, a group of conservative Christian scholars coined the term "complementarianism" as a euphemism for patriarchy in the 1980s.[52] According to this ideology, males and females are divinely ordained to be structured as a hierarchy, with males at the top of the hierarchy; however, they claim, males and females are still equal.[53]

This highly influential group in White evangelicalism claims to reject the term hierarchalist; however, it precisely assures that traditional gender hierarchies stay in place, mystified now by claims of equality. Here again, we see traditional efforts to maintain hierarchies by reframing them in new epistemologies. The "equality" claimed by complementarians nevertheless assures that, both in the church and

---

48. See, for instance, Aristotle, *Politics* 1.2.

49. Martin, "The *Haustafeln*," 206–31.

50. Barr, *The Making of Biblical Womanhood*, 71–99.

51. Barr, *The Making of Biblical Womanhood*, 107.

52. Denny Burk, "What's in a Name? The Meaning and Origin of 'Complementarianism,'" *The Council on Biblical Manhood and Womanhood*, August 1, 2019; https://cbmw.org/2019/08/01/whats-in-a-name/.

53. John Piper and Wayne Grudem, eds., *Recovering Biblical Manhood & Womanhood: A Response to Evangelical Feminism* (Wheaton, IL: Crossway, 1991) xv; cited in Denny Burk, "What's in a Name."

in the home, women are subordinate to men. In the end, what emerges is a form of biological determinism: women are biologically determined by God to submit themselves to their husbands (thus maintaining the subordination ensured by the cult of domesticity developed during the post-Reformation period) and to remain silent in the churches (thus maintaining the subordination ensured by Aristotelian anthropologies in the Household Codes). Once more, we see a discursive move by White evangelicals to make claims of moral excellence and virtue while masking and cloaking efforts to retain social hierarchies.

Conclusion

White evangelical elites make certain claims to reinforce their regulatory norms and ideological interests. Those claims are that they represent "Christianity" in an unqualified manner. This is not to say that they imagine themselves as perfectly synonymous with the values of previous Christianities. Nevertheless, they do purport to model an unchanging moral core of Christianity that expresses excellence and virtue and that rejects previous social hierarchies in favor of the equality of all human beings. Despite this, however, their churches are racially homogeneous and advocate positions that support White interests at the expense of the interests of BIPOC and many women in the U.S. They often make claims to support Israel while praying for the destruction of two-thirds of its Jewish populace and the entirety of its Palestinian populace. Finally, they claim that they "certainly reject the term 'hierarchicalist'" while preserving an almost impermeable gender hierarchy. All the while, White evangelicalism has insisted on the power to "name" what it is to be Christian, convincing many of that power, but not all. Many adherents are leaving because they cannot reconcile what they were perceiving in their White evangelical churches with what they read in the New Testament. To counter the political gains made by White evangelicals and the damage done to people who assume that there are no other options in Christianity, we must learn our history and resurrect suppressed social memories; we must continue to advocate for critical theories that help us unmask these efforts at cloaking and masking; and we must point out the logical inconsistencies repeatedly and unceasingly. This will be a decades-long challenge.

Nevertheless, tragically, White evangelicals are demonstrating an uncomfortable reality, which is that racialized, Judaized, and gendered hierarchies are built into the warp and woof of Christianity throughout its history. Can any form of Christianity be epistemically committed to reject such hierarchies? To be sure, there are many forms of Christianity today that seek to do just that. Can those forms of Christianity ultimately have the kind of sway of White evangelicalism? It does not appear that they have been able to gain the mass appeal of such hierarchized structures. This is a reality over which we grieve and lament. May change come soon; however, I do not see it occurring in my lifetime.

RESPONSE TO SMITH

Bret M. Widman

I want to start off by thanking Dr. Smith for her excellent work that she submitted for symposium. "What's in a name?" What is in a name—INDEED! Her contribution to this symposium deconstructing the blind naming of white evangelicals hopefully will be read widely after this symposium. I found myself responding to her paper with "AMEN"; which was scribbled on my notes in the margins of her paper as well as what repeatedly sprang out of my heart.

I would be remiss to not name my social location before I respond. As a white, cisgender, straight male discipled in an evangelical, white context, it is not lost on me the endless points of blindness and ignorance that still lurk within me, that I embody, and how I may have "named" in ignorance in my past. In other words, I am very conscious about my incompetence. I have served in various pastoral roles within the church, all on the West Coast, before landing in academia. In fact, it was the 2016 election that revealed so much troubling fruit within the church, that I sensed an invitation and call to engage the discipleship of a younger generation that are leaving the churches they were nurtured in . . . primarily because of the blindness and ignorance of said church.

Dr. Smith lets us know exactly where she is headed in the second paragraph of her work. She states:

> By the twenty-first century, White Evangelicals have coopted the name "Christian" and have successfully employed it politically to re-inscribe a racialized, gendered, anti-Jewish hierarchy on their form of Christianity while fostering ignorance among their congregants of the contingent and limited nature of their form of Christianity, on the one hand, and of its hierarchical genealogy, on the other. They have done so by re-defining the name while asserting that their definition is comprehensive for all Christianities. They have been equally adept at masking the racialized, anti-Jewish, and gendered nature of the hierarchies they put forth. These developments have now crystalized into a movement whose social violence and, at times, physical threats of violence, can be well documented.

She ends her work with the following:

> White evangelicals are demonstrating an uncomfortable reality, which is that racialized, Judaized, and gendered hierarchies are built into the warp and woof of Christianity throughout its history. Can any form of Christianity be epistemically committed to reject such hierarchies?

Is there hope for white evangelicals?

This is the question she invites us to wrestle with after reading her thesis. She develops her work by talking about the power of naming and the subsequent consequences when naming is done by blindness or "white ignorance." Dr. Smith quotes Charles Mills on page seven with italicized emphasis.

> To begin with, *white ignorance* as a cognitive phenomenon has to be clearly historicized.

Which is exactly what she does in this paper. Dr. Smith rightfully states that naming is political, hierarchal, and results in dehumanizing people and creating violence. Her charting the history of white evangelicalism reminded me of Kristin Kobes du Mez's work *Jesus and John Wayne: How White Evangelicals Corrupted a Faith and Fractured a Nation*.[1] I highly recommend this text to be read alongside Dr. Smith's work.

For the sake of supporting her claims, I found myself wandering in Genesis. In Gen 1:26–27, we are taught that male/female are both image bearers. We read the familiar:

> Then God said, "Let us make humankind in our image, according to our likeness; and let them have dominion over the fish of the sea, and over the birds of the air, and over the cattle, and over all the wild animals of the earth, and over every creeping thing that creeps upon the earth." So God created humankind in his image, in the image of God he created them; male and female he created them.[2]

God names that both male/female are image bearers with a purpose of stewarding creation. Both bear God's image; both to be stewards of creation.

In Genesis 2 the narrative gets more specific about the male/female creation. We read the following:

> Then the LORD God said, "It is not good that the man should be alone; I will make him a helper as his partner." So out of the ground the Lord God formed every animal of the field and every bird of the air, and brought them to the man to see what he would call them; and whatever the man called every living

---

1. (New York: Liveright, 2020).
2. Scripture citations are all from the NRSV.

> creature, that was its name. The man gave names to all cattle, and to the birds of the air, and to every animal of the field; but for the man there was not found a helper as his partner. So the LORD God caused a deep sleep to fall upon the man, and he slept; then he took one of his ribs and closed up its place with flesh. And the rib that the LORD God had taken from the man he made into a woman and brought her to the man. Then the man said, "This at last is bone of my bones and flesh of my flesh; this one shall be called Woman, for out of Man this one was taken."

It is interesting to note that God did not instruct the man to name the woman. God instructed the man to name the animals. The word choice is notable in that the man uses the phrase "This one." "This one" that was presented to me in the same way that the animals were presented. God brought her to me in the same way that God brought animals to me. Man named animals, man named woman. While it is easy to romanticize this passage with the man's song and/or poetry, his naming of Woman after naming the animals is troubling. It should make us pause and take notice.

Pulling on this thread a bit more, we see after Genesis 3 the man deflecting from himself and blaming the woman. He scapegoats her to God, thus absolving himself of any responsibility. "This one," by the way that you brought to me, gave me the fruit and I ate it. As we read along, we see what the man does which reinforces the power of naming her in Gen 3:20: "The man named his wife Eve, because she was the mother of all living." While this is often chosen to preach during a Mother's Day sermon, I find it alarming that the man chooses to name her when he was never instructed to do so. She, "this one" will be named "Mother" . . . not image bearer. "Mother" . . . not co-heir and co-steward.

Thus, the patriarchy takes root without paying attention to it. Man names, at will, what he names and the woman does not get the privilege of naming. She does not name in either creation narrative. She is named . . . as lower than man . . . dare I say on par with the animals that man was naming. This is *dehumanizing*.

We know that it is important to acknowledge the narrative nature of the creation account and so I am daring to connect this narrative to what happens later. In Gen 6:1–2 we read:

> When people began to multiply on the face of the ground, and daughters were born to them, the sons of God saw that they were fair; and they took wives for themselves of all that they chose.

In some passages the men are called "sons of God" and these beautiful women are called "daughters of men." Upon research, I discovered there are many complexities about who the sons of God are believed to be. Some say they are divine beings, or angels, that came and took beautiful women as wives . . . hinting at sexual intercourse.

What is problematic about that is Jesus's teaching about sexuality after death—that it does not exit. There is no "giving/receiving" in marriage in heaven. For the sake of my point, I believe that these "sons of God" signal powerful divine-like men. Elevating the men as very close to God; almost divine, in a hierarchal way, over women. THESE men were sons of God . . . whereas, women were not offspring of God, but were offspring of men.

This narrative precipitates the flood. The great wickedness spreading over the earth is directly connected to what was happening here. These "sons of God" were taking wives most likely without their consent. Rape is a likely possibility. God sees this and it's a great injustice . . . a great evil.

The naming of woman/Eve in a hierarchal way from man, dehumanizing her lower than himself as with others he named, lead to a great evil that grieved God.

If I were to meme this, I would say this is the very first "Name it, claim it." Because the male named the woman "Eve," he could enact violence against her or CLAIM her as wife without her consent. Or many other women as wives. *Naming, as Dr. Smith rightfully states, can be a power that is abused, creating a hierarchy, dehumanization, and violence.*

When Europeans descended on the land we now stand on, we see the power of naming and the dehumanizing violence that ensues. My descendants named themselves "Christian" and named those they encountered as "savages"; less than human. They continually named others that were not white as less than human (three-fifths perhaps?) and built institutions, systems, and a culture of violence stemming from wrongly naming in willful white ignorance of what they were doing. In the same way that the man, in Genesis, scapegoated and gaslit the woman and violence ensued, white evangelicals have a recorded history of scapegoating and gaslighting BIPOC communities and not taking any responsibility for the wrongful naming that they have done. I believe God sees this as a great evil within the white evangelical church.

These weeds, on this soil, were allowed to grow among the wheat and now have burst forth their noxious fruit. The reckoning of hundreds of years of improper naming, and the violence that has ensued, is at our doorstep. This is the reason why Dr. Smith poses her question to us about white evangelicals and the precipice we find ourselves on. Can any form of Christianity be committed to reject violent hierarchies?

I would like to end my comments with a small mustard seed of hope. Because the kingdom of God is like yeast—a small amount affects the whole—I would like to pivot and say that NAMING, which done in ignorance and blindness creates hierarchies and dehumanizing violence, can also be used for good. Dr. Smith, and a plethora of other theologians and Christian leaders, are rightfully naming. Naming our histories. Naming the pain. Naming the violence. Naming the truth. There will be a cost to doing that which we are witnessing. Naming the truth about white evangelicalism and the chaos in its wake will not be popular amongst white evangelicals that are willfully ignorant of our history. However, courageously telling the truth will help us to walk in the light of that truth to new wineskins that we may/may not see the completion of.

My other title at North Park has been the Director of CRUX—an intentional living-learning discipleship cohort for first year students in the undergraduate side of our campus that is intentionally intercultural and city-centered, and where I am seeing seeds of hope growing as students are told the truth. It is painful for some of them, yet by the end of the year and following forward, it becomes life-giving; a way to engage others without violently naming them. This little cohort provides enough hope for me for what will be . . . Lord, have mercy.

SELECT ANNOTATED BIBLIOGRAPHY ON POLITICS

Agamben, Giorgio. *The Omnibus Homo Sacer*. Meridian: Crossing Aesthetics. Stanford: Stanford University Press, 2017. This one-volume collection of a previous nine-volume series by the Italian philosopher Giorgio Agamben is one of the most significant works ever written to challenge and rethink the legacy of Christian theology. From economics to politics, Pauline letters to Platonic myths, this series touches on virtually every aspect of Western metaphysics and is essential reading for those trying to understand the nature of religion and politics today.

Bacote, Vincent. *The Political Disciple: A Theology of Public Life*. Ordinary Theology. Grand Rapids: Zondervan, 2015. This brief exploration of Christian doctrines connected to public life and discipleship is a good place to see one expression of a neo-Kuyperian approach to faith and public life.

Balibar, Étienne. *Secularism and Cosmopolitanism: Critical Hypotheses on Religion and Politics*. Translated by G. M. Goshgarian. New York: Columbia University Press, 2018. Calling for a "secularization of secularity," Balibar's short study on religion and politics offers critical insights and challenges to religion from a political theorist of the highest order. His aim to rethink the concept of the secular as not fully secularized enough is a wake-up call to those working in theological circles who are trying to conceive of the "postsecular" as a re-entrance of the theological.

Capon, Robert Farrar. *Kingdom, Grace, Judgment: Paradox, Outrage, and Vindication in the Parables of Jesus*. Grand Rapids: Eerdmans, 2002. Capon's provocative treatment of the metaphor of the kingdom of God in Jesus's parables elucidates why white Christians' project of "advancing the kingdom of God" through their own political power is so problematic.

Caputo, John D. *The Insistence of God: A Theology of Perhaps*. Indiana Series in the Philosophy of Religion. Bloomington: Indiana University Press, 2013. From the master of "weak thought," this work captures the heart of his theo-poetics while sacrificing none of the wit and insight that characterize his deconstructivist take on theology. Always searching to revitalize the "event" that is the name of God and its impact upon our thought and world, Caputo provides a series of challenges to traditional theological notions of sovereignty and divine being—all with major political and communal implications following in their wake.

Carter, J. Kameron. *Race: A Theological Account*. New York: Oxford University Press, 2008. Kameron Carter's searing account of how western Christianity became the religious foundation of white supremacy and imperialism reveals the depth and breadth of white Christian dominionism.

Crockett, Clayton. *Radical Political Theology: Religion and Politics after Liberalism*. Insurrections: Critical Studies in Religion, Politics, and Culture. New York: Columbia University Press, 2013. Crockett's approach to political theology as a field offers an admittedly "radical" take on how best to proceed in the wake of liberalism's failures. In many ways, he lays the blueprint for so many who follow his lead. This book gives a good sense of how to rethink sovereignty, law, community, and the historical operations of theology in light of the "death of God" we are still trying to comprehend.

Du Mez, Kristin Kobes. *Jesus and John Wayne: How White Evangelicals Corrupted a Faith and Fractured a Nation*. New York: Liveright, 2020. Du Mez's sweeping history of white evangelicals' worship of rugged masculinity and militarism illuminates how Trumpism captured the hearts of so many among their ranks and legitimized their self-interested approach to political power.

Dunkelman, Marc J. *The Vanishing Neighbor: The Transformation of American Community*. New York: Norton, 2014. Dunkelman's account of the "missing middle" in contemporary U.S. society.

Dunn, James D. G. "Echoes of Intra-Jewish Polemic in Paul's Letter to the Galatians." *JBL* 112 (1993) 459–77. Discusses the relationship between Peter and James and how the political background in Judea at that time may have influenced Peter's decision to withdraw from the gentiles in Antioch.

Eskola, Timo. *A Narrative Theology of the New Testament: Exploring the Metanarrative of Exile and Restoration*. WUNT 350. Tübingen: Mohr Siebeck, 2015. Investigation of the meaning of "exile" in the NT.

Esler, Philip F. *Galatians*. New Testament Readings. New York: Routledge, 2013. Provides a thorough engagement of cultural concerns and background to Galatians with particular attention to terminological and literary evidence.

Felder, Cain Hope, ed. *Stony the Road We Trod: African American Biblical Interpretation*. Minneapolis: Fortress, 1991. This collection of essays includes chapters that convey the historical trajectory of African American biblical interpretation.

Grabbe, Lester L. *Ancient Israel: What Do We Know and How Do We Know It?* Rev. ed. London: Bloomsbury T. & T. Clark, 2017. Evaluation of historical evidence for reconstructions of ancient Israel.

Gushee, David P., and Glen H. Stassen. *Kingdom Ethics: Following Jesus in Contemporary Context*. 2nd ed. Grand Rapids: Eerdmans, 2016. Gushee and Stassen focus their approach to Christian ethics on Jesus's Sermon on the Mount, pointing readers to a Christian ethical framework based on Jesus's teachings about the kingdom of God's justice and peace.

Hauerwas, Stanley. *The Peaceable Kingdom: A Primer in Christian Ethics*. Notre Dame: University of Notre Dame Press, 1983. Hauerwas is one of the most important persons to introduce an Anabaptist type of approach to Christian faith and life, particularly to those not of Mennonite heritage. Of his many volumes, this is one of the first that conveys the theological and ethical commitments that are expressed as a "counter-polis" or alternative witness.

Hauerwas, Stanley, and Will Willimon. *Resident Aliens: Life in the Christian Colony*. Expanded 25th anniversary ed. Nashville: Abingdon, 2014. Influential theological account of the meaning of "exile" for the contemporary Christian church.

Hendricks, Obery M., Jr. *Christians against Christianity: How Right-Wing Evangelicals Are Destroying our Nation and our Faith*. Boston: Beacon, 2021. Biblical scholar Obery Hendricks contrasts the political theology of right-wing white evangelicals with his black liberationist read of Jesus's politics, showing the bankruptcy and harmful consequences of the former.

Hill, John. *Friend or Foe? The Figure of Babylon in the Book of Jeremiah MT*. BibInt 40. Leiden: Brill, 1999. Exegetical analysis of Babylon motif throughout the book of Jeremiah.

Select Annotated Bibliography on Politics

Jones, Robert P. *White Too Long: The Legacy of White Supremacy in American Christianity.* New York: Simon & Schuster, 2020. Religion scholar Robert Jones offers an astute perspective in the much-needed effort to reckon with the atrocious legacy of white supremacy in American Christianity.

Knowles, Melody D. *Centrality Practiced: Jerusalem in the Religious Practice of Yehud and the Diaspora in the Persian Period.* ABS 16. Atlanta: Scholars, 2006. Investigation of the interactions between postexilic Jerusalem and Jewish communities outside the land of Israel.

Kotsko, Adam. *Neoliberalism's Demons: On the Political Theology of Late Capital.* Stanford: Stanford University Press, 2018. Following Max Weber's famous study of capitalism and religion, Kotsko's short work demonstrates effectively how political theology must take seriously its economic implications and entanglements. Ranging widely across a number of economic and political-theological texts, this work gives a general orientation on neoliberalism and its negative effects on our world from a political theological point of view that yet takes theology to task for its indebtedness to neoliberalism's ways and means.

Leithart, Peter J. *The Theopolitan Vision.* West Monroe, LA: Theopolis Books, an Imprint of Athanasius Press, 2019. This is the best place to see a clear articulation of Leithart's biblical and theological strategy in connection with a distinctive vision of church and politics.

Lindbeck, George A. *The Church in a Postliberal Age.* Edited by James J. Buckley. Radical Traditions. Grand Rapids: Eerdmans, 2003. Essays on the status and mission of the church in the world.

Lischer, Richard. *The Preacher King: Martin Luther King, Jr. and the Word that Moved America.* Updated ed. New York: Oxford University Press, 2020. Exploration of the ecclesial dimension to King's work.

Lopez, Davina C. *Apostle to the Conquered: Reimagining Paul's Mission.* Paul in Critical Contexts. Minneapolis: Fortress, 2010. Explores the dynamics of power involving gender and empire using a large *comparanda* of visual and textual evidence to resituate Paul's arguments in light of cultural preconceptions of conquest.

Maier, Harry O. *Picturing Paul in Empire: Imperial Image, Text and Persuasion in Colossians, Ephesians and the Pastoral Epistles.* London: Bloomsbury, 2013. Outlines various ways in which Paul and his later tradition negotiated identity by utilizing power language and imagery of Roman imperial paradigms.

Margolis, Michele F. *From Politics to the Pews: How Partisanship and the Political Environment Shape Religious Identity.* Chicago Studies in American Politics. Chicago: University of Chicago Press, 2018. Margolis's book is helpful for understanding how the relationship between politics and religion in contemporary American society is a two-way street.

McCauley, Esau. *Reading While Black: African American Biblical Interpretation as an Exercise in Hope.* Downers Grove, IL: IVP Academic, 2020. McCauley's book is an accessible volume that displays patterns of biblical interpretation connected with the lives of African Americans.

Milinovich, Timothy, and T. J. Rogers. *The Campaign Rhetoric of Paul.* Lanham, MD: Lexington/Fortress Academic, forthcoming. Evaluates Paul's arguments regarding himself and his opponents in 2 Corinthians, Galatians, and Philippians as campaign rhetoric and underscores how arguments about the law and the cross may not have been central to Paul's theology but were developed in response to the political challenges he faced from external threats to his authority in his communities.

Nancy, Jean-Luc. *Dis-Enclosure: The Deconstruction of Christianity*. Translated by Bettina Bergo et al. Perspectives in Continental Philosophy. New York: Fordham University Press, 2008. Ostensibly a work devoted to deconstructing Christianity and its legacy in the West, this work by a prominent French philosopher acknowledges the centrality of the Christian heritage to today's political landscape while also challenging those in the West to go beyond it. Christianity points toward the secular because what it gives to the West is far more complex than one might suspect. Breaking toward an openness without horizons to foreclose upon it, Christianity has more to offer the West, even as it appears to be in significant decline.

Nugent, John C. *The Politics of Yahweh: John Howard Yoder, the Old Testament, and the People of God*. Theopolitical Visions 12. Eugene, OR: Cascade Books, 2011. Evaluation of Yoder's exilic approach to the Old Testament.

Oakes, Peter. *Galatians*. Paideia: Commentaries on the New Testament. Grand Rapids: Baker Academic, 2015. Utilizes the house church model to consider how the implied audience of Galatians receives Paul's arguments from their own logistical and cultural perspectives.

Phillips, Elizabeth, et al., eds. *T&T Clark Reader in Political Theology*. London: T. & T. Clark, 2021. This recent volume is one place to encounter the growing conversation around the different approaches to political theology.

Putnam, Robert D. *Bowling Alone: The Collapse and Revival of American Community*. 20th anniversary ed. New York: Simon & Schuster, 2020. Classic account of how civic life in the U.S. contracted during the twentieth century.

Santner, Eric L. *The Royal Remains: The People's Two Bodies and the Endgames of Sovereignty*. Chicago: University of Chicago Press, 2011. A gem among political-theological texts, Santner's contemporary unfolding of the study of the king's two bodies—a medieval concept made famous by Kantorowicz's book *The King's Two Bodies*—allows us to see how significant the concept of sovereignty remains today, and how we might begin to address it more directly. If we are to think new democratic forms in light of this long political-theological history, we must begin to rethink the modern subject in light of the (theological) forces that have brought it into being.

Schiess, Kaitlyn. *The Liturgy of Politics: Spiritual Formation for the Sake of Our Neighbors*. Downers Grove, IL: InterVarsity, 2020. Reflections on the political dimensions to Christian formation.

Sisson, Jonathan P. "Jeremiah and the Jerusalem Conception of Peace." *JBL* 105 (1986) 429–42. Study of the key term "peace" in Jeremiah 29:7.

Taylor, Charles. *A Secular Age*. Cambridge: Harvard University Press, 2007. Taylor's wide-ranging treatment of secularization processes in the West elucidates how religious and political ends and identities intermingle among various constituencies

Warnock, Raphael G. *The Divided Mind of the Black Church: Theology, Piety and Public Witness*. Religion, Race, and Ethnicity. New York: New York University Press, 2014. Warnock's volume provides context for the range of biblical and theological approaches in the Black church, providing helpful complexity that helps explain differences in public posture and political commitment.

Warren, Nicolas de. *Original Forgiveness*. Northwestern University Studies in Phenomenology and Existential Philosophy. Evanston, IL: Northwestern University Press, 2020. This book is a strong analysis of numerous philosophical takes on forgiveness, mainly approached from a Levinasian point of view. His numerous literary, dramatic, and philosophical references provide a solid foundation for considering an "original forgiveness" prior to any single act of individual forgiveness, without having to claim that such a ground beneath us is yet of divine origin. What he ends up illustrating are the significant social stakes for rethinking forgiveness beyond theology and as a political category much in need of taking up publicly.

Whitehead, Andrew L., and Samuel L. Perry. *Taking America Back for God: Christian Nationalism in the United States.* New York: Oxford University Press, 2020. Whitehead and Perry's landmark study of Christian nationalism shines a light on many features of this influential movement.

NORTH PARK THEOLOGICAL SEMINARY SYMPOSIUM ON THE THEOLOGICAL INTERPRETATION OF SCRIPTURE

SEPTEMBER 2021

Politics

PRESENTERS

Stephen B. Chapman
Associate Professor of Old Testament, Duke Divinity School

Timothy Milinovich
Professor of Theology, Dominican University

Colby Dickinson
Professor of Theology, Loyola University

Jules A. Martinez Olivieri
Visiting Professor, Interamerican University of Puerto Rico

Vincent Bacote
Professor of Theology, Wheaton College

Janel Kragt Bakker
Professor of Mission and Culture, Memphis Theological Seminary

Kay Higuera Smith
Professor of Biblical and Religious Studies, Azusa Pacific University

RESPONDENTS

Christy Randazzo
Affiliate Faculty, Department of Religion, Montclair University and University of St. Joseph

Kaitlyn Schiess
Doctoral Student, Duke Divinity School

Rose Lee-Norman
Adjunct Assistant Professor of Reconciliation Studies, Bethel University

Presenters and Respondents

Jonathan M. Wilson
Adjunct Instructor of Church History, North Park Theological Seminary

Christopher W. Skinner
Professor of New Testament and Early Christianity, Loyola University

Bret M. Widman
Associate Professor of Ministry, North Park Theological Seminary

www.ingramcontent.com/pod-product-compliance
Lightning Source LLC
Chambersburg PA
CBHW080248170426
43192CB00014BA/2600